THE WORLD OF GURUS

REVISED EDITION

A critical look at the philosophies of India's influential gurus and mystics

by
Vishal Mangalwadi

CORNERSTONE PRESS
Chicago, Illinois

Originally published by Nivedit Good Books Distributors Pvt. Ltd., New Delhi, India.
© *1987 Vishal Mangalwadi*

To Ruth
To Nivedit and Anandit

Cornerstone Press is the publishing arm of Jesus People USA Evangelical Covenant Church, which is a community of Christians serving the poor, the homeless, and the elderly in the Uptown neighborhood of Chicago. If you would like more information about the community and its various outreaches, write to: JPUSA, c/o Cornerstone Press, 939 W. Wilson Ave., Ste. 202C, Chicago, IL 60640.

All Scripture quotations are from the Revised Standard Version *of the Bible,* © *1952 by the Division of Christian Education of the NCCC, U.S.A., and are used by permission.*

The World of Gurus, Revised Edition
ISBN 0-940895-03-X

Printed in the U.S.A.
99 98 97 96 95 94 93 92   9 8 7 6 5 4 3 2 1

Library of Congress Cataloging in Publication Information

PREFACE

At first the voices startled L.T., even though they sounded so melodious. The mahatma who bestowed the esoteric "knowledge" on L.T. had assured him that he would hear the divine sound if he closed his ears to the outer noises and meditated on the inner silence.

Initially, he thought that he heard the sound of sitar music being played by an angelic Ravi Shankar. A little later he heard some voices calling to him from the fathomless void of his inner self. They startled him, yet he rejoiced, for he thought that he was now close to achieving the goal of moksha, for which he had labored so long—for countless ages during his previous eighty-four hundred thousand lives. His heart was overwhelmed with gratitude toward his mahatma and guru Maharaj Ji. The disciple had surrendered his life to the service of the "perfect master." But then Maharaj Ji's mother removed the sadguru from the leadership of the mission because of his "unspiritual way of life." The older and younger brother went to court to decide who the "perfect master" was.

L.T. began to wonder if the voices he heard, the light he saw, the nectar he tasted, and the word on which he concentrated were really divine. Could these be merely human experiences generated by physical manipulation of the senses and autosuggestion? Doubts and questions haunted him for days and weeks until his heart sank to such depths of despair that he began to contemplate suicide.

He had grown up in an affluent home in Canada. True, his parents had spent more time earning money than with him, yet he knew that they were sincere people who loved him. After his first year studies in psychology and philosophy at the University of California, he declared that he no longer believed the Bible.

His parents hadn't taken him seriously, but he broke their hearts when he dropped out in 1966 as a drug addict.

The university had destroyed his faith but had given him no alternative philosophy to live by. When he realized that the best of his professors were in as much darkness about the meaning of life as he was, he saw no point in continuing as their student. He felt that only a person who knew the truth was worthy of being a teacher.

Between 1966 and 1970, while there was a philosophical void in his mind, L.T. listened to the voices of many gurus. He took initiation into Transcendental Meditation, which helped him give up drugs, but didn't satisfy his quest for truth. He chanted "Hare Krishna" for a few days but saw little sense in it. He learned yoga, indulged in occult practices, lived in nudist communes, and travelled around in search of truth. Finally, an Indian mahatma (an authorized preacher of the Divine Light Mission) in London initiated L.T. into DLM in 1971. The experience of blinding light during the initiation ceremony blew his mind, and L.T. gave up everything for the guru. Serving the guru became his life, and the guru's word his philosophy of life.

But now the fall of the perfect master challenged his faith. For weeks he continued to ignore the challenge. The security of belief seemed a lot better than the adventure of an honest search. What was the guarantee that he would find the truth? Hadn't he looked at all the possible answers? University professors had been the blind leading the blind. He had tried many other gurus before joining DLM and had talked to followers of other gurus since. What was there to live for now? What was the point in living? Would death not be a better alternative than senseless existence? But no. Ever since his grandmother died, he had always wanted immortality, not death. Was there no one who could give him eternal life? It was in October 1975 that L.T. heard another voice that offered what he sought. L.T. says he found the truth in the sadguru Jesus Christ.

This is not a traveller's account of gurudom but a researcher's quest for truth in guruism. Peter Brent's *Godmen of India*, Marvin Harper's *Gurus, Swamis and Avataras*, and Khushwant Singh's *Gurus, Godmen and Good People* are accounts of the significant names and happenings in gurudom. This volume examines the social and historical background, the intellectual impulses, and the religious and cultural aspirations of humanity that have produced the institution of gurudom. It takes the truth claims of some of the prominent gurus seriously and examines their validity. It proposes a criterion for truth and applies it vigorously to the teachings of the individual gurus.

I have sought to be fair and accurate in my presentation of all the gurus, including those whose teachings I reject. My approach is critical, because one has to reject falsehood while seeking truth.

Since writing the first edition, I have lived in a rural area of Madhya Pradesh, serving the poor. Therefore, it has not been possible to keep up with all the developments of each of the sects. My only justification in issuing an American edition, without giving the latest information on each guru, is that the book was meant primarily to assist those who seek the truth—for those who desire reliable foundations for their lives and for society.

It would have been impossible to write this book without the help of many of my beloved friends in and outside the TRACI community. I am deeply grateful to them. Special mention must be made of Dr. B. Khan, who initiated me into the study of gurus while I was his student; Bob Jono, who spent several months travelling with me to various ashrams; Miss E. Brattle, who graciously typed the manuscript; and my best friend Ruth, who married me while this work was in progress and helped edit it.

This edition has been painstakingly scrutinized and edited by Kurt Hoeksema at Cornerstone Press, Chicago, with subsequent proofreading and re-indexing by Jennifer Mullen, Leah Grover, Nanci Fahey, Corey Fitz, and Sally Watkins. Kathryn Frank did the typesetting, with Sally Watkins' assistance. Thanks to Chad Wolf who helped with the final layout of the book, and to Noah Krogh for the front cover illustration.

VISHAL MANGALWADI

CONTENTS

Preface   *iii*

Part I. The Perspective

1. Understanding Guruism   3
2. The Intellectual Impulses Behind Guruism   19
3. Criterion for Evaluating Guruism   29

Part II. The Traditional Gurus

4. The Divine Life Society and Chinmaya Mission   41
5. Hare Krishna   55

Part III. The Modernistic Gurus

6. Transcendental Meditation   73
7. Acharya Rajneesh   87

Part IV. The Thaumaturgic Gurus

8. Sathya Sai Baba   107
9. Swami Muktananda Paramahansa   123

Part V. The Audio-Luminous Gurus

10. The Divine Light Mission   135
11. Radhi Soami Satsang (Beas)   141

Part VI. Evaluation and Alternative

12. Evaluating Monistic Gurus   155
13. The Sanatan Sadguru   167

Notes   185
Index   195

PART I

THE PERSPECTIVE

WHEN THE BRITISH came to India, Hinduism was at its lowest ebb. To many observers it seemed virtually synonymous with caste, untouchability, female infanticide, child-marriage, and sati (widow burning). With Raja Ram Mohan Roy and the Brahmo Samaj it began its great renaissance which culminated in the lives and works of men like Mahatma Gandhi and Dr. Sarvapalli Radhakrishnan. The present phase of Hinduism can be described as the revival of guruism. The contemporary gurus have made Hinduism a worldwide force.

Before one can fully appreciate or evaluate a particular guru it is necessary to form a clear perspective for looking at this phenomenon. We will start in the first two chapters by examining the historical, sociological, and intellectual dynamics, along with the context of modern guruism.

But there are more basic questions. Why does one want a guru, or for that matter, a religion? What is, in fact, religion? Can we possibly judge it to be true or false? How?

Chapter One

Understanding Guruism

GURUS HAVE BEEN with us for a long time. Today they are popular everywhere. Millions of people, young and old, rich and poor, illiterate and sophisticated, bow before them and obey without question.

The impact of the gurus has already become a significant force worldwide. It is shaping the civilization of tomorrow's India. In the West it is not simply a passing fad, and guruism may become increasingly influential as Western culture decays.

In both East and West the popularity of gurus symbolizes at least two things: first, a resurgence of the perennial spiritual quest of man; and second, a struggle for new forms of culture. More specifically, in India it is part of the struggle for cultural independence, and in America the struggle for a counterculture.

India and Guruism

India achieved political independence in 1947, but because our national leadership was a product of Western civilization, the cultural dominance of the West continued. Except in the dress of some of our leaders, we continued, as many felt, to ape the West. Our language, education, politics, economy, judiciary, science, technology, medicine, and entertainment were all heavily Westernized. Perhaps this was inevitable and necessary and in some cases even good. No doubt we need much more humility to learn from traditions other than our own.

Political independence, though, gave us tremendous self-confidence. The search for our cultural heritage, which had begun in the previous centuries,

3

became more vigorous. Today, indigenous art, sculpture, music, dance, medicine, and language are being rediscovered, as are those things that are more foundational to culture: philosophy, religion, politics, and education. There are voices asking us to be indigenous. The revival of guruism is an important part of this process.

Many gurus consciously seek to mold our culture in the light of their philosophy. Swami Sivananda dedicated his *Bliss Divine* to "the promotion of a happy new civilization and culture built on the blissful atman that pervades all." Swami Krishnananda entitled his three lectures, given at Allahabad University in November 1960, "Resurgent Culture."

Unquestionably, the trend to incorporate indigenous culture into our social life is a good one, but it can and already has been exploited by evil and selfish forces. The path to cultural awareness should not be followed blindly. There is much that is great in our past but also much that is ugly. Like everything else, the institution of guruism, with its teachings and implications, needs to be understood and analyzed. Its strengths should be appreciated and its weaknesses seen. Only then should we accept or reject guruism as a cultural phenomenon.

Guruism and the West

In the West during the preceding centuries, three great ideological forces have shaped civilization: Catholic theology, the Protestant Reformation, and the Enlightenment. From the sixteenth to the nineteenth centuries, the forces generated at the Reformation dominated the culture of the northern European and North American people. During the last hundred years, however, due to internal decay in the Western church and the onslaught of rationalism, Christianity has lost its throne to naturalistic humanism, or secularism, as it is often called in the West.[1]

With a rationalistic epistemology (knowledge to be attained through reasoning and empirical experience) as its cornerstone, secularism developed a worldview which denied God and deified man. It looked upon the universe as a materialistic machine. Not only the universe but soon every person was considered to be a biochemical, sexual, or economic machine by the secular scientists, psychologists, economists, and sociologists. Such an ideology, which views both the universe and man as mere machines, produced a mechanistic society in the post-Christian West. Humanness was lost. "One-dimensional man" replaced the multidimensional person. Individuals began to be treated as "cogs in the wheel." Naturally, they rebelled against this dehumanizing society.

The protest against technocracy first came from serious thinkers such as Jacques Ellul, David Riesman, William H. Whyte, Paul Goodman, Cyril Wright Mills, and Aldous Huxley.[2] In the 1960s the protest was headed by thinkers such as Herbert Marcuse. By 1964 the more sensitive sections of society, especially the students, had joined in. Mario Savio stood on the steps of the administrative building at the University of California at Berkeley and amplified the thesis of Marcuse and the feelings of his comrades when he declared:

> There is a time when the operations of the machine become so odious, make you so sick at heart, that you can't take part, you can't even tacitly take part. And you've got to put your bodies upon the gears and upon the wheels, upon the levers, upon all the apparatus, and you've got to make it stop. And you've got to indicate to the people who run it, to the people who own it, that unless you're free, the machine will be prevented from working at all.[3]

This sounded the battle cry. Some members of the young generation launched the famous "free speech movement." The New Left sought to produce a counterculture even if this required violence. Others dropped out of society, preaching love, sex, drugs, and alteration of consciousness in order to change the culture. We saw a variety of hippies, yippies, junkies, freaks, dropouts, and flower children in India.

In this climate, when the younger generation in the West was searching for something new—a new worldview, new values, new consciousness, and a new culture—the appearance of the gurus attracted their immediate attention. Maharishi Mahesh Yogi visited California in the autumn of 1965. Only forty students responded then to the publicity for a course on his principles and the practice of Transcendental Meditation. By 1971 the numbers had risen from forty to seventy-three thousand. By 1972, the Maharishi's followers had put forward a world plan to change society.

Swami Prabhupada went to New York in 1965, and by the next year he had enough converts to form the International Society for Krishna Consciousness. Many gurus, of course, had preceded them, and many who have also made the headlines have been there since. Their impact, at least in America, can best be summed up in the words of Marvin Henry Harper. He begins his book *Gurus, Swamis and Avataras* with the statement that "Hinduism has invaded America" and concludes it by saying, "Hinduism is striking its roots deep into American soil." Many gods of the counterculture have already failed, such as the New Left, drugs, sex, and the occult.[4]

To many, guruism still seems to be a viable alternative to secularism and rationalism. But is it? If it is, which guru? Ever since the dawn of civilization, man has cried out in the words of *Brihadaranyaka Upanishad*:

> Lead me from the unreal to the real
> Lead me from the darkness to light
> Lead me from death to immortality.

All through history humanity has sought for God; for His guidance, protection, and favor; and for union and communion with Him. Humans have sought to discover the source, purpose, and meaning of their existence. We have longed for the forgiveness of our sin and for immortality. This religious thrust seems to be an integral part of our being.

However, since the rise of secularism it has become fashionable for the "enlightened" of the world to scoff at the ideas of religion, spirituality, or God. Some tolerated religious ideas as comfort for weak people. Those in the intellectual world who still felt the need for God practiced religion privately. They often were dualistic: secular in the university, and religious at home, church, or ashram.

But within the past twenty years the trend has been completely reversed. Everybody is now talking about spirituality, God, religion, and values. Of course, those with more brilliant minds saw the inadequacy of the secular worldview much earlier. Aldous Huxley, who had a completely humanistic upbringing, wrote in 1944:

> For those of us who are not congenitally the members of any organized church, who have found that humanism . . . [is] not enough, who are not content to remain in the darkness of spiritual ignorance, the squalor of vice or that other squalor of mere respectability, the minimum working hypothesis would seem to be about as follows: That there is a Godhead or Ground, which is the unmanifested principle of all manifestation. . . .[5]

Indian thinkers like Dr. Sarvapalli Radhakrishnan had also been arguing for a rediscovery of faith within academic circles for several decades. Their efforts are now paying dividends.

However, not all religious faith is true or helpful. Nor is all "religious experience" genuine or edifying. If there is mysticism that is sacred, there is also that which is profane. As gurus, swamis, and bhagavans flood society with religiosity and spirituality, they need to be calmly analyzed and to have reasonable criteria applied to them to distinguish true faith from false, divine from demonic, genuine from spurious.

Hinduism and Guruism: A Thumbnail History

Several etymological meanings of the word *guru* have been given. By some it is thought to be derived from *gur* (to raise, lift up, hurt, kill, make effort, eat, go) with the noun-making termination *u*. Accordingly, a guru is so called because he tortures, kills, or eats up the ignorance of his disciples, elevates or makes effort to elevate their character, and ultimately leads them to the path of salvation.[6]

Early Vedic literature (the holy writing of Hinduism) does not have the word *guru*. Even the idea of *guru* is absent because Vedic religion was chiefly sacrificial. The word was first used and the concept developed during the Upanishadic times when the emphasis shifted from sacrifice to jnana (knowledge) as the means to liberation. Someone who knows is needed to impart jnana.

During the Upanishadic era the ashram system was also established. The acharya who taught the students in the first ashram of life was different from the acharyas of the other three ashrams. The first was called acharya-guru. The word guru was and is used for many different people, but most commonly and traditionally it has been applied to a teacher, particularly to the one who gives religious instruction.

The advent of Pauranika and Tantrika religions (A.D. 300) added new connotations to the word guru. He was no longer only a teacher. The founder or inventor of a sect or creed also began to be called guru. His followers who preached and propagated his doctrines were also referred to as gurus.

Thus in the time of the *Puranas* the fundamental essence of guruship was preaching rather than teaching. For the followers of Tantrika sects the giver of a mantra was guru.[7]

These secret mantras were communicated in the ears of the disciples and were called bija, bijaksara mantra, or the guru-mantra. It was in these Pauranika and Tantrika sects that the lineage of guruship began to be established. For the line to continue it was considered essential that the guru be married and have sons. Apparently it was because of this consideration that the father of Balyogeshwar of the Divine Light Mission married a second wife. His first wife, who is still alive, is not worshiped because she is not the "mother of God" or the "divine mother."

The Upanishadic acharya-guru could teach students of any class (except Shudra) without considering caste or creed. But Tantrika gurus could give a mantra only to the members of their own sect. Naturally a sectarian mentality developed, each group claiming its guru to be supreme.

Sant Kabir (A.D. 1440-1518), born in the family of a Muslim weaver, raised the status of the guru more than his predecessors. He was influenced by both the Sufis (Muslim mystics) and Hindu gurus (especially Ramananda). These two influences caused him to reject the doctrine of avatara (incarnation), idolatry, rituals, and the authority of all scriptures, whether the *Koran* or *Vedas*. He substituted the authority of the guru in place of scriptures or incarnations. He preferred to worship the guru in place of idols. In fact, he would touch the guru's feet before God's:

> Guru and God are both standing, whose
> Feet shall I touch first?
> I shall touch yours O guru, for
> You revealed God to me.

Gurus According to Sikhism

Kabir's influence did not last as long as Nanak's, his younger contemporary. Guru Nanak (A.D. 1469-1538), the founder of Sikhism, was reared in the same religious atmosphere as Kabir and was influenced by the same ideals. He insisted on extreme reverence to the guru. Consequently, after his death there arose nine gurus in his line, gradually transforming his disciples into a powerful religio-military community. It was Sikhism that paved the way for the development of the idea of guru to that of Godman.

Sikh scriptures proclaimed God as the unattributed absolute or as formless (nirankar). But they also described it as guru—in an attributed and personalized sense the object of worship and devotion and the revealer of light. The human preceptors, Guru Nanak and his nine successors, were also called gurus. The tenth, Guru Govind Singh, however, unable to find a suitable successor, declared their scripture *Adi Granth* to be the guru. He also called the community of the Sikh believers "guru." A committee of five elected leaders was to be the final authority in the community after him.

But these various usages of the term *guru* have resulted in confusion. If God alone is the guru, then in which sense were the ten human beings gurus? Sikh theologians have answered it by saying that not the body of these men but their bani (word) was the guru. They are called guru because they experienced the merging of self into the divine reality. Professor Gurbachan Singh Talib writes:

> That "guru" should have been employed for "God," as also for the human preceptor, arises from the mystical postulate of the merging of the perfect preceptor's self into the divine reality in which it is immersed.[8]

But if this is so, then why can't other human beings who experience merging of their self in the divine reality also be called gurus? Why limit the title only to ten? Sikh theologians don't have any adequate answer to this question.

Consequently, though the orthodox Sikh still limits the use of the term guru to God, the ten gurus, the scriptures *Guru Granth,* and the Guru Panth sect, there have arisen among Sikhs a number of human gurus in the last century or so. This is particularly true in the northwest where Sikh influence is the greatest. The orthodox Sikhs have rejected them as heretics, but some of these gurus have gathered large followings. Some of these sects have solved the confusion of the use of the term *guru* both for God and human preceptor by declaring the human leader to be God. Satsangies of Radha Soami at Beas (Punjab) believe that

> a Guru is man and God at the same time. While taking the ordinary form of a human being, the guru in his awareness and consciousness is total and, therefore, God himself.[9]

This is very logical in a monistic worldview where the belief is that the human soul and God are identical. Because of this new trend, several of the new gurus, such as Sri Neel Kanth Thataji, Acharya Rajneesh, and Sathya Sai Baba, have chosen the title of Bhagavan (God) for themselves. We can expect that many more will follow their example. Outsiders also have given the title Godmen to the gurus because of the identification of guru with God.

It is significant that from Guru Nanak (b. 1469) to Bhagavan Rajneesh (b. 1931) there is a gap of about five centuries. During these centuries guruism was overshadowed by Islam, Christianity, and the Hindu Renaissance. True, the Vaishnavite and Shaivite sects of the Hindus as well as Sikhs continued to worship or at least revere their gurus, but they did not identify the guru with God. Islam and Christianity taught strict monotheism. This influence prevented even the most consistent monists from identifying the human guru with God.

The institution of guru was held in various degrees of esteem in the great religious movements of the nineteenth and twentieth centuries. The earliest and the most outstanding movements such as Brahmo Samaj,[10] Prarthana Samaj, and Arya Samaj rejected both idol worship and man worship. Groups like Radha Soami (Agra), the Chetramis, and the members of Dev Samaj rejected idolatry but reinstated guru worship. But even they did not identify guru with God.

Swami Vivekananda and his followers worshiped their Guru Ramakrishna Paramahansa, and they believed that man was essentially God, yet because of Christian influence they did not go as far as identifying guru with God. Vivekananda said:

> We look upon the Master as a Person who is *like* God. We offer him worship *bordering* on divine worship.[11]

The religious leaders and thinkers who exerted the greatest influence in the first part of our century, such as Aurobindo, Gandhi, Radhakrishnan, and Krishnamurti did not teach guru worship either. Now, as the influence of these leaders is declining, guruism has reemerged. Hindu monism, which has always taught that man is identical with God, has now worked itself out logically and declared that guru is God.

The obvious but profound problem with this teaching is that we are given no way of verifying whether a person has attained so-called "total consciousness" (to qualify to be a Godman) or not. We have only the claim to this end. Of course, each guru gives his criterion to test the truth of the claim. But the criterion itself is unverifiable: we are simply to believe it, and often it is given merely to defend one guru's claim and to destroy the claims of others.

Logically, on the basis of monism, it is obvious that there can be millions of Godmen at any given moment. Anyone who is "merged in the divine reality" or has attained "unity consciousness" is a Godman. By that definition, no one can claim to be the only one or the "Perfect Master."

But many sects do claim their guru alone is the true Godman for this age, which is clearly indefensible on their own premises. If we accept the claims of one sect simply on the guru's authority, we must accept the claims of everyone. No one can be a fake. At least we can't know if anyone is a fraud. Likewise we can't know if anyone is legitimate.

Of course, a more basic question is: How can we know that "pure consciousness" is the ultimate reality or God? Could it be that ultimate reality is beyond consciousness or distinct from it? Even if the guru has attained "unity consciousness," how can we know that this consciousness is God? For if it isn't, then the guru can't be a Godman.

Godman, Monist, Dualist

So not all sects consider their leader to be a Godman, though there does appear to be basically three different concepts of a guru. The first is this Godman concept which declares that the guru is God. Swami Sivananda writes:

> The guru is God Himself manifesting a personal form to guide the aspirant. . . . The Sadguru is Brahman Himself.[12]

Swamy Shyam Sunderdass of Hardwar says:

> The Guru is God, the Guru is the director, the Guru is supreme.[13]

And Swami Akhanananda of Vrindaban (Mathura) says:

> Although the Guru is identified with absolute God, in order to teach the disciple he has to bring himself down to the level on which the disciple can follow.[14]

The second concept is that of the traditional monistic view. The more traditional monistic sects aspire to become one with the Absolute (God). They don't claim that their gurus have actually attained the highest realization. The guru is just further ahead on the road than the others. Subramanya Sharma says:

> At the time that he is learning, the student should think of the Guru as God. The true Guru is like God; he is not God himself.[15]

The third is the dualistic view of the guru. Those sects which hold to Ramanuja's qualified monism or various forms of dualism don't think that human beings ever become God or merge into the ultimate reality. Though they may worship the guru as equal to or greater than God, being his revealer, they never claim divinity for him. Swami Prabhupada of the International Society for Krishna Consciousness says that the disciple should honor

> the Spiritual master with the honour due to God because the Guru is the . . . representative of God who distributes unalloyed love of God.[16]

But anyone claiming to be God must be considered a "dog"[17] or a "murderer."[18]

The Nature of Indian Education and the Origin of the Guru Concept

The life of an individual in Indian society was theoretically divided into four ashrams. During the first ashram of life, Brahmacharya, one was a student and lived under a teacher. Usually many students lived under one acharya-guru, who taught them the *Vedas* and related subjects such as grammar, interpretation, pronunciation, performance of sacrifices, astronomy, and sometimes subjects like mathematics and literature.

In the absence of printed books and other modern facilities, the student was wholly dependent on the teacher for knowledge. Being young, a student could neither critically evaluate a teacher's opinions nor generally check the opinions of one teacher against the opinions of another as can be done in modern universities. This almost total dependence on the guru was given scriptural sanction. In fact, the student was virtually a servant to the teacher. Prof. A.L. Basham writes:

> The student was . . . expected to treat his master with the utmost reverence, ministering to all his needs and obeying all his commands implicitly.[19]

Dr. Chaubey writes that, according to later scriptures,

> Guru is to be worshipped specially because he alone shows what is Dharma and what is Adharma. Even when god Siva is wrath [sic..], the Guru is the saviour, but when the guru . . . is angered there is none to save. Ruin follows from the anger of the Guru; bad death from the criticism of the Guru, catastrophes from the displeasure of the Guru. It may be possible for a man who has entered the fire to remain alive; possible also to be alive after drinking poison or even caught in the hands of death; but not if he has offended the Guru. One should not lend one's ear to any censure of the Guru; where such criticisms occur one should close one's ears. One should not disrespect the retinue of the Guru; one should not criticize his tradition, whether based on *Vedas* or scriptures or *Agamas*.[20]

Today's secular education has unfortunately gone to the opposite extreme— total disrespect for the teachers. But the former Hindu concept of slavish acceptance of and obedience to the guru's teachings was unsatisfactory, too. It stifled both the critical faculties of students and their creative ability to break new ground. It can easily be seen that in this environment the teacher would attain an unquestioned authority. He was needed in society, so the condition he generally put forward was "all or nothing." Either you accepted everything he said or you received nothing. His interpretations, not the scriptures, became supreme and infallible.

Esoteric Character of Indian Religions

The word *Upanishad* literally means a "session," "sitting near the feet of a master who gives secret teachings." Since the Upanishadic times, many religions that arose in India were esoteric in character. The teachings, or mantras, were given secretly to the initiated disciple. Such knowledge, or jnana, was essential to liberation.

Even when liberation was achieved through action (karma) or devotion (bhakti), knowledge was still a prerequisite. Sri Krishna, in the *Bhagavad Gita*, gives knowledge regarding bhaktimarga and karmamarga to Arjuna. This need of knowledge, and often "secret" knowledge, made a living guru indispensable. Being so disposed, the guru also tended to become supreme, even above the scriptures. When he declared the scriptures to be above reproach, he usually meant his interpretation of the scriptures, which he meant for the disciples to accept without question.

With no objective reference point in the esoteric religions of India against which the guru's teaching could be checked, the doors were left wide open for any charismatic personality to arise and start a new sect. His own authority, derived from his private mystical experience, was final. The scriptures and reason were used (or misused) to defend and justify his claims. Even in those sects where the knowledge was not so secretive, as in some forms of yoga, the help of a competent guru was indispensable for practicing the techniques correctly.

Class System, Brahmin Dominance, and Guruism

The division of Indian society into four basic classes (or castes, as they are usually called) and the notion of ritual purity separated the priests from the masses. Priesthood was confined to the Brahmins, who generally looked down upon the masses and claimed a monopoly in socioreligious affairs. According to C. O. McMullen,

> a combination of three consequences of this seem to have facilitated the origin and development of the institutions of Guruship. The first consequence was a protest, if not revolt, against the Brahmin supremacy and dominance. Second, . . . the services of the priest in the traditional Hindu organization were denied . . . or . . . became extremely difficult for [the masses] to secure. Third, the *varnashrama* scheme denied the right of salvation and religiosity to those sections of society who were not twice-born. The institutions of guruship developed in response to these conditions. It met the religious needs of the masses and especially in the *bhakti* period, and in the *sant* tradition showed a definite protest against the Brahmin dominance.[21]

The breakdown of the class system in our own era, under the influence of Christian missions, Hindu reformers, and the industrialization of society, has also opened the doors for the gurus to come in and replace Brahminism with guruism. The class system has been the chief strength and an important distinguishing mark of traditional Hinduism. It is closely linked to the authority of the scriptures, which itself is another of the main characteristics of Brahminism besides the class system and idol worship. All three of these, which are interlinked, have been losing their hold on Indian society.

Traditional Hinduism was weakening, an alternative was needed, and the gurus provided it. The authority and worship of the guru is subtly replacing the authority of scriptures and idol worship. The four classes are being reduced to two: initiates and noninitiates.

Authoritarian Structure of the Indian Family

Peter Brent, the author of *Godmen of India*, points in his analysis to two psychological motives—authoritarianism and puritanism—that may explain why Indians, more than any other people, seek gurus. He suggests that the first of these is the overauthoritarianism of Indian fathers:

> I suspect that there are very few countries other than India, where one could find an advertisement in the matrimonial columns of the newspaper beginning, "Youth of forty seeks wife . . . " From almost his earliest days, . . . the young Indian is expected to conform absolutely to his father's wishes and commands. . . . For the rest of his life the average Indian is almost incapable of doing anything of which his father disapproves. In this situation, the guru can appear as a rescuer. For, with him, the whole conditioned mechanism of happy slavery can come into operation without conflict. He is the father who has been chosen; in this way, the disciple remains free in his bondage, bound in his freedom. Taught to be non-attached, he can cut himself off from his family without guilt.[22]

How true. In the ashrams of the Divine Light Mission at Hardwar and New Delhi I have seen young men doing manual labor almost slavishly but happily. They cannot step out of the ashram nor answer the questions of visitors like myself without permission. Yet they testified that they had peace and contentment, which they hadn't had before. I suspected, though, that some of this peace came from the fact that their three meals a day were guaranteed in the ashram and were not necessarily guaranteed at home.

Repressive Puritanism of Indian Society

The Indian conception of human sexuality led to the strict segregation of the sexes and to the repression of normal emotions. These normal feelings were instead offered in intense devotion to the guru. To quote Peter Brent again:

> In the West, we are free to work for the approval of those we love or respect and whom we would like to love and respect us. Not so the Indian, who fits into his family situation and his social stratum as inevitably as a part of a machine. . . . For the average and particularly the middle-class Indian, there are often only two directions he can go to prove that he can love, that he can be loved. One is towards homosexuality, the other towards the guru. (These are not, of course, mutually exclusive.)[23]

Here, again, I think Brent is right. Initially, I was shocked to hear that some of the most widely respected gurus in India had sexual relationships with their young devotees. Even where no homosexuality is involved, the intensity of love between guru and disciple is often the result of the transference of the sexual urge; this becomes especially obvious in groups such as the International Society for Krishna Consciousness.

Sociological Factors in the West and the Guru Concept

The great European Indologists of the eighteenth and nineteenth centuries, such as Sir William Jones, Charles Wilkins, and Max Mueller, were the first to rediscover and advocate the glories of ancient Indian civilization to the West.

Thinkers such as Goethe, Schopenhauer, Emerson, and Thoreau were among the earliest to welcome the insights of India into their thought and society. The first outstanding impact Hinduism made in the West, however, was through Swami Vivekananda. Since then the preaching of movements like the Ramakrishna Mission and the Theosophical Society, the prestige of personalities such as Mahatma Gandhi and Rabindranath Tagore, and the philosophy of thinkers such as Dr. Radhakrishnan, Aurobindo, and Krishnamurti have given intellectual respectability to Hinduism in the West and have opened the way to its propagation.

Popularization must be credited to the present gurus and yogis. Their remarkable success was not so much due to the Western mind becoming convinced of the truth of Hinduism, but to the conviction that the intellect was incapable of knowing the truth. The West was living in an intellectual vacuum after having rejected Christianity in the early part of this century and more recently having been exposed to humanism and its utter philosophical nakedness.

People had no purpose to live for, no particular ideology to believe in. Doubt, cynicism, and pessimism prevailed. The gurus and Godmen spoke into this void and showed a direction, which—though nonrational—was nevertheless attractive because of its novelty.

Erosion of Religious Authority

The countries in the West where guruism has greatest influence today were mostly Christian countries until the turn of this century. Christianity provided meaning and values and the basic impulses for the development of modern science, education, medicine, democracy, and capitalism.

The influence of the Enlightenment was also considerable, and its philosophical assumptions worked against Christianity. Atheistic philosophers such as Hume, Voltaire, and Nietzsche attracted the attention of their generations.

Not just philosophy but modern science, which was Christianity's child, also changed. After Newton, science began to view the universe as a closed machine of cause and effect, in which the idea of God as sustainer was unnecessary. After Darwin, the idea of chance replaced the idea of a transcendental creator. Instead of an invisible and intangible God being the ultimate reality, matter (later energy) itself began to be considered supreme. Theology was replaced by psychology. Economics explained individual and social behavior. The result was that naturalistic humanism emerged as the predominant ideology in these countries.

The intellectual attack on Christian presuppositions wasn't so strong that the Church couldn't have withstood it. The humanists have themselves seen the philosophical bankruptcy of their own position during the last few decades. But the reason for Christianity's overthrow was its own internal decay and weakness. The influence of pagan philosophies and the rise of pietism had destroyed the intellectual vitality of the Reformation era.

The Church became preoccupied with personal salvation and morality alone. So when the rationalistic attack came, the Church surrendered the intellectual, academic, and cultural arena to the humanists with little, if any, resistance.

Christian thinkers were largely dwelling on theological subjects and so were incapable of handling the rationalistic attack. The apologists defended Christian dogmas without seeking to expose the folly of rationalism, scientism, and humanism. Once humanists took over academic and cultural leadership, they were easily able to mold the beliefs of young minds.

This was not all. If the orthodox Christians retreated from the cultural arena, the more liberal ones surrendered to secular premises and compromised their beliefs. Christian faith began to be interpreted in Darwinian, Hegelian, existentialist, or Marxist terms. By the mid-twentieth century the West even saw atheists and agnostics becoming bishops and theologians, preaching a "new theology" and practicing a "new morality."

Liberals prided themselves on being intellectual and contemporary, but their children saw them as hypocrites—reciting creeds in church and denying them in their books and lives. Due to the theological confusion, the Church ceased to have a clear voice on the perplexing issues of the day. Because it allowed people of any or no persuasion to remain its leaders, it had no credibility. When it did speak, the Church showed to the world that it no longer believed anything was true.

Reaction to Hollow Materialism

Christianity had always taught that material benefits in themselves can't satisfy human longing. Jesus urged his disciples not to lay up treasures for themselves on this earth, but rather to "seek first the kingdom of God and His righteousness and all these things will be added unto you." St. Paul wrote that "love of money is the root of all evil, but godliness with contentment is great gain."

But the post-Christian, secular West had become too materialistic. Hedonism became the philosophy by which most people lived. Everything began to be judged materialistically—whether or not a thing was economically valuable or sensually pleasurable. Unfortunately, a great part of the Western church allowed this non-Christian materialism to enter and take control. The values of the church were no longer different from those of a hedonistic society.

When people became dissatisfied with materialism, they looked around for spiritual values and lifestyle. Turning to the Church, they found it engulfed by the same hollow materialism they hated. But the gurus—preaching essentially an otherworldly philosophy of life,[24] spiritual peace, and bliss—captured their imagination. However, many of the devotees who rejected Western materialism saw nothing wrong with the extravagant lifestyle in which many gurus live.

Frustration with Futile Reactionism

Sensitive souls in the West reacted not only to materialism but also to the forms and conventions of society. This often led them into deeper bondage. It caused them to revolt against themselves and to seek escape from both the world and themselves.

Aldous Huxley's conversion to Hinduism illustrates this contention. He confesses in *Ends and Means* that the second rebellion—against oneself—developed out of the first—against society. Huxley and his friends reacted against an unjust political and economic system but had nothing to put in its place. It was a revolt into meaninglessness. They rebelled against conventional sexual morality, but it only entangled them further in the material world which nauseated them. Professor Zaehner points out:

> Huxley's whole career . . . predisposed him to conversion to a type of religion that would provide him with a way of escape from a world into which he had found it so extraordinarily difficult to fit himself. He had, it seems, not been a happy man; and because he was both unhappy and introspective, he needed a philosophy or religion that would deliver him from both his unhappiness and himself.[25]

Naturally he turned to Hinduism and Buddhism—two great religions which in their classic form offer escape from the world and elimination of ego, a merging into the cosmic self.

Admittedly, not all modern Indian gurus preach escapism. But many do, and it has an attraction for many Westerners like Aldous Huxley, frustrated with both society and their own revolt against society.

Disillusionment with Barren Rationalism

The rationalistic search for truth that began with the Enlightenment did not bring a knowledge of truth. Immanuel Kant showed that beginning with reason alone one could never know the "noumenal" reality—reality as it is in itself. It was impossible then to know about God, the meaning of life, values, or morals.

Other philosophers realized that humans couldn't know anything for sure by reason. The big questions of life went unanswered: Who am I? What is the meaning and purpose of life? Is there a God? What are morals? As rationalism failed to provide credible answers to their questions, people began to give up rationalism and accept experiential philosophies like existentialism to find answers.

The existentialists such as Kierkegaard, Sartre, Jasper, and Heidegger became the intellectual gurus because they taught anti-intellectualism. But the experience they taught lacked sufficient mystique and authority. Their popularity is being superseded by that of the Indian gurus, who have greater tradition, mystique, and charisma.

Disillusionment with the rationalistic approach to knowledge and the search for an alternative method for obtaining truth form the basic philosophical impulse behind the rise and popularity of guruism. Many look upon the Indian gurus as a viable option and feel that they have found their answer.

Chapter Two

The Intellectual Impulses Behind Guruism

EPISTEMOLOGY DEALS WITH the theories of the method or ground of knowledge. It seeks to answer the questions: How do we know and how can we be sure that we know? Beginning with the ideas of Descartes and Locke, modern Western philosophy assumed the premise that humans could and had to know the truth by their own reasoning and empirical experience. This ruled out revelation or intuition as a valid means of obtaining knowledge. The British philosopher Berkeley indicated that by ourselves we can't even know that this book objectively exists.

How do we really know that other people or objects exist? Perhaps they are there only in our mind. The mystic, drunkard, and psychedelic drug user all "see" various things. Alone, one can only know that ideas of people and things exist in the mind. Starting with the rationalistic premise of modern philosophy, one can never know whether or not things actually exist objectively outside of the imagination. David Hume went further and showed that people can't even know if *they* exist. Hume argued that "when I go within myself, I do not find Mr. Hume there."[1] If we assume that knowledge must be attained through reasoning and empirical experience, then the only thing that can be known for sure is that ideas exist.

Many Western philosophers, until the logical positivists a few decades ago, did all sorts of intellectual acrobatics to get away from the conclusions of Berkeley and Hume. But with the presupposition that we have to attain knowledge by ourselves without revelation from God, no one has succeeded or can logically succeed in hiding from these conclusions. Not all philosophers face this problem squarely. Immanuel Kant made a dichotomy between noumenal (reality in itself) and phenomenal (reality as it appears, that which is open to sense verification). God, morals, values, and meaning lie in the realm of noumena, and phenomena consist of all that we can see, touch and feel. But Kant merely assumed without verification that things objectively exist.

Ludwig Wittgenstein followed Kant's dichotomy and argued that language is meaningful only in the sphere of phenomena. Realizing that one can't verbalize that which is unknown and unknowable, he then concluded that "whereof one cannot speak, thereof one must be silent." God, morals, values, and things that give meaning and purpose to life are in this realm of "silence." For Wittgenstein this was a mystical silence, but some of his followers, like A. J. Ayer, turned it into the silence of atheism. For Ayer no sentence about God or morals can have any meaning. A sentence like "God is good" is neither true nor false but is just meaningless "blah-blah." Os Guinness writes:

> This leaves the Western discussion of God with only two possibilities . . . the sheer silence of the atheist or the mere symbolism of the mystic. The latter is the virtual conclusion of much liberal theology. Theological language is not what God means about himself to man, but rather what man has made of meaning about God. It is symbolic truth, silence qualified by parables.[2]

So, whether you accept the radical conclusions of Berkeley and Hume (that you can't know anything) or the limited conclusion of Wittgenstein (that you cannot know anything about things that really matter—like values and meaning of life), you are still faced with the problem of the meaning of language.

If nothing can be known for sure, then what does language mean? If I can't correlate the word "book" with a particular book I'm familiar with or the word "God" with a Being who actually exists, then what do these words mean? Many conclude that they don't mean anything. Linguistic analysis, a recent fad in academic philosophy, finds that words only lead to words which lead to more words and never to reality. Words have no ultimate meaning. Silence alone is real. Indian gurus have been saying this for a long time. Swami Sivananda, the founder of Divine Life Society, writes:

> God or Brahman is Supreme Silence. Soul is Silence. Peace is Silence, or simply is God.[3]

Western thinkers have realized that beginning with the assumption that knowledge is to be attained by reason, we can't know anything, or at least anything that is in the realm of noumena. If we can't know a thing, we can't talk about it meaningfully. We are shut up in silence. Silence has therefore been a key word of recent Western thought. Ingmar Bergman made the famous movie, *Silence*. John Cage, the great chance musician, called his biography *Silence*. There have been plays, novels, lectures, discussions, and much talk about silence.

Many words have been spoken to communicate the meaning of silence.[4]

But humans can't be silent. The mark of personality is the ability to communicate knowledge in meaningful words. If we can't know the truth by reason, we try to find it through nonrational experience—by feelings or intuition. The youth revolution of the 1960s and 1970s which sought to build a counter-culture (a culture different from the Western mechanistic society) searched for truth through nonrational means.

Suzuki taught Zen Buddhism, Huxley added soma, and Leary advocated LSD as the means to knowledge. Others of the counterculture tried the occult, sex, and a "Jesus trip" in search of truth. Some almost accidentally met Mahesh Yogi, Bal Yogeshwar, Swami Prabhupada, and other gurus and Godmen. They thought they had now found techniques to transcend reason and know the truth through the mystical experiences which the gurus offered. The Indian gurus had temporarily filled the vacuum created by the epistemological crisis of the West. "Thou shalt not think" was a command common to all of them. They taught direct nonrational, irrational, or suprarational experience of truth.

Truth As Unreason: Indian History Revisited

The word *guru* is absent in the early Vedic literature. Early on those in India were trying to find the truth through reason and rational speculation. Consider this wonderful "Hymn of Creation" from the *Rig Veda*, its sophisticated speculation, philosophical doubt, and abstract thinking:

> Then even nothingness was not, nor existence.
> There was no air then, nor the heavens beyond it,
> What covered it? Where was it? In whose keeping?
> Was there then cosmic water, in depths unfathomed?
>
> Then there was neither death nor immortality,
> Nor was there then the torch or night and day.
> The One breathed windlessly and self-sustaining.
> There was that One then, and there was no other.
>
> At first there was only darkness wrapped in darkness.
> All this was only unillumined water.
> That one which came to be, enclosed in nothing,
> Arose at last, born of the power of heat.
>
> In the beginning desire descended on it—
> That was the primal seed, born of the mind,
> The sages who have searched their hearts with wisdom
> Know that which is kin to that which is not.
>
> And they have stretched their cord across the void,
> And know what was above, and what below.
> Seminal powers made fertile mighty forces.
> Below was strength and over it was impulse.
>
> But, after all, who knows, and who can say

Whence it all came, and how creation happened,
The gods themselves are later than creation,
So who knows truly whence it has arisen?

When all creation had its origin,
He, whether he fashioned it or whether he did not,
He, who surveys it all from highest heaven,
He knows—or may be even He does not know.[5]

This rational search ended in the despair of doubt. These thinkers realized that they couldn't know the truth through the intellect. As Swami Sivananda writes:

Everyone who has endeavoured to account for the empirical world has been confronted by ignorance at every step, and has been obliged to confess that human wit could go only so far and no further.[6]

Professor Basham writes:

Some teachers, like the Buddha, taught that speculation on first causes was a futile waste of time. There were out-and-out Pyrrhonists, denying the possibility of any certain knowledge at all, and materialists, who rejected the existence of the soul and all other immaterial entities, while some teachers proclaimed that the world was made of eternal atoms. The intellectual life of India in the seventh and sixth centuries B.C. was as vigorous and pullulating as the jungle after rains.[7]

Doubt about how to know the truth by reason alone led directly to the mystic silence. The silence of Buddha on metaphysical questions is well known.

When our ancestors realized that truth couldn't be known by reason, they too sought truth by nonrational experience. It is said of the sage Vasishtha that, unable to solve his spiritual problem by a rational samaya (proper) path, he went to Maha-China to learn the secrets of tantra. There he found people indulging in wine, meat, fish, dancing, and sexual orgies. It is claimed that the Lamas taught him the way to spiritual salvation through these secret indulgences. Besides sex, others tried soma, ganja, bhanga, as well as various crude or refined physical and mental exercises to seek mystic experience. What they found was considered the ultimate truth.

Those mystics who formulated metaphysical theories to explain and propagate their experiences became gurus. You can't ask whether their theories are true. You just believe and have faith. The guru is a "realized soul." He is on a transcendental plane, in touch with the infinite. He can serve lepers or feed his elephants chocolate or have sex with his male and female followers. But he can't be judged—he is God. Infallible. Inscrutable. You simply bow before the mystique!

The epistemological dilemma of those who want to discover the truth purely by their own efforts is that if they begin by reason, they end up with knowledge but also with doubt. The guru offers an escape. He teaches a nonrational way to a knowledge of truth. How do you know whether it is true? You don't.

Obviously this is unsatisfactory because reason is the distinguishing gift of our species. How can we blindly believe and commit intellectual suicide? Is nonrational mysticism the only alternative to barren rationalism?

Not exactly. Even though most gurus preach nonrational mysticism, some gurus teach a third possibility, that of divine revelation. If there is a Creator, couldn't He reveal the truth to us? Generally, revelation is considered to be propositional in the case of words of scriptures or personal in the sense of incarnation. Often mystical experience is called "divine revelation" as well.

But mystical experience is nonrational and subjective, whereas revelation is rational and objective, something which all can read and understand. Mystical experience is often the result of human effort and not divine initiative. In it one may experience the divine, but it is also possible to mistake an experience of nature, of the "collective unconscious," of one's own subconscious, or of the devil for an experience of God.

Once we assume that the knowledge of truth can't be obtained by an objective study of natural phenomena, but that truth can only be known by a subjective exploration of one's own mind, then the next logical step is to believe that consciousness is the only reality. It alone can be known through this methodology. What then is the external world? Either it is considered outright maya (illusion) or explained as the transformation of consciousness, which transforms itself as energy and then becomes matter and then life.

Consciousness becomes the ultimate reality, and all the diverse things that we perceive are seen as one and the same. This is monism: the belief that consciousness is identical with God. When it is said that everything is one and that it is all divine, this is pantheism.

But monism and pantheism are by no means simply logical deductions based on mystical epistemology. When humans go within their consciousness, whether through meditation techniques or with the help of drugs, they often experience an extraordinary perception of the oneness of all things. Describing his experience of intoxication through nitrous oxide, William James wrote:

> One conclusion was forced upon my mind at that time, and my impression of its truth has ever remained unshaken. It is that our normal waking consciousness, rational consciousness as we call it, is but one special type of consciousness, whilst all about it, parted from it by the filmiest of screens, there lie potential forms of consciousness entirely different. We may go through life without suspecting their existence; but apply the requisite stimulus, and at a touch they are all there in all their completeness. . . . Looking back on my own experiences, they all converge towards a kind of insight to which I cannot help ascribing some metaphysical significance. The keynote of it is invariably a reconciliation. It is as if the opposites of the world, whose contradictoriness and conflict make all our difficulties and troubles, were melted into unity.[8]

This inner experience of "unity" is the basis of the teaching of most gurus. However, there are many other factors in the intellectual climate of our day that have prepared humanity to receive the teachings of the religious gurus with unprecedented enthusiasm.

Foundations of Modern Science

Modern science began in the cultural milieu of Christianity. The fathers of modern science, such as Francis Bacon, Galileo, Faraday, and Newton all had a Christian worldview. They believed that there was a reasonable God who had created a reasonable universe. Therefore, they used their reason to find out the nature and laws of the material universe, since they took both the supernatural and the natural world as real. Their high view of created material reality and its reasonableness propelled them into scientific inquiry. Many have pointed out that the intellectual giants of ancient India and Greece couldn't have produced modern science because they lacked this view of physical reality.

During the last two centuries, along with the slow erosion of the Christian faith in the West, modern science has changed its presuppositions and become what Francis Schaeffer has called "modern modern science"—a secular, naturalistic science. The empirical methodology was absolutized, and it began to be thought that whatever could not be known by the methods of physical science could not be real. Therefore God couldn't exist. The material universe alone was deemed real and ultimately eternal. Because the world acts according to definite laws, it is a machine. Man has evolved from matter, and therefore he too is a machine. This naturalistic and mechanistic worldview is being seriously questioned and challenged in our day. The famous psychoanalyst R. D. Laing calls the mechanistic view of man "crazy." In *The Divided Self,* Laing writes of

> people who experience themselves as automata, as robots, as bits of machinery, or even as animals. Such persons are rightly regarded crazy. Yet why do we not regard a theory that seeks to transmute persons into automata or animals as equally crazy? The experience of oneself and others as persons is primary and self-validating. It exists prior to the scientific or philosophical difficulties about how such experience is possible or how it is to be explained.[9]

As more thinkers are rejecting the mechanistic worldview, they are turning to mysticism. Guruism has adapted well to this climate. Current Western speculation in physics, biology, psychology, parapsychology, and ecology give evidence of this trend towards mysticism.

From Physics to Monism, Idealism, and Irrationalism

Matter is no longer the solid substance it was for the nineteenth century scientist. It has dissolved into energy, something which is not known by itself but only by its effect. One form of energy can be converted into another (heat into light), which suggests that energy may be only one.

Some monists have indeed asserted that energy is one and that its ultimate nature is consciousness. All things, according to them, are but different aspects or manifestations of a single consciousness. This gives apparent solutions to some riddles in biology, and it also seems to solve the mind-body problem. If we accept the dualistic position that mind and body are two qualitatively distinct entities, then the problem is: How and why do they relate? No naturalistic philosophers seem to have any satisfactory answers. Many have said that these are not two but one and the same.

The most prevalent opinion until recently has been that mind or consciousness is simply a function of the brain—the product of the combination of physiochemical properties in our head. But this explanation has been found inadequate. Wilder Penfield, in his paper for the International Congress of Brain Researchers (held at the Vatican in 1966), said:

> If we are good scientists we cannot claim that science has already explained the mind. . . .[10]

C. H. Waddington wrote in *The Nature of Life:*

> [W]e have not the faintest idea what this awareness [consciousness] means.[11]

Sir Charles Sherrington, the father of modern neurophysiology, didn't think the mind was simply a function of the brain. In his classic *Man on His Nature,* he confesses that he is baffled by the way the mind acts on matter and vice-versa:

> Mind for anything perception can compass, goes therefore in our spatial world more ghostly than a ghost. Invincible, intangible, it is a thing not even of outline; it is not a "thing." It remains without sensual confirmation and remains forever.[12]

If the dualism of mind and matter is unacceptable and the reduction of mind to brain impossible, then can the brain be explained as mind? This is what some scientists are now attempting to do. The physicist Erwin Schrodinger, Nobel Prize winner for the discovery of wave mechanics, writes in his book *My View of the World,* which he confesses to be derived from Vedanta:

> The external world and consciousness are one and the same thing. In abandoning the dualism of thought and existence, or mind and matter, the condition for our doing so is that we think of *everything* that happens as taking place in our *experience* of the world, without ascribing to it any material substratum as the object of *which* it is an experience.[13]

If scientists said earlier that "there is no mind, only body," scientists like Schrodinger are now saying that "there is no body, only mind." In *Mind and Matter* he writes:

> [S]ubject and object are only one. . . . The reason why our sentient, percipient, and thinking ego is met nowhere within our scientific world picture can easily be indicated in seven words: because it is itself that world picture. It is identical with the whole.[14]

The *Advaita Vedanta* of course teaches this, and gurus proudly claim that their teaching is in line with modern physics.

Some physicists like Heisenberg and others who accept the Quantum Theory, though, have made randomness instead of reason ultimate in the universe. Moreover, the old conception of three-dimensional space passing simultaneously moment by moment through time has been given up. It is no longer considered an adequate explanation in the light of more recent speculations. "Time" has now become a mystery having within it an ingredient of space. The universe is now being viewed as a "four-dimensional space-time continuum," a continuum being defined as a series of component parts passing into one another. Scientists today don't consider this impossible, but because of the difficulty of conceiving this rationally, some have begun to doubt whether the natural world is, in its deepest recesses, rational or understandable beyond a certain point.

The gurus have asserted that truth can't be known through the lower faculty of reason. Truth, according to them, is irrational or suprarational. The gurus also claim a willingness to teach techniques for intuitive knowledge, and many men of science are now prepared to try these methods out.

From Biology to Mysticism

Once the belief in creation by a personal God is given up, then one or another form of materialistic evolution is accepted as the only plausible alternative. Until recently it was imagined that matter was the ultimate reality, and in higher animals a complex arrangement of molecules had resulted in consciousness. Now the opposite is being suggested as more probable—that consciousness has been controlling or directing the evolutionary process from the very beginning. It is argued that in the process of evolution there has been a steady increase in interiorization—an enlargement of the psyche or consciousness. Organisms become more vital and conscious as they become more complex. From this observation it is supposed that in every particle, however simple, there exists a psyche or consciousness in an embryonic, undeveloped form.

The psyche becomes more and more predominant as evolution proceeds. This is the "pattern of organization" inherent in the whole evolutionary process, the dynamic urge—whatever its origin—impelling the organism to develop in certain directions. This shift can easily lead to mysticism, as evidenced in the writings of Pierre Teilhard de Chardin. Since the process of "interiorization," or development of consciousness, is the fundamental principle of evolution, the next step in the process would be achievement of a still higher or spiritual consciousness of which the mystics are forerunners. This is exactly what Sri Aurobindo Ghose taught in India, and some of the present gurus, like Maharishi Mahesh Yogi, are attracting Westerners by teaching the techniques of attaining "higher" forms of consciousness in order to evolve further.

From Psychology to Vedanta

Many leading psychologists and psychotherapists have also been led in the direction of mysticism in recent decades in their search for adequate theories for their practice.

If behaviorists like B. F. Skinner have had to reduce humanity to the level of a machine due to their commitment to a quasi-biological creed, psychotherapists like Jung and Fromm have tended to turn to mystic views in attempts to understand consciousness. Dr. Carl Jung, who has been described by Christmas Humphreys as "building a bridge between essentially Chinese thought and Western psychology," writes:

> The psychotherapist, however, who is seriously concerned with the question of the aims of his therapy cannot be unmoved when he sees what ultimate result an oriental method of spiritual "healing"—i.e., "making whole"—is striving for. It is a well known fact that this problem has been seriously occupying the most venturesome minds of the East for more than two thousand years, and that in this respect methods and philosophical doctrines have been developed which simply put all Western attempts in the same line into the shade.[15]

The problem before a psychotherapist is: What am I seeking to do with the patient? If the therapist answers that he is helping the patient to become a normal person, then the questions arise: Who is normal, and what does normality require? Christianity teaches that there is a personal God who has created humans in His own image—as a personal being—and revealed our nature in the Bible. If this is given up, then we have to find out who we are by ourselves and decide what a normal person is. If we also reject Skinner's notion that humans are machines (which is a logical implication of materialistic science) and that the normal person is one who fits in well with society, then we are left with little choice. Could it be that the Eastern Hindu-Buddhist ideas of man and his healing are right? If a great psychologist like Jung has opened the door to reveal this, many others have stepped in through the door by faith. The guru for some has become an Eastern substitute for a psychoanalyst. Dr. J. S. Neki, head of the psychiatric department of the All-India Institute of Medical Sciences, argues in a paper that

> a personality revolution often underlies those religious transformations in which an autocentric personality organization gets suddenly transmuted into a theocentric organization. . . . The guru is considered to be the prime alchemist of the soul who brings about this great mental and personality change.[16]

Gerald Sykes writes in *What Vedanta Means to Me* that one of the things that attracted him to Vedanta was the discovery that many of the Western psychological theories were reflections of Upanishadic concepts.

From Parapsychology to Gurus

Experiments by Dr. J. B. Rhine and others in the field of parapsychology have convinced many of our agnostic generation that humans indeed possess some psychic powers of extrasensory perception and action, which are developed to a greater extent in some than in others. Many yogis in India have claimed extraordinary siddhis, through which they can accomplish supernatural feats. Gurus like Sri Sathya Sai Baba and Bhagavan Neel Kanth Thataji claim to perform miracles today. This has attracted much attention to guruism. Some people are simply drawn by curiosity; others actually seek similar powers and are willing to stay in ashrams and to work hard for "higher spiritual attainments."

I met Michael, son of a Presbyterian clergyman from New Zealand, in an ashram at Rishikesh. He told me that he had been disillusioned with materialism even when he was young and realized vaguely that the mechanistic worldview must be wrong because it didn't explain parapsychological phenomena such as telepathy, telekinesis, astral travels, horoscopes, and astrology. He believed in these things intuitively and read about them. He heard of the Theosophical Society and of Sai Baba and came to seek explanations for these things in the ancient wisdom of India.

From Ecology to Pantheism

Because of its greed and ecological ignorance, the industrial society of the West has exploited and raped nature. Many thinkers such as Aldous Huxley have argued that this has happened because we have so far considered humanity to be distinct from and superior to nature. Such a view naturally leads us to exploit nature. One answer to this exploitation is pantheism. It is hoped that if we begin to think of ourselves as one with nature, we might treat nature with respect. "Elementary ecology leads straight to elementary Buddhism," writes Huxley.[17]

Chapter Three

Criterion for Evaluating Gurus

HOW CAN WE know if the claims and teachings of a guru are true? Do gurus have valid answers to our aspirations? As I visited several ashrams, talked to many gurus, and read many of their books, I noticed that the universal lack of any reasonable criterion for evaluation became very apparent.

Most of the gurus and their followers claim that their experience is self-validating and that this justifies their faith. They claim that truth can't be known through reason. Potential devotees allegedly need to drop all doubts and practice the technique of meditation prescribed by the gurus in order to know if their teachings are true: they will then experience the truth of their teachings directly.

The followers of the Divine Light Mission insist that they have seen the Divine Light within them and do not need any further proof that their guru is the "perfect master." Radhasaomis "see" the visions described by their master, and they even "see" him in his radiant form while meditating. Therefore, they "know" his teachings are true. Mahesh Yogi and Rajneesh offer instant experiences of transcendental consciousness and claim that anyone can know the truth of their teaching through direct experience.

No one is denying that mystical experiences are usually so vivid that they carry their own authority; a person who has experienced them rarely doubts their genuineness. Just as we insist that what we have perceived with our senses is true, so mystics insist that what they have perceived with intuition is true. In fact, Professor Zaehner writes that beside the mystical experience

the ordinary world of sense experience seems pathetically unreal. . . . [T]hese experiences which sound so ridiculous when transferred to a printed page always leave one with an impression of greater reality than anything supplied by ordinary sense perception.[1]

William James, also reflecting on his own experience, wrote:

> Looking back on my own experiences, they all converge towards a kind of insight to which I cannot help ascribing some metaphysical significance.[2]

However, even though it is true that mystical experiences are often vivid and transforming, it doesn't follow that the interpretations given to these experiences are also true. People may think that they are experiencing God when instead they may be experiencing the unity of nature or of their souls, or they may have altered their consciousness through drugs, or they may have become lunatics. There is no lack of examples of people who have come out of a "mystical experience of God" but in a saner moment denounced it either as self-deception or a lie.

The great Jewish philosopher Martin Buber records how he mistook the experience of the unity of his soul for an experience of unity with God. He writes:

> Now from my own unforgettable experience I know well that there is a state in which the bonds of the personal nature of life seem to have fallen away from us and we experience an undivided unity. But I do not know what the soul willingly imagines and indeed is bound to imagine (mine too once did it)—that in this I had attained to a union with the primal being or the godhead. . . . Nevertheless, in the honest and sober account of the responsible understanding this unity is nothing but the unity of this soul of mine, whose "ground" I have reached, so much so . . . that my spirit has no choice but to understand it as the groundless.[3]

The famous French poet and mystic Arthur Rimbaud yearned for God so deeply that he exclaimed, "I wait on God like a glutton." In his mystic experiences his "gluttony" seemed to be satisfied, and he said, "God constitutes my force, and I praise God."[4] But later he realized that what he had experienced was not God but nature. He recants by saying, "At last I shall ask to be forgiven for having fed myself on lies."[5]

The case of John Custance is more interesting. He often suffered from acute mania and was a certified lunatic. During the manic stages he had many experiences which seemed to him a "great deal more real than the majority of things that pass for fact in everyday life." Professor Zaehner writes that

> Custance has an uneasy conviction that during his manic periods he obtains a more profound insight into reality than he does when he is merely sane; and this is the common experience of all Nature mystics.[6]

What did he experience? In *Wisdom, Madness and Folly: The Philosophy of a Lunatic,* Custance writes:

> I feel so close to God, so inspired by His Spirit that in a sense I am God. I

see the future, plan the universe, save mankind; I am utterly and completely immortal; I am even male and female. The whole Universe, animate and inanimate, past, present and future, is within me. All nature and life, all spirits, are co-operating and connected with me; all things are possible. I am in a sense identical with all spirits from God to Satan. I reconcile Good and Evil and create light, darkness, worlds, universes.[7]

Many Indian gurus might well make a statement like this today. And if Custance had claimed these things in India, he would certainly have been worshiped as God. However, he realized that even though this experience of divinity seemed so real and self-validating to him, it was not true. Later he wrote:

Of course, it is all a dream, a vision, pure imagination. . . . I know perfectly well in fact that I have no power, that I am of no particular importance and have made rather a mess of my life. I am a very ordinary man and a miserable sinner.[8]

These illustrations show that however intense an experience may be, it still doesn't prove the reliability of any particular philosophy or religion. Abu Hamid al-Ghazili, the great Muslim mystic and theologian, compares mystic ecstasy with drunkenness:

When the mystics reached the heavens of reality, they no longer had the capacity to recollect aught but God, nor could they in any wise remember themselves. Nothing was left to them but God. They became drunk with a drunkenness in which their reason collapsed. One of them said, "I am God (the Truth)." Another said, "Glory be to me! How great is my glory," while another said, "Within my robe is naught but God." But the words of lovers when in a state of drunkenness must be hidden away and not broadcast. However, when their drunkenness abates and the sovereignty of their reason is restored—and reason is God's scale on earth—they know that this was not actual identity, but that it resembled identity as when lovers say at the height of their passion: I am he whom I desire and he whom I desire is I; we are two souls inhabiting one body.[9]

Here in a mystic's own words—"reason is God's scale on earth"—we have the basis for formulating a criterion. In order to see how reason can be used in evaluating a guru's religious teachings, we need to ask some fundamental questions such as, What is religion, why are we drawn to it, and when is a religion true?

A guru preaches a particular message. Some people are convinced that what's said is true. They also take initiation, practice the technique or discipline taught, join the flock, and try to mold their lives according to this technique. These four elements, which seem to be true for all religions, can also be discerned in modern guruism:

(a) Gurus teach something definite about God or the ultimate reality. God may be a personal spirit, an impersonal consciousness, light, or sound. Something is taught about the origin, nature, and destiny of the universe and of the individual.

They teach some way or technique to help humans reach their destiny. There is a definite teaching, doctrine, philosophy, theology, or worldview which forms the theoretical basis of the religion proclaimed by a guru.

(b) In regard to this philosophical system, an experience is taught by the guru and sought by the disciple. The guru may assure seekers that they don't have to believe any doctrines before they can experience the truth; it is possible for a skeptic to experience first and believe later. Nevertheless, philosophical presuppositions determine and justify the nature of religious experience. The sects that believe that God is light in fact claim that through the practice of proper technique you can see this light. In the sects that teach that the self or God is Pure Consciousness, you are invited to experience this consciousness. In Christianity, because you are distinct from God and an alienated sinner, the religious experience consists of being forgiven and reconciled to God. In any case, the experience is derived from and justified by the underlying philosophy or theology.

(c) Besides the philosophical system and religious experience, an additional factor in religion is fellowship with believers. The devotee joins a social group (satsang) with its own structure, rules, and hierarchy of authority.

(d) The final essential ingredient in religion is a characteristic lifestyle that results from its presuppositions, values, morals, and social codes. The devotee may or may not become a vegetarian, may pray or meditate, may become permissive in sexual behavior or instead be celibate.

At the root of religion is a definite system of thought. Religious experience, fellowship, and lifestyle are derived from this base and are justified in the light of it. The nature of experience and moral codes differs in different sects because of the basic distinctions in worldviews. Therefore, while asking which religion or guru is true, we can't legitimately ask which religious experience or ethic is true or which guru has the most charisma or the greatest following. We have to ask which worldview is true. If we can determine that a particular worldview can't be true, it follows that the guru who teaches it is not true, nor is the religious experience derived from it a real experience of God. If humanity isn't sinful, then the experience of forgiveness of sin can't be true. Or if God is silence and not sound, then the experience of hearing the divine sound can't be an experience of God, even though one may actually hear something.

This is not to imply that those who hold the view that God is sound have not experienced anything; we can accept their testimony that they have heard a sound, but their interpretation of the experience—that this sound is divine—obviously can't be accepted. We have to reinterpret it in light of a worldview which is true.

In the modern climate of total relativism, there are many who wonder if any worldview can be called true: Don't all religions have some truth and falsehood? This itself is essentially a matter of presuppositions. If we suppose that all religions are man-made, then we have to assume that they are all a mixture of truth and falsehood. But if a religion is actually revealed by God, then it can be and has to be true.

Every religion has a distinct philosophy, though some religions prefer to call it theology. But all philosophical systems are not religions. A philosophy becomes a religion when it ceases to be merely an abstract system of thought, claims to be true, and demands that we live by its precepts and implications. As Swami Krishnananda says, "philosophy is the rationale behind religion. Philosophy and religion are inseparable."[10] Or as Swami Chinmayananda writes:

> Philosophy is the theoretical aspect of religion which, with scientific and rational analysis, elucidates the why and the wherefore of life and the universe and contains a coherent system of thought for interpreting Reality.[11]

An atheistic worldview, for instance, can become religious if people accept it as true, derive their values from it, and seek to live by it. This again indicates that in examining whether something is true, we must examine whether its philosophical or theological basis is credible.

The Need for Religion

Why does humanity need religion? That we have always wanted religion and want it today is indisputable. But why? If we answer this question adequately, we have a means for evaluation. That religion would be true which truly fulfills our needs.

As children grow, they experience people and things. In this encounter, they develop self-consciousness. Soon they begin to ask, Why do things exist? How did I come about? Why? What is the meaning of life? What is the origin and destiny of the universe? Why the contrast between good and evil, joy and sorrow, birth and death, beauty and ugliness? Are some things to be preferred over others? Which? How can I choose?

Parents, family members, and older friends answer these questions. Children accept these answers. If the answers do not seem to fit the question, the child challenges them. Usually children are subdued by social pressures, but at times they muster enough courage to seek more satisfying answers. If no given answers seem satisfactory, they decide to think on their own. Whatever system they finally decide to live by becomes their religious worldview.

This is admittedly a simplistic analysis of our religious impulse. Longings for forgiveness of sin and for immortality, the emotional need for security in someone stronger, the moral need for judging between right and wrong, the ultimate aesthetic need for adoring and worshiping someone absolutely perfect in goodness and beauty, the social needs for a family and culture—these play a part and influence choices. But the intellectual quest, one for meaning and for a worldview, seems to be the most basic, even though it may remain subconscious in many religious seekers. One can't realistically deny its existence.

The Freudian analysis that our need for religion is based on a need for a father-figure as a shelter and comfort is superficial. It is often used to destroy the claim that a religion is true, but it neither adequately explains the religious impulse nor destroys its claim to be true. I may think about a girlfriend and derive much satisfaction from the thinking. The fact that this is psychologically satisfying to me does not rule out my actually having a girlfriend. Likewise, the fact that the contemplation of God as Father gives me comfort doesn't automatically rule out the possibility that He may be there.

Such a psychological analysis of religion fails to explain the religious impulse because at best it can only explain the impulse behind the Christian faith, which views God as a loving, caring Father. What about religions which believe in an impersonal God or no God at all? But actually, the father-figure idea does not even explain a Christian's faith. If this analysis were true, it would follow that Christians would be the most insecure people. But most Christians have almost always been examples of great courage and boldness, unafraid even of death.

Like the psychological analysis, the sociological ones, which attempt to explain religions as sociological cement or opium are also invalid. They often propose that the elite of society preach religion as a tool for maintaining the status quo. No doubt religion is often patronized by the elite and misused to manipulate the masses. But far from maintaining the status quo, religious innovations have always been instruments of radical change. Many of the major historical religions such as Judaism, Christianity, and Sikhism started as daring political movements for justice. A short-term sociopolitical movement, when guided and inspired by eternal values, often becomes a long-term religion.

Far from providing opium, saints have often stood for truth and justice even at great cost. They have shown a passion for humanity. Their zeal has been fired by a knowledge of truth. This is not to deny that some of the present gurus have a zeal for religion. But even a superficial glance at the religious history of the world makes it clear that the impulse behind religion is the same as that behind philosophy except that it goes beyond philosophy and involves a commitment of the whole being to an intellectual system of thought and program for action.

So we desire religion because we need to have an intellectually satisfying worldview to help us combat the struggles of life. It is like this: when you step out of the railway station in New Delhi for the first time and want to go around sightseeing, you need a guidebook and a map that give a bird's-eye view of the whole city. So also people who find themselves in the world and don't know what it is all about want a guidebook and a map to help them make sense of life and to live it meaningfully. Just as only that person who knows the whole of Delhi can write a guidebook, draw a map, or become a guide, so also only that person who knows the whole of life and reality can give a worldview, draw a map of reality, and become a guide or guru.[12]

When Is Religion True?

A map of Delhi may be fairly accurate, but if it is contradicted by the reality of Delhi at any point, we call it inaccurate. A map will never be exhaustive in its description, but it must be true in what it does describe.

Let us pose a problem: Why is there food scarcity in India?

If someone suggested that our food problem came from the fact that we are an agricultural country, we would likely scratch our heads. It is true that we are an agricultural country, yet the statement doesn't make sense. Why should an agricultural country lack food? It is self-contradictory. The hypothesis can't be true. Swami Vidyavanya, the great philosopher-saint of ancient India, said that "truth is that which stands the test of the principle of non-contradiction."

Suppose a second person suggests that we lack food because we waste a great deal, and a third says that we lack food because we produce too little. Both the theories seem plausible. To determine which one is actually true, we would have to do a factual survey. The theory which is true to life, which corresponds to the reality of India, would be the true one.

Because worldviews are theories—either humanly conceived or revealed by God[13]—that attempt to answer basic questions about life and the cosmos and seek to give a map of the totality of reality in which we have to live, it would seem that for a religious worldview to be true, we must be able to understand every question of life and reality within its presuppositions as well as be able to live by it. The worldview must be true in all that it affirms. This doesn't rule out the possibility of mystery in a given worldview. If a system presupposes that truth comes to us through a revelation from God, it could consistently hold that some questions can't be answered because God has not revealed their answers to us. But in order to be acceptable, the area of mystery will have to be consistent with the rest of the revelation.

Some will object that this criterion is too rational, whereas religion is suprarational. Indeed, religious experience can be mystical or personal and therefore transrational. But all worldviews are rational in nature even if they attack reason; their defenders must have the courage to face rational inquiry. Aldous Huxley, comparing science with religion in *What Vedanta Means to Me*, states clearly:

> Research by means of controlled sense-intuitions into material reality—research motivated and guided by a working hypothesis, leading up through logical inference to the formulation of a rational theory and resulting in appropriate technological action. That is natural science.
>
> No working hypothesis means no motive for starting the research, no reason

for making one experiment rather than another, no rational theory for bringing sense or order to the observed facts. . . .

Among other things, religion is also research. Research by means of pure intellectual intuition into non-sensuous, non-psychic, purely spiritual reality, descending to rational theories about its result and appropriate moral action in the light of such theories.

To motivate and (in its preliminary stages) guide this research what sort and how much of a working hypothesis do we need? . . .

For . . . us . . . the minimum working hypothesis would seem to be about as follows:

That there is a Godhead or Ground, which is the unmanifested principle of all manifestation.

That the Ground is transcendent and immanent.

That it is possible for human beings to love, know, and . . . to become actually identified with the Ground.

That to achieve this unitive knowledge, to realize this supreme identity, is the final end and purpose of human existence.

That there is a Law or Dharma, which must be obeyed, a Tao or Way, which must be followed if men are to achieve their final end.[14]

Huxley admits that this summary of Vedanta is certainly a rational hypothesis. It is open to evaluation. If this experience of unity is beyond the reach of reason, it will have to be reinterpreted if the hypothesis which justifies the experience is unacceptable.

The secular worldview, for instance, which has been the predominant international "religion" of recent decades, has asserted that there is no God or supernatural reality. Matter or energy is all that there is. All life has evolved out of matter, purely by chance. The whole universe, including humanity, is a machine. We have no soul; consequently there is nothing like free will: we are totally programmed, either chemically or psychologically.

This worldview is self-consistent in its main outline. But because it presupposes that the ultimate reality is impersonal energy, it fails to explain how and why personality has emerged out of impersonality, consciousness out of unconscious matter. To be consistent, the naturalists have to say that we are a machine; personality, freedom, love, meaning, beauty, morals, sin, and guilt are illusory, meaningless concepts. They explain these problems by explaining them away, but naturalists can't live with this view as though they have no personality. They crave the things their philosophy denies.

If the universe has come about by random chance, what is beauty? Why is an evergreen tree or a flower beautiful? The naturalist has to say that these things are not beautiful in themselves, because in an impersonal universe the concept of beauty doesn't make sense. We perceive them as beautiful; it is our thinking that makes them beautiful. Naturalists have to deny aesthetic value and give a utilitarian explanation. They have to convince themselves that during the process of evolution plants knew that millions of years later there would be insects flying around, so the plants developed flowers in advance to attract insects. Or perhaps when insects appeared, the plants thought they should develop flowers to attract insects for the purpose of cross-pollination.

Even if naturalists can manage to satisfy themselves intellectually by explaining away beauty as something which is not in the universe but only in the imagination, they still can't live with this theory. They still look for a "beautiful" spouse when considering marriage or a "beautiful" painting when considering means of decorating a home.

Considering the question of love, a naturalist is usually forced by the logic of these impersonal premises to conclude that love is only a blind encounter of atoms or a psychologically determined emotion. But aspirations for love mock this philosophy. The French philosopher Diderot wrote to his beloved Sophia Volland, "I am furious in being entangled in a confounded philosophy which my mind cannot refrain from approving and my heart from denying." Freud, who explained away love because of his psychological determinism, wrote to his fiancee, "When you come, love me irrationally, dear."

Both Bertrand Russell and Jean Paul Sartre, considering their naturalistic premise, were forced to conclude that the universe is amoral. Nothing is intrinsically good or bad, right or wrong. Yet Sartre was one of the first to condemn the Algerian War, and Russell kept making moral judgments in connection with his campaigns for nuclear disarmament. He also believed, practiced, and taught that adultery was not immoral, but when his first wife sought to live by his teachings, he divorced her.

The naturalistic worldview fails to explain many vital areas of our being and experience and also fails to give a philosophy for living. Naturalists themselves can't live by its code. It fails to pass the second and third conditions of our criterion. Its impersonal presupposition doesn't square with the reality which we know to be both personal, moral, and aesthetic—as well as impersonal and mechanistic. The naturalistic map of reality is false because it neither correlates correctly with the reality of life nor guides us in the personal dimensions of life.

PART II

THE TRADITIONAL GURUS

TO PUT VARIOUS Hindu gurus into neatly defined categories has to be somewhat of an arbitrary process. Each guru is unique.

"Traditional" gurus are those whose teachings and practices have long traditions in classical Hinduism. Shaivism and Vaishnavism are the two chief sects of traditional religious Hinduism. The former offers the highest worship to Shiva, whereas the latter reserves it for Vishnu and his incarnations such as Rama and Krishna. Philosophically, orthodox Hindus fall into three broad categories: Advaitins—who, following Shankaracharya, believe in non-dualism or absolute monism; Vishishtadvaitins—who, following Ramanuja, believe in some form of qualified monism; and Dwaitins, who follow Madhava's dualism.

Partners in these movements are the Divine Life Society, Chinmaya Mission, and Hare Krishna. The first two are Shaivite and monistic sects and are stronger in India. The third is a dualistic (bhed-abhed) Vaishnavite sect with a stronger base in the West.

All three movements are traditional in that they accept authority of the scriptures and teach idol worship and guru worship. The first two identify the guru with God but don't make idolatry and guru worship compulsory. Hare Krishna categorically rejects that the guru is God, but it makes both guru worship and idolatry compulsory.

Chapter Four

The Divine Life Society and Chinmaya Mission

THE FOUNDER OF the Divine Life Society, Kuppuswamy Iyer, who upon initiation became Swami Sivananda Saraswati, was born on September 8, 1887, in Tamil Nadu, in a religious home. He graduated from the medical college at Tanjore and started his private practice at Trichy.

After his father's death in 1913, he went over to Malaya and spent ten years as a doctor in charge of a hospital at a large rubber estate. He treated the poor free of charge, yet earned enough to live a very affluent life. It was a book given him by a wandering sadhu that started him on a spiritual quest. He began studying various Hindu scriptures and religious books as well as the Bible and *The Imitation of Christ*. In 1923 he resigned from the hospital, renounced the world, and returned to India. The change in his lifestyle was dramatic. Giving away all his riches, he chose poverty. He spent one year visiting holy shrines, sleeping on the ground, and eating wild berries. Towards the end of that year he reached Rishikesh. He spent the first few weeks under the porch of an inn. It was in Rishikesh that Swami Viswananda Saraswati, a noted guru, initiated Kuppuswamy into the Sannyasa order.

After initiation, Kuppuswamy, now Swami Sivananda, travelled across the river to Swargashram and made his abode in a dilapidated, scorpion-infested hut. There he began practicing extreme austerities and meditation. Along with these he slowly resumed his practice of medicine, visiting sick sadhus and pilgrims. In 1927 he started a charitable dispensary with some money from an insurance policy. He looked upon his service as worship. After many years of intense sadhana, he reached his goal of self-realization or nirvikalpa samadhi (the thoughtless superconscious state).

Many visitors had started coming to Swami Sivananda for spiritual counsel at Swargashram. Because people told him that they had benefited by his advice, he decided to write out many of his answers for wider circulation. Thus came his first booklet "Brahm-Vidya," on the knowledge of God. Those who found it helpful urged him to write more and undertook to bear the cost.

As he became known, several opportunities arose for lecture tours. He especially liked to conduct the religious group singing known as Sankirtana. In 1932 he returned to Rishikesh and founded the Sivananda ashram. It started with an abandoned cowshed, but as the number of disciples grew so did the accommodation. The Divine Life Society was formed in 1937; now it has about three hundred branches around the world. The society has developed a thriving preaching, publishing, and medical program. The impulses behind Sivananda's spirituality, which become obvious as one reads his books, seem to provide the motivation for many gurus and their followers who stand in his tradition. The first thing that strikes readers forcefully is Sivananda's pessimistic view of life. Life to him is "ignorance, pain, and misery." It is not worth having a positive attitude towards life because "a mustard seed of pleasure is mixed with a mountain of pain."[1] Hating the supposed joys of this life, Sivananda is especially an enemy of sex:

> Sex-pleasure is the most devitalizing and demoralizing of pleasures. Sexual-pleasure is no pleasure at all. It is a mental delusion. It is false, utterly worthless, and extremely harmful.[2]

He mocks at the foolishness of men:

> You know that the body of a woman is made up of all sorts of impurities, flesh, bone, urine, and fecal matter, and yet you rejoice in embracing her.[3]

The whole world to him "is nothing but sex and ego,"[4] which he hates and wants to flee.

Escape describes the impulse behind his spirituality. He is what William James calls the "sick soul" who longs to escape from both self and environment. The aim is to transcend the very consciousness of the world and self. This attitude becomes alarming when he recommends to his followers that they should "never, never join those offices which are amenable to corruption."[5] Among these he lists the police officer, advocate, and businessman.

He longs for escape from the self and from the world because he is looking for a utopia. He is seeking perfection, infinite bliss, and immortality—none of which will have even a trace of pain in them. And because this can't be attained in this present world or life, he wants release.

With his sacrificial spirit, his combination of preaching with medical service, and his wide scholarship and authoritative eloquence and writing, Sivananda laid a strong foundation for the Divine Life Society. After his death on July 14, 1963, the leadership passed into the able hands of Swami Chidananda. The credit for the rapid spread of the Society in the West goes to him.

Few gurus have impressed me with their sincerity and humility as did Swami Chidananda. He was born in the affluent home of a landowner in South India on September 24, 1916, and was named Sridhar Rao. Deeply interested in the Hindu scriptures from an early age, he decided to become a rishi. His education in Christian schools and particularly in Loyola College, Madras, provided opportunity to study Christianity. The life of Christ, the apostles, and Christian saints made a great impression on his gentle personality. Like Jesus, he took great interest in the sick. On the vast lawns of his home he built huts for lepers and attended them personally. His compassion reached out to sick animals as well. The teachings of Sri Ramakrishna, Swami Vivekananda, and Swami Sivananda were most influential in determining his faith and life. Leaving home in 1943, he became a member of Sivananda Ashram. Soon he was initiated into the order of Sannyasa. Sridhar Rao became Swami Chidananda ("one who is in the highest consciousness of bliss").

His foreign tours began in 1959. Since then he has been to most of the main cities of India, Asia, Europe, South Africa, Australia, and North and South America.

After Swami Chidananda became the President of the Divine Life Society, Swami Krishnananda was made General Secretary. Author of many books, Krishnananda is greatly respected for his scholarship within and outside the ashram.

The ashram continues to draw many foreigners and Indians (mainly from the South), even though it already shows all the problems of a large organization—a lack of discipline and spiritual fervor. Of the three hundred residents, only five to ten were attending lectures, and only about fifty gathered for the satsang during our stay. Intellectually, it is one of the most respected ashrams in that area. Even in mundane things like cleanliness and food, it is quite impressive. The day begins with meditation at 4:30 A.M. and ends at 9:00 P.M. with satsang. It continues to draw seekers. More and more buildings are being put up, yet many have to stay in the nearby Government Tourist Bungalow.

In recent years frictions developed between Chidananda and Krishnananda. According to local reports, the latter was able to outwit the former in ashram politics. Using his position as General Secretary, he engineered the exit of some of Swami Chidananda's supporters from the ashram. Consequently, the medical work has closed down. Swami Chidananda has also moved out to Uttar Kashi where he now spends most of his time.

Chinmaya Mission

Chinmaya Mission, founded by Swami Chinmayananda—a disciple of Sivananda, is growing faster today than the Divine Life Society. In essence its teachings are the same as those of the Divine Life Society, but it has some distinctions as well.

Swami Chinmayananda, who makes great attempts to relate Advaita philosophy to national life, was born in Kerala in May 1916. He grew up in an atmosphere steeped in learning and culture. A man of sharp intellect, he has an academic background in science, Sanskrit, and law. Before becoming a Sanyasi he obtained a master's degree in English literature and worked for some time as a journalist.

The patriotism that is reflected in his preaching and writing has been with him since his early days. It is said that he even underwent privation and suffering at the hands of the police because of his participation in India's struggle for freedom.

It was doubts and questions that drew him irresistibly to Uttar Kashi, where finally in 1943 he found some comfort and knowledge at the feet of his revered Gurudev, H . H. Swami Tapovan Maharaj. The other great influence on him was that of Swami Sivananda, the founder of the Divine Life Society.

Even though he chose sannyasa renunciation, he decided not to spend his life in the tranquil heights of the Himalayas but rather in the humdrum of the cities with the masses, communicating the message of the scriptures to them. He evolved a unique technique, "gnana yagna," in order to preach his message. A gnana yagna, in his own words,

> is a cooperative endeavour of a community of understanding people, joining together to organize a field for its own inner growth, personality and character.[6]

During the yagna, Swamiji daily expounds the scriptures while the audience meditates on their significance in order to kindle within themselves the fire of knowledge:

> Into this fire an intelligent seeker offers within himself as his oblation his own false values and negative tendencies.[7]

The first yagna was conducted for a hundred days in Poona between December 1951 and March 1952. After Poona a second one was conducted in Madras in April 1953. It was here that some persons, impressed by his talks on *Mundakopanishad,* formed the association called the Chinmaya Mission. From this small beginning in Madras has grown a worldwide Chinmaya family with about a hundred centers in India and many more in foreign countries. Owing to his brilliant oratory, Swami Chinmayananda appeals especially to the intelligentsia. He has preached his message in major academic centers in the United States, such as Harvard, Yale, Stanford, Berkeley, UCLA, New York

University, Columbia, MIT, and Boston College.

Swami Chinmayananda's basic teachings are the same as those of his master Sivananda, but he has a very soft and winsome way of communicating his message to laypersons. He takes great pains to assure his audience and readers that Advaita Vedanta (the non-dualism or monism of Shankara) is an absolutely scientific and rational philosophy. Such phrases keep recurring to the point of becoming boring, defensive, and useless:

> After carefully analyzing our weaknesses, the masters in the religious fields advise us . . .
> Philosophy is a pure science of life . . .
> After a scientific analysis . . . the religious masters discovered . . .
> Rishis made a thorough study and scientific analysis of the structure of a human being . . .

In contrast to Swami Sivananda, Chinmayananda also keeps assuring his readers that religion isn't a negation of life and its joys but its fulfillment:

> The world of objects is meant for us to enjoy and the scriptures do not deny us the freedom to enjoy them. They merely advise us to be masters of our enjoyments.[8]

He preaches self-control but does not support traditional renunciation:

> An unintelligent and abrupt denial of sensual pleasures and a blind following of spiritual values results in suppression in an individual, and this suppression for a period of time leads him to bitterness, frustration, and cynicism in life.[9]

Instead of suppression of desires he teaches sublimation—a rejection of lower values following higher understanding. This naturally makes religion easier for potential devotees. Chinmayananda takes great pains to assert that religion is not dead or outdated. It is essential both for individual joy and national prosperity:

> Our ancient benefactors formulated certain basic regulations of self-restraint and discipline for gaining a more permanent joy, out of our relationship with the world of objects.[10]

Regarding the social value of religion, he stresses individuality:

> A nation is built by the individuals comprising it and when each individual in the society or nation puts forth his effort in the direction indicated in the scriptures and reconstitutes his personality, then that society or nation grows dynamically, permeating peace and glory to one and all. . . . Civilization flourishes with the promotion of culture, but when cultural values deteriorate, the civilization of a society breaks down as we have seen in the fall of Egyptian, Greek and Roman Empires. . . . The need of the hour is forthwith to arrest the deterioration by reviving the great philosophical and religious values of life.[11]

In its desire to combine social action with preaching, the Chinmaya Mission has opened welfare centers. In Madras it runs a home where five hundred children are fed daily. In Indira Nagar (Bangalore), a hospital with twenty-two beds is being run with financial aid from the government. A housing project has been launched in Andhra Pradesh with the help of other charitable organizations. In Bombay it runs two clinics. Swamiji has written thirty books and commentaries and has started a postal tuition course to teach Vedanta to foreigners. The mission lays particular emphasis on imparting religious instruction to children in homes and balviharas.

The most important and innovative institution started by Swami Chinmayananda is Sandeepany Sadhanalaya. This institution, patterned after Christian seminaries, was founded in 1962 in Bombay to train young men and women in Advaita philosophy for missionary activity.

The beautiful seven-acre campus, in the neighborhood of Powai Lake, was donated by a wealthy Indian lady. Large hostels for men and women, a library, lecture hall, dining hall, and temple have been built with the donations of other devotees. Usually the course is for two years, but the course of 1973-74, when I visited there, had been extended. There were about sixty-five students, including twelve foreigners. The students are given free boarding, lodging, tuition, and books. Swami Dayananda Saraswati, a brilliant speaker, was the main teacher in the institute, assisted by some others. Later, however, Dayananda parted company with Chinmayananda. He has now opened his own ashram in Rishikesh and taken away some of Chinmayananda's disciples.

Main teachings of the Divine Life Society and Chinmaya Mission

Both the Divine Life Society and Chinmaya Mission follow the Advaitic or non-dualistic philosophy of the ninth-century philosopher Shankaracharya. According to them, God (Brahman) alone is real. God is not a person or spirit but consciousness. He, or rather "It," is "pure consciousness"[12] in the sense that It is beyond thinking, feeling, willing, and even ideas of good or evil.

God, through Its own power of maya, deludes Itself into thinking that It is an individual personality (jivatma). Under the influence of maya, God also considers the world and its plurality to be real, even though the world is simply a projection of Its own mind.

Once God falls into ignorance, considering Itself to be human and the world to be real, It begins to desire enjoyment in the world. Because of these desires, God acts (thinking Itself to be human). Due to a universal law of karma (according to which every action must have a reaction), It has to be repeatedly reborn in order to take the consequences of Its karma. Sometimes God is reborn as man, other times as an animal, plant, or even an inanimate object.

When this man-who-is-God realizes that this world is illusory and that "It" really is God, not man, It attains moksha (liberation). This realization occurs when through one of the several yoga techniques, man alters his usual rational consciousness and experiences a state of pure consciousness—in which all perceptions of duality and plurality melt away into unity, where all thoughts, including the thoughts of good and evil and of individual personality, are transcended, where one is conscious only of consciousness and bliss. This realization is called God-realization or self-realization, because self is God. Because this experience of pure consciousness is blissful, It (God) is called Saccidananda—that is, being, consciousness, and bliss.

The Divine Life Society and Chinmaya Mission teach a synthesis of yoga. Mainly they emphasize five yogas: karma, bhakti, jnana, raja, and japa.

Karma yoga is for the activist. Karma yogis must be detached from the fruit of their actions and dedicate all their activities to God in entire self-surrender. Selfless service of others is the highest form of karma yoga. And as one turns every act of service into worship, one is led to the goal of self-realization.

Bhakti yoga is for those of a devotional temperament. In bhakti, love is the golden thread that binds a devotee to his lord. In surrender, singing, and worship the devotee begins to get lost in the consciousness of God.

Jnana yoga is for the meditative type. But ultimately it is the most essential. Sivananda writes:

Atma-Jnana alone can give *mukti* or salvation. *Jnana* (knowledge of the self) is the only direct means to freedom. *Srutis* [Upanishads] emphatically declare . . . [that] without wisdom, there is no liberation. . . . Works or actions can't liberate a man. Works cannot dispel ignorance, because they are not antagonistic to each other. *Brahma-jnana* undoubtedly annihilates nescience or ignorance, just as light destroys the densest darkness. Works of a disinterested kind purify the mind and prepare it for the reception of the light of the Self.[13]

Raja yoga is for those with a disciplined temperament. As taught by Patanjali, it has eight limbs (ashtanga): yama (self-restraint), niyama (religious observances), asanas (posture), pranayama (restraint of breath), pratyahara (abstraction of indriyas), dharana (concentration), dhyana (meditation), and samadhi (super-conscious state). The purpose of yoga is to dissolve one's mind in God through concentration and meditation.

Yoga is complete suppression of the tendency of the mind to transform itself into objects, thoughts, etc. . . . The highest summit is *Asamprajnata Samadhi* . . . where all the *Samskaras* [impressions], which bring about successive births, are absolutely dried up.[14]

Japa yoga is a repetition of mantras or the name of the Lord. According to Swamiji, "om" is the best mantra. He writes:

You must repeat Om at least 21,600 times daily. This will take 3 to 4 hours. The more the better. Have a sitting in the morning from 4 to 6 and at night from 8 to 10. Keep up the bhava [feeling] even during work. Have "Om" as the background of thought with the feeling "I am the immortal self. I am all pervading consciousness or intelligence." This will eventually result in

Self-realization and *Nirvikalpa Samadhi*. You will realize unity of consciousness, unity of life, oneness everywhere. The dividing principle mind will be dissolved in Brahman.[15]

Just as when one awakes out of dreaming, one realizes that the dream was illusory, so also when one reaches this transcendental state of consciousness called turya, one realizes that that so-called "real or waking life" was also illusory, that these bondages, births, and deaths were all illusory, that "It" really is ever-free God. Swami Chinmayananda explains this philosophy by the following story:

> One newly initiated anchorite, during a pilgrimage, felt tired and weary one hot day in the burning sun, and he, seeing a shaded arbour near the Ganges bank, took shelter there to rest. There was a narrow piece of rock upon which he stretched himself and composed himself for a restful nap.
>
> As he was dozing off, in those moments between waking and sleeping, his attention was attracted to two village girls who had come to the Ganges to collect water. They filled their pots and went away quietly. But the vision generated a line of thinking in the half-sleepy anchorite.
>
> "Why not? Certainly there is no harm. Supposing I marry one of them. Then I shall keep a small little house; certainly there must be three spacious rooms at least. And I shall be a very severe and grave husband too.
>
> "Working in my own fields I shall live a happy life of contentment and joy. Then the first born . . . yes, a fat, beautiful son. Of course, I must name him Somadatta. And we shall all three sleep in the same bed.
>
> "But is there enough space for my son? Devi, please give some more space for our son; he might fall down."
>
> "Lord, how can I move?" answers she. "Move? To where? You move a bit to your end."
>
> "Alright." Splash.
>
> Poor Somadatta's father had moved a little towards his side and the stone was narrow. He lost his balance and rolled down into the Ganges waters. Awakened, the anchorite swam out, and reached the shore.
>
> Now, friends, what made this anchorite fall? And after his awakening, where should he go to regain his young wife and only child? The poor Brahmacharin created the world of Somadatta in himself, and identifying completely with it, came to live the dream life as though "real" and thus suffered the fall.
>
> So too, Pure Eternal Self [God] we all are. The Self in a dream has forgotten Itself, and dreams of Its own Samsar.[16]

Salvation or moksha means waking out of this dream and realizing that one is God and that this world is an illusion, a projection of one's own mind.

Is Advaitin Philosophy True?

The strongest point in favor of this philosophy is that the experience of pure consciousness is a well-attested fact. Those from many cultures and creeds have testified that they have had vivid mystic experiences in which they seem to have transcended all dualities and personality and have experienced an undifferentiated, blissful consciousness. Then, when compared with this experience, the "ordinary world of sense experience seems pathetically unreal."[17]

The testimonies of the Jewish philosopher Martin Buber, the Catholic scholar R. C. Zaehner, and the secular philosopher William James—showing that these men have had similar experiences and interpreted them very differently from the Divine Life Society and Chinmaya Mission—indicate that the experience in no way proves Advaitic philosophy.

In fact, the non-dualist Advaitins have themselves borrowed the experience and the technique of attaining pure consciousness from the dualistic philosophy of samkhya yoga. The theory on which classic yoga is based is not dualistic Vedanta but dualistic samkhya. Samkhya believed that the universe consists of two eternally existing and qualitatively different things: purusha (spirit) and prakriti (nature). Purusha has no qualities, but prakriti consists of three gunas or qualities—sattva (goodness), rajas (energy or activity), and tamas (darkness, sloth, and desire).

According to samkhya-yoga philosophy, somehow purusha gets enmeshed with prakriti, and that is what we call humanity. The soul's destiny is to return to its original state of isolation, to be free from all associations with prakriti and its attributes. Yoga classically is the technique of dissociation—of withdrawing one's senses entirely from their respective objects and one's mind from all discursive thought. When this is achieved, the soul knows only itself and not prakriti, though the latter continues to exist.

Swami Sivananda admits that the experience of a dualistic raja yogi is the same as that of an Advaitin.[18] It may well be an experience of one's own soul and not of God or of the totality of existence.

Even more interesting is that the techniques of yoga are not the only means of attaining pure consciousness. Because it consists of alteration of our consciousness, it can be attained by artificially altering one's consciousness with drugs. Huxley, himself a Vedantin, said so in his book *The Doors of Perception* after he had experimented with mescaline. Bhagavan Rajneesh teaches that this state of consciousness can also be reached through sexual intercourse.

Why do these gurus think that an artificially altered state of one's consciousness is God? Not because the experience itself proves it, but because they presuppose that a person's own atman or consciousness is God. And why do they presuppose it? Essentially, on the authority of scriptures, particularly of the *Upanishads*. These are the last portions of the *Vedas*, consequently called Vedanta ("end of *Vedas*"). The gurus themselves are called Vedantins.

But do the Hindu scriptures unanimously teach Advaita philosophy? By no means. Hindu scriptures, including the *Upanishads*, contain many—at least superficially—contradictory passages. One can equally well justify monism or dualism from them. One has to accept a philosophical position for other reasons and then read Hindu scriptures in its light. The Hare Krishna movement, for instance, accepts dualism as the main teaching of the scriptures and interprets everything in the light of that.

Because neither the experience nor the scriptures verify the non-dualistic philosophy of the Divine Life Society and the Chinmaya Mission, they are making attempts to prove their position from modern discoveries and speculations in physics. But any attempt to prove that which is real—Brahman—through a study of that which to them is illusory—the empirical world—appears ludicrous even when put forth in sophisticated language by such individuals as Sir James Jeans, Arthur Eddington, or Albert Einstein. It becomes amusing and irritating when Advaitins, who take great pains to try to prove their philosophy is rationally true, are shown that it isn't. Then they turn around and call the mind the "arch enemy."[19] They say, "Don't try to reason out faith; practice yoga and experience the truth of this philosophy yourself." When shown that the experience doesn't prove their philosophy any more than it proves the philosophy of dualistic samkhya yoga philosophy, then they often go a step further and ask one to believe blindly the authority of the guru, who is a realized soul and knows better.

Inconsistencies of Advaitin Teachings

Many scholars have pointed out that when Advaitins describe their "attributeless" God as Sat-cit-ananda, they admit differentiation within the Godhead and contradict their absolute monism:

> If beside Being [sat] there is also thought [cit] and bliss [ananda], then there must be something that can be thought and something that can be enjoyed.[20]

However, even if the Advaitins respond that consciousness and bliss being attributes of attributeless God doesn't imply real differentiation, they still have the problem of harmonizing belief in karma and transmigration within their monism.

If God (or unity consciousness) alone is real and is beyond good and evil, then how can the law of karma, which distinguishes good from bad action, also be true? Sivananda insists that the law of karma is "self-evident truth." He says that every sensible person has to accept it.

A monist can't consistently believe in the dualism of an eternally existing amoral God and an eternally existing moral law. Either one has to believe in a moral God whose own character is the eternal moral law and give up the view that God is impersonal, attributeless being; or one has to concede that the doctrine of the law of karma is not really true, that it is just part of the illusory dream. When pressed to be logically consistent, Advaitins usually choose the latter alternative and agree that there really is no law of karma and ultimately there is nothing good or evil. Sivananda writes:

> The world is neither good nor bad. The mind creates good and evil. Thinking makes it so. . . . The evil is not in the world. It is in the mind. Man sees only

the reflection of his mind. If you become perfect, the world will appear good.[21]

Chinmayananda also believes that in order to realize God, we have to go beyond good and evil[22]—even the idea of good is illusory.

If no deed is actually good or evil, then the belief in transmigration, namely that one has to be reborn repeatedly to take consequences of good and bad acts, is also absurd. Both the Divine Life Society and the Chinmaya Mission insist that the doctrine of transmigration is true. Sivananda claims that it is as old as the *Vedas* and that today "it is accepted by the majority of humankind."[23] Yet during the moments when they are logically more consistent with their essential philosophy, they do vaguely acknowledge that the doctrine of transmigration is an illusion.

> *Moksha* is not an attainment of liberation from an actual state of bondage, but is the realization of the liberation which already exists. It is freedom from the false notion of bondage. . . . Birth and death, bondage and freedom . . . are mental creations. . . . You were never born; you will never die.[24]

God never really falls into the bondage of transmigration (samsara); It ignorantly thinks It is in bondage. The belief in transmigration is illusory.

The Divine Life Society and the Chinmaya Mission also believe that

> the Guru is God himself manifesting in a personal form to guide the aspirant. The grace of God takes the form of the Guru.[25]

The guru is not God incarnate but someone who has realized God, thereby becoming "identical with Brahman or supreme self," and is now helping to liberate others.

This view involves many contradictions: if individuality is false and there is only one consciousness in the universe which has come under the spell of maya, then when one person realizes truth, the whole consciousness ought to realize it since there is only one consciousness. If all the other individuals still continue in ignorance, this implies that they are separate individuals having their own distinct consciousness. This obviously contradicts the basic Advaitin premise.

Moreover, if the guru has realized the truth that the world is illusion and individuality is illusory, then why is he going all over the world to preach to individuals who, from his enlightened point of view are, by definition illusory? Indeed, within the framework of Advaitic philosophy, the guru is not an expression of the grace of God but a logical absurdity. In fact, within impersonal monism, the very idea of the grace of God is meaningless. Advaitins have borrowed this idea from theistic sects within Hinduism. Logically they can't believe in a personal God (Ishvara) who is gracious towards individual souls, for if Ishvara thinks that individuals are there, he too is under illusion and needs mercy! It does not make any sense to believe that God, who is under false notions of bondage, would send gurus to deliver Itself from this false notion.

Can We Live With This Philosophy?

Swami Chinmayananda realizes that a prosperous civilization is impossible without science and hard work. He rejects the popular criticism against Vedanta that it admonishes us to be indifferent to the sorrows of man, to social injustices, and to progress:

> [This is an] unjust criticism made by those who are interested in this blasphemy. And . . . [it is] applauded only by the gullible and the ignorant.[26]

He declares that our secular plans, scientific knowledge, and materialistic values by themselves are insufficient. A civilization built on them alone would crumble. Therefore, he argues that

> the redemption seems to be in the happy marriage between the secular and the sacred, the scientific and the religious.[27]

However, he does not tell us how the illusory, dream-like world of science can be wedded with the real world of religion. His passionate plea for marriage between the unreal world of maya and the real world of consciousness seems impossible to fulfill, because in his philosophy these are not two mutually complementary worlds but are mutually contradictory worlds. The pursuit of science demands deep interest and involvement in the physical world. The pursuit of the Advaitic goal demands detachment from the world. Sivananda quite logically says:

> The more you think of the objects the more this world will appear to you as real. The conception of the reality of the universe will increase if you think of sense-objects often.[28]

The low view of the physical universe that is inherent in Advaitic philosophy undercuts the very basis for science.

Not only their view of the world, but also their view of mind destroys the basis for science. Science presupposes that through our mental efforts we can discover the secrets of nature. At times, the Divine Life Society and the Chinmaya Mission view the mind as God's supreme gift to us, but their overall teaching is clear. The whole experience of duality, made up of perceiver and perceived, is pure imagination. There is no world apart from the mind; on destruction of the mind all is destroyed.[29]

Thus we must not study the world with the aid of the mind but seek to "consciously destroy the mind by Sadhana and Samadhi"[30] so that the world may vanish:

> Do not use your reason too much in the selection of your guru. . . . Keep your intellect at a respectable distance when you study mythology. Intellect is a hindrance. . . . That which separates you from God is mind.[31]

Swami Krishnananda, who argues in *Resurgent Culture* that Vedanta alone can bring about the best civilization, gives his case away when he confesses:

> All types of objective thinking are considered in our system of yoga as certain diseased conditions of consciousness.[32]

Adherents of the Divine Life Society or the Chinmaya Mission might well argue that involvement in science is involvement in bondage, yet it is essential for those who are living in ignorance. Those who consider the illusory life and world to be real may as well make it comfortable through science and technology. But if Advaita is true, then this advice is cruel. Why should we ask the ignorant to become more comfortable in their ignorance and illusion?

In his three talks to the Secretariat Workers in New Delhi on the "Secret of Action," Swami Chinmayananda correctly indicates that the basic cause of India's poverty is that people don't work honestly and diligently. He rightly sees that our national progress is impossible without a "new philosophy of action." He regrets, however, that the government and the industrialists are employing specialists from America and other countries to motivate our people to work, "as if it is not in our culture or in our scriptures."[33]

But when it comes to actually showing how a philosophy of work can be derived from Advaita, he fails. The motivation to work that he gives is that if we want to make a great name for ourselves we have to work hard like Mahatma Gandhi and Gautama Buddha. The truth of the matter is that Advaita, which presupposes that God, or the supreme bliss is pure (inactive, unthinking) consciousness, can't derive a philosophy of action from its premise. Sivananda is more consistent when he says:

> You must be prepared to abandon the work at any time, however interesting the work may be, however much you like the work. . . . Attachment to any work will blind you.[34]

Work presupposes duality in—and the reality of—the material universe. Though Sivananda also asks us to work hard, he acknowledges that the ultimate aim of life is to go beyond work, especially for those who have attained salvation. Those who are

> absorbed in Brahman . . . will not be able to work. . . . Only the man of renunciation with knowledge attains Brahman, and none else.[35]

How can Advaita Vedanta bring material prosperity to the country when it ultimately destroys the philosophic basis for science, technology, and work?

Sivananda, Chidananda, Chinmayananda, Krishnananda, and Dayananda are right in saying that a materialistic philosophy of life doesn't give any moral values and can't provide a basis for a humane and just society. But what they usually fail to point out is that their philosophy too rejects the distinction between good and evil as unreal.

If this is true, then a pessimistic view of life doesn't mean that the world and its pleasures are evil but that the Advaitins who consider it evil have projected evil on the world. They also have no objective basis for calling anything good or bad. Sivananda would have us see God everywhere:

> It is *Hari* [God] who is playing the part of the prostitute, the thief, the dacoit, the scavenger.[36]

To a thief who enters our house, Sivananda would have us say:

> O thief! take this ring also. Your duty is to steal things. Thou art Krishna. Keep up this Lila.[37]

This is not to say that Advaitins don't believe in morality. They say that so far as we live at a relative level of ignorance we have to believe in morals and preach morals, even though ultimately there is nothing good and evil. But this faith in morality and the preaching of ethics is the same as asking children to believe in ghosts even though we may not believe in them ourselves, for fear of ghosts can make children behave better. What kind of society will this kind of amoral philosophy produce? Sivananda answers the question himself:

> Wholesale preaching of Vedanta to the masses is not advisable. It will result in chaos, bewilderment, and stagnation.[38]

His followers will do well to heed him.

Chapter Five

Hare Krishna

FIFTH AVENUE, NEW YORK. 1966. All of a sudden your way is blocked by a crowd watching a group of American Hindus chanting "Hare Krishna" and dancing with transcendental ecstasy. Young men—in saffron dhotis, with or without a kurta, their heads cleanshaven except for the tuft of their chutia, and wearing sandals—are playing drums, cymbals, and the harmonium; women—in beautiful, though clumsily draped sarees, lost in Krishna consciousness, dancing to the hypnotic beat of the drums—are completely oblivious of the crowds. You will indeed have witnessed a spectacle fit for sensational evening headlines: "America Invaded by Hinduism." When the scene is reenacted at Trafalgar Square, London, and in front of the city hall in Hamburg, Germany, it becomes world news.

The man who introduced the chanting of "Hare Krishna" as a way of salvation in the West was A. C. Baktivedanta Swami Prabhupada. He was born in Calcutta in 1896 and was named Abhay Charan De. A graduate of Calcutta University, with majors in English, philosophy, and economics, he was active in India's independence movement in 1922 when he first met his guru, Srila Bhaktisiddhanta Saraswati Maharaj. He took initiation from him in 1933 and was ordered to spread his teachings in the West, but Prabhupada instead continued to work as a manager of a chemical firm until his retirement in 1954.

He didn't completely renounce the world until 1959, though as early as 1944 he had begun to express his religious ideas in English through a magazine called *Back to Godhead*. It was not very successful, but because of these efforts he received the title of Bhaktivedanta (devotional knowledge) from the Gaudiya Vaishnava Society, which was founded by his guru's father. The opportunity to spread the message in the West did not come until 1965 when Prabhupada won a patron in Sumati Morarji, the owner of India's largest shipping firm. She not only gave him a berth on one of her ships but also some money to get him started on the mission. Prabhupada sat under a tree in Tomkinson Square, New York, and began chanting his maha mantra:

Hare Krishna, Hare Krishna
Krishna Krishna, Hare Hare,
Hare Rama, Hare Rama
Rama Rama, Hare Hare.

This attracted some passers-by, who began to come to hear discourses. Some of them took initiation, and the International Society for Krishna Consciousness (ISKCON), popularly called the "Hare Krishna" movement, was formed.

ISKCON claimed that Swami Prabhupada was "the acharya for this age."[1] He was said to be the only true, authorized teacher or guru who stood in a line of disciplic succession going back directly five hundred years to the time when Lord Chaitanya appeared in India, and from there still further—back five thousand years to the time when Krishna first spoke the *Bhagavad-Gita*.[2]

The movement asserts that because during the preceding centuries the *Bhagavad Gita* has been misunderstood and misinterpreted, the Lord came as Chaitanya Mahaprabhu to set things right, to teach the principles of devotional service (bhakti), through which alone a man can attain salvation in this evil age (kali yuga). Chaitanya Mahaprabhu, born in Navadvipa, Bengal, in 1486, was no "human" guru. He was the "Supreme Personality of Godhead, Krishna Himself, appearing in the role of devotee."[3] ISKCON claims that at the age of sixteen Chaitanya "became the greatest scholar in all of India"[4] and began the Sankirtana movement of chanting the "Hare Krishna" mantra. His teachings now come to us in their original purity through an unbroken line of disciplic succession.

It's difficult enough to prove that Swami Prabhupada was the "authorized" successor of his guru, Bhaktisiddhanta, and the claim that the "disciplic succession" goes back five thousand years to Krishna himself has to be accepted purely on faith, without any evidence.

After the death of Bhaktisiddhanta, there was some controversy in Gaudiya Math as to who his successor was. Goswami Maharaj, who Bhaktisiddhanta is said to have selected as successor, didn't feel worthy to assume the position of his master, but now the majority of the organization acknowledges him and not Prabhupada as the legitimate successor of their guru. After the latter's death in 1977, Goswami Maharaj began to draw many of Prabhupada's followers away from ISKCON to Shri Chaitanya Math.

Even though Prabhupada couldn't prove that he was the "authorized" successor of his own guru, much less of Chaitanya, it is true that his teachings are the same as theirs. However, Chaitanya's teachings by no means go back five thousand years to the times when Krishna is claimed to have lived. For Chaitanya belongs to the bhakti (devotional) schools of the thirteenth and fourteenth centuries. The Alvars (seventh century) in South India were the pioneers of the Bhakti movement. Ramanuja, in the twelfth century, gave a philosophical basis to the devotional path of attaining God-realization, emphasizing absolute self-surrender as the quickest path to liberation. He was a qualified monist, believing that the soul and matter are distinct from though completely dependent on God. Later, Madhava, in the thirteenth century, interpreted the *Bhagavad Gita* and other scriptures to teach dualism (dwaita) of God and souls. Chaitanya's philosophy is a slight modification of Madhava's dualism.

Ramanuja and Madhava were philosophers, but there arose after them a number of saints who practiced and taught devotion to God as the means of salvation. There were two parallel streams of Bhaktas—those who worshiped Shiva (Shaivites) and those who worshiped Vishnu (Vaishnavites). The latter movement spread more in North India. It also split into two streams—the worship of Rama and the worship of Krishna, both of whom were considered to be incarnations of Vishnu. Those who worshiped Krishna also split into two streamlets. The saints of Maharashtra such as Jnaneshvar, Namdev, Eknath, and Tukaram worshiped Krishna and his wife Rukmini, but the sects founded by Nimbaraka, Vishnuswami, Vallabha, and Chaitanya worshiped Krishna and his beloved, Radha. Some made Radha his wife. The two groups differed as well in their mode of worship. D. S. Sharma writes:

> Naturally, the Bhakti that takes as its symbol the love of the husband is pure and serene, while that which takes as its symbol the love of the lover is passionate and tempestuous.[5]

Even the gurus that worshiped Radha and Krishna differed in their philosophy. Nimbaraka taught that the relationship between God and the world was one of identity in difference (bhed-abheda). Vallabhacharya (1475-1531), on the other hand, taught pure monism. Chaitanya was at first influenced by the dualism of Madhava and later came under the influence of Nimbaraka and others. Prabhupada also accepts Nimbaraka's form of dualism called bhed-abheda.

History of the Hare Krishna Movement

Chaitanya Mahaprabhu (1486-1534) started the Sankirtana movement—the group chanting of the "Hare Krishna" mantra—in Bengal and Orissa. An extremely emotional—though also intelligent—man, he "won his success by a tempest of devotion."[6] Through his nagar sankirtana, the public chanting in the streets of the city, he added thousands of converts to his movement.

Some of Chaitanya's close devotees articulated and wrote down his philosophy after his sudden disappearance in 1534. Soon after Chaitanya's disappearance, his movement "degenerated to carelessness and uncleanness."[7] In the seventeenth century, there was a renewal of faith in Chaitanya due to the influence of three men: Srinivasa Acharya, Narottama Datta, and Shyamananda Das. But during the eighteenth and nineteenth centuries, Chaitanya's Vaishnavism again declined. Some features, such as public sankirtanas with the use of traditional drums and cymbals, were revived in the mid-nineteenth century by the Brahmo Samaj.

Toward the end of the last century, in 1886, Bhaktivinode Thakur established the Gaudiya Vaishnava Mission. His son Bhakti Siddhanta Goswami, who had been a professor of mathematics and astronomy before his renunciation, continued his father's work, revitalized Vaishnavism, and informed the English-speaking world of Chaitanya's message. It was he who initiated Swami Prabhupada and ordered him to preach this message to the West. The International Society for Krishna Consciousness, founded by Prabhupada, has made Chaitanya's message—or at least the mantra—popular in the West. ISKCON has no formal relationship, though, with the parent body, the Gaudiya Vaishnava Society.

ISKCON was formed in 1966; six years later it claimed sixty-eight centers and about three thousand followers spread throughout the USA, Canada, Mexico, the West Indies, Japan, Hong Kong, India, Sweden, France, Germany, Holland, Switzerland, England, Scotland, New Zealand, and Australia.

Though the membership of the movement is relatively small, its influence is much greater. They claim a circulation of about three hundred thousand copies of their monthly magazine *Back to Godhead*. It is reported that Swami Bhaktivedanta's translation of and commentary on the *Bhagavad Gita As It Is* sold about fifty thousand copies in the first six months of publication. They have a large factory for manufacturing incense in Los Angeles and another is planned for Mexico. The one in Los Angeles gives great financial stability to the movement because it employs devotees and enables those who have renounced the world to live by selling its products.

By sending Western missionaries to preach the glories of Krishna in India and to chant his name in our cosmopolitan cities, the society has naturally attracted a great deal of attention in India. Initially, however, it had great difficulty in winning Indian followers. In 1974 it had only four or five centers in India. Ganga Muni, president of the ISKCON temple in Calcutta, estimated at that time that they hadn't converted more than twenty-five or thirty Hindus to their ranks.[8]

When Bob Jono and I visited the center in Bombay in 1974, we found twenty-five Westerners and eight Indian devotees. When I went out searching for their temple in Delhi in early 1975, I found that it had already closed down due to the lack of response there. The Western devotees who came to India as missionaries were not even allowed to enter any of the major Vaishnava temples because the orthodox Vaishnavas still believed strongly in the caste system. Traditionally all foreigners are considered outcasts. Prabhupada and his Western followers also believed fully in the Hindu caste system as taught in the scriptures, but they also added that anyone who is in Krishna-consciousness is to be regarded as a Vaishnavite Brahman even if he is a low-caste by birth.

Even though the movement was not growing rapidly in India, it developed industries and other devices that could ensure its sustenance. At the end of the seventies, the movement suddenly started growing in India.

The Appeal of the Hare Krishna Movement in the West

The Hare Krishna movement has largely been limited to the young people who joined in the early phase of the counterculture. They had reacted against the materialistic values, dehumanizing technology, meaningless education, valueless politics, and hypocritical morality of much of the West. They challenged the basic presuppositions of its rationalistic philosophy which fails to give any meaning or value to life. Some protested against the dominant culture by seeking to destroy it through violence, and others protested by dropping out of society and seeking an alternative philosophy, consciousness, and lifestyle in drugs, sex, the occult, or mysticism.

Philip E. Slater has suggested that there are three basic sociological needs that must be fulfilled in order to have a stable culture—those for community, engagement, and dependence. The individualistic culture of the West had failed to provide this, and this is what the pioneers of the counterculture were looking for.

The *desire for community* is the wish to live in cooperation and close fellowship with others instead of in the constant competition that marks so much of the Western culture.

The *desire for engagement* is the wish to deal directly with social problems instead of setting up committees and commissions to study our problems and recommend impractical suggestions with which nobody does anything.

The *desire for dependence* is the wish to share with others the responsibility for controlling one's impulses and guiding one's life.

True, the establishment failed to meet these needs, but the early protest movements of the counterculture such as the New Left and hippyism also failed. Most of the Hare Krishna converts came from hippyism. Some were deeply involved in it, others casually, but they found neither a coherent philosophy there, which could give positive meaning to life, nor an authoritative leadership that could make community living possible. Though drugs did give occasional "religious" experiences, their evil effects soon became apparent. Many hippies who tried various forms of yoga and had "religious experiences" still kept looking for a loving and warm community religious experience and lifestyle based on a coherent philosophy. To this group, which had given up the establishment-culture already, found the hippie phase of the counterculture inadequate, and was desperately looking for an alternative, the Hare Krishna movement had an instant appeal. It met their obvious needs.

The Hare Krishna movement met the needs for community and dependence by welcoming the new converts to live in its centers and share the discipline and privileges. It provided the totalitarian but loving and personal authority of Krishna which was integral to its philosophy. Young people who had rebelled against the impersonal authority of the state and the unloving authority of their parents found an authority to which they could joyfully surrender. The material-istic values of the establishment and the hedonistic values of hippyism were replaced by the more spiritual values of serving Krishna. Once surrendered to Krishna, people in the movement undertook to provide for each other's material needs and to take away all personal worries and care. "Routinized experience of religious enthusiasm and discipline shared with like-minded individuals"[9] helped them to validate and internalize their new-found faith. It met their need for engagement by helping them to spread Krishna consciousness with the assurance that spreading it was the best and only genuine way of solving the world's problems. Swami Prabhupada believed that

> only a person who is in Krishna Consciousness is truly engaged in welfare for for all people. . . . Physical welfare work is not helpful, since it gives only temporary relief.[10]

Though this kind of lifestyle has been helpful for alienated, disillusioned hippies, it has been too extreme for the average person, especially the average Indian who has not felt these needs so acutely. For an unemployed, wandering hippie to join the community means free board and lodging amidst like-minded people, but for an average employed man or woman to join the community means having to share half their income with the community. For hippies who have become sick of their lonely freedom, the submission to authority means new security, dependence, and freedom within strict discipline. They have to get up at 3:00 A.M. and continue loving service of Krishna till 9:30 P.M. in joyful fellowship with others. They are not allowed to gamble, which is extended to include all frivolous sports and games. Nor are they allowed to use any intoxicants, including alcohol, drugs, tobacco, coffee, or tea. All non-vegetarian food and "illicit sex" are also taboo. "Illicit sex" includes all sexual acts which are indulged in for pleasure. Sex is permitted only for procreation of children, which means that the use of contraceptives is also banned. This is obviously too big a price for the average person.

Even though the affluent Indian youth have aped the Westerners in hairstyle and dress, have shown a desire for drugs and loose sexual ethics, have expressed anti-parental and anti-establishment feelings, they haven't reached total isolation from the predominant culture, its humanistic philosophy, materialistic values, and hedonistic ethics. They haven't had the courage to completely break away from their parents and haven't come to the place where Hare Krishna can have an appeal for them. In fact, most college-going Indian youth haven't given up faith in reason and science. They can't easily accept a teaching that asks for blind belief and experiential verification. That is why ISKCON didn't appeal to them as it appealed to the Western youth.

Towards the end of the seventies, however, ISKCON changed its appeal in India from the dropouts of society to those successful in business. Consequently, by 1982 ISKCON had fifteen centers in India plus two farms, two schools, and two posh vegetarian restaurants.

The Hare Krishna establishment in Bombay became the star attraction. Built on the prestigious Juhu Beach, it has already become a pilgrim place and the heart of Krishna culture. In the ISKCON Center for Devotional Arts, guests are daily exposed to classical drama, dance, and music. There are daily discourses and idol worship. The complex includes a two-story book depot which sells literature by the ton every day. Their literature, which has only been in English so far, is being translated into Hindi, Gujarati, Telegu, Sindhi, and other Indian languages. The complex also has a guest house with two seven-story towers, which offers four-star hotel services to life members of ISKCON and a vegetarian restaurant which they claim is Bombay's most popular.

However, observers question whether this growth of the Hare Krishna movement is a genuine spread of religious culture in India or merely the economic success of a sect. In 1982, as I walked into the Rs. 50 lakh temple-cum residential complex of ISKCON in Greater Kailash I, New Delhi, I was flabbergasted by its affluence, coming as I did from a village in the backwoods of Madhya Pradesh. Three telephones, two cars, dozens of rooms furnished with Persian carpets and equipped with sophisticated intercom facilities at first spoke very highly of the depth of devotion and generosity of the patrons, but in a few minutes of conversation with the Brahmacharies there, the affluence ceased to dazzle me. It was saddening to see that ISKCON had slipped into the trap of materialism which its founder never ceased to condemn. It has become the religion of the rich.

The fee for life membership in ISKCON was Rs. 4,444. They said that four thousand people had paid the fee in Delhi, a hundred thousand in Bombay, and thirty thousand in the whole of India. Beside the bliss of Krishna consciousness, life members also had the privilege of staying in ISKCON guest houses in the business centers of the world. Was that the main attraction? It seemed to me that ISKCON's real strength in India came from the fact that it provided spiritual consolation to the affluent of our nation, many of whom are burdened with the guilt of economic offenses. The demands that ISKCON made on its original Western followers were severely legalistic, but on Indian businessmen, who were prepared to pay a fee higher than that of the Rotary or the Lion's Club, ISKCON put no religious or moral demands. Instead, it guaranteed a removal of moral guilt. Having achieved Krishna consciousness, they could go on accumulating black money if they wanted to, without worry, because Krishna consciousness canceled out the accumulation and consequences of bad karma against them.

One wonders if the reason ISKCON doesn't speak out against moral and economic offenses is because it thrives on them—just as our political parties that thrive on the nation's black money are incapable of doing anything about it except for levying a political tax on it.

However, the fact is that ISKCON drew initial recruits from among sincere young men and women who, disgusted with the evils and hypocrisy of Western society, wanted to build a counterculture based on religious truth and philosophy. It's difficult for some of these sincere people to accept the fact that instead of creating a counterculture ISKCON has been swallowed up by Bombay's economic culture, which even sells religion. The life membership fee of Rs. 4,444 is a modern version of the selling of indulgences by the medieval Church, which triggered the Protestant Reformation. These people, who wanted to build a new society, may be happy to reap the benefits of the religious tax on black money, but they also need a way out to ease their conscience.

They have done this by extending service to the poor. A new department, ISKCON Rural Development (IRD), has been established. Understandably, the initiative and leadership for this has come from the Western devotees, the chief architect of it being a Swiss devotee, Citrakara. This attempt, though inconsistent with their low view of the physical universe, is nevertheless praiseworthy. However, it remains to be seen whether the Hare Krishna movement can provide a genuine philosophy for social action. Earlier, Swami Prabhupada asserted that physical welfare work was unhelpful because it brought only temporary relief.

His Divine Grace A. C. Bhaktivedanta Swami Prabhupada died in 1977. The movement had difficulty finding a successor, even though this appointment is said to be God's responsibility because the line of succession goes back five thousand years to Krishna himself.

One of the basic problems was that the real leadership of the movement was in Western hands, yet the Indians insisted on having an Indian figurehead. Besides this, the movement had exalted Swami Prabhupada so highly during his lifetime that it was virtually impossible to find a person who could inspire the same awe and provide the same cohesiveness and discipline which an ambitious movement like the Hare Krishna needed. Also, because Krishna consciousness had become an economic gold mine, the conflict of vested interests couldn't be easily handled. After five years of struggle, a mediocre figurehead was appointed as the spiritual master in 1982, and twenty-five governing body commissioners took control of the strings behind the scenes. The new leader, Shri Gopal Krishna Maharaj, was earlier looking after the literature business of ISKCON in Western India.

The Teachings of the Hare Krishna Movement

The International Society for Krishna Consciousness claims to accept the authority of Hindu scriptures entirely and asserts that all its teachings are derived from the scriptures. In practice it doesn't give much importance to the *Vedas* or to the *Upanishads*. Its favorite scriptures are the *Bhagavad Gita* and the *Bhagavad Purana,* which ISKCON claims were written twenty-five hundred years before the time of Buddha, who lived in the sixth century B.C.! Most Western scholars and respected Indian scholars such as Dr. Radhakrishna and Prof. D. S. Sharma date the *Bhagavad Gita* around the fifth century B.C. and the *Bhagavad Purana* around 900 A.D.[11]

As its basic premise, the sect accepts Nimbaraka's form of dualism called bhed-abheda, according to which God and the human soul are distinct yet similar and related. Even though the sect claims to be nonsectarian—"any man, Hindu or Christian, will become better in his faith by chanting the Holy Name of the God"[12]—it considers monists and Buddhists to be its greatest rivals.

Swami Prabhupada taught that God is personal but that the human soul is not God. Anyone claiming to be God must be anathema—"the philosophers who maintain that God is impersonal energy or impersonal nothingness and that everything and everyone is therefore God, are murderers."[13] Yet the sect accepts Buddha as an incarnation of Krishna himself and Shankaracharya as a great scholar sent by God. Theories are advanced that Buddha taught voidism and Sankara impersonalism for specific reasons. Animal sacrifice was widespread during the time of Buddha. The sacrifice derived its authority from the *Vedas,* but because the correct art of sacrifice had already been lost, God incarnated himself as Buddha to stop the sacrifices. In order to stop the sacrifice, he superficially rejected the authority of the *Vedas* and taught ahimsa, or nonviolence. So even though Buddha "outwardly rejected the Vedas and preached an atheistic doctrine, he is an incarnation of the personality of Godhead himself, the original propounder of the Vedic knowledge."

How can Buddha, in spite of being God, teach that there is no God? Or how can he, being the revealer of the *Vedas,* reject their authority? ISKCON argues that

> the Supreme Lord is supreme in everything, and therefore He is also the supreme cheater.[14]

He appeared in disguise as the Lord Buddha, rejected the *Vedas*, and taught atheism simply to stop sacrifices. Likewise, Shankaracharya came superficially preaching that the material world or human individuality is an illusion and that God is an impersonal, formless oneness. But actually, according to ISKCON, Shankaracharya was "among the greatest of the theists."[15] He preached impersonalism simply to counteract the influence of Buddhism and to reestablish the authority of the *Vedas*. "By skillfully misinterpreting the Vedic verses" he succeeded in his mission. So even though Buddha is Krishna himself and Shankaracharya his greatest instrument, their philosophies "are manifestations of the darkest materialistic ignorance."[16]

According to Swami Prabhupada, the material world is not an illusion. It actually exists. The illusion is that we accept this world to be a permanent home although it is temporary. Also, when the *Upanishads* say that the Supreme Lord is formless, it only means that he does not have a material form like ours. He has a form but is made up of Spirit. Also, man is distinct from God. Even the guru is not God. He is God's representative, his external manifestation. He is as good as God and should be worshiped as God, but he must not be identified with God.[17]

Even though God is a distinct person who is not to be identified with matter, the human soul, or a guru, he is considered identical with his idols by Swami Prabhupada.[18] Idol worship is therefore an essential part of the devotional service in ISKCON.

The ultimate reality is a personal God—Krishna. He has many incarnations and expansions, but in his original form he incarnates himself as the cowherd deity of Vrindavan. Therefore, the pastimes—adventures and love affairs—of "Krishna's life in his original form are of great importance to the young Vaishnavas of the Hare Krishna movement. They are tenets of the living faith."[19] More time is spent in studying the pastimes of Krishna than in studying philosophy as such. Krishna's affairs with Radha are of supreme importance because Radha's love for Krishna shows how we ought to love him.

Just as the Advaitins who believe in an impersonal God include "personalism" within their framework by postulating the inferior personal god, Ishwara, so does ISKCON make concession to the impersonalists by including an inferior impersonal aspect of Krishna, Brahman, within its teachings. Krishna has three paramount attributes—sat, cit, and ananda. Realization of impersonal Brahman is the realization of the aspect of Krishna's sat, or being. Classical yoga's realization is that of Krishna as cit, or knowledge. But Krishna is also an ocean of bliss (ananda). The highest goal of Krishna consciousness is to realize this ecstasy.

Krishna has traditionally been regarded as an incarnation of Vishnu. ISKCON, however, considers Vishnu to be a "plenary expansion" of Krishna.

Therefore, strictly speaking, ISKCON is a Krishnite sect and not Vaishnavite. Krishna consciousness is the original, pure state of the soul as she lives in a blissful, loving relationship with her Lord Krishna. Through contact with the material world the soul gets contaminated, but the chanting of the Hare Krishna mantra purifies the soul and brings the original Krishna consciousness back to it. The soul develops various loving relationships with Krishna—friend, child, lover, master—and realizes itself. Self-realization does not mean merging into God but realizing oneself as a part of God, his loving servant. According to Swami Prabhupada, the famous Vedic phrase "Aham Brahmasmi" does not mean "I am Brahma" but is a realization that "I am not this body; I am spirit, soul, part and parcel of the Supreme Brahman."[20]

Humanity is not the only entity that has soul. All animals and plants also have souls. These souls are in bondage, and they migrate from one body to another until they become established in Krishna consciousness—their original state.

How did these souls fall into bondage? Prabhupada doesn't clearly tell us why the souls fell from Krishna consciousness:

Somehow or other we have fallen into this material existence.[21]

At times he holds us responsible for our fall:

Man becomes impure because he wants to enjoy material pleasures.[22]

At other times he holds God responsible:

All living entities have come under the control of the illusory energy by Your will.[23]

In more rational moments, he suggests that souls have fallen from Krishna consciousness because they misused their free will, but this view is not consistent with the rest of the system.

Swami Prabhupada doesn't talk about moksha or liberation because "devotional service surpasses all liberation." He takes up the popular analogy of the monists and says that they are like the river that slowly spills into the ocean, merges with it, and loses its identity forever. Those who render devotional service to Krishna are like the aquatic creatures that live in the ocean and enjoy it forever. "The devotees eternally live in the ocean of devotional service, and they do not care for the rivers."[24] This is salvation—to live forever in the joy of Krishna's service. Devotional service to Krishna in this life includes chanting his name (because Krishna and his name are one and the same thing); surrendering whatever talent one has to him—a painter should paint him, a writer should write about him; hearing about the pastimes, adventures, and love affairs of Krishna; eating prasad, or the foodstuff that is offered to him; and dressing, feeding, and caring for the idols (called statues) of Krishna.

In order to be properly established in the devotional service, one first has to establish a relationship with Krishna. This is only possible "by connecting oneself with the bona fide spiritual master who is the direct representative of Krishna in disciplic succession."[25] We connect ourselves with the guru through initiation, without which the cultivation of Krishna consciousness is impossible. From the devotee's side, initiation means that he accepts the guru as his spiritual master and agrees to worship him as God. From the guru's side, it means that he takes the karma, or sinful reactions of the disciple, on himself.

The initiation ceremony in ISKCON is not secret. It consists of a fire ceremony in which the disciple receives a set of 108 beads strung together on a thread, and a Sanskrit name. The devotee is required to fast before the ceremony and is given prasad (offered food) to eat during it. There is much chanting and dancing. Devotees vow to refrain from illicit sex, meat eating, intoxication, and gambling. They are asked to chant the "Hare Krishna" mantra 108 times, once for each bead, and then to repeat the whole process at least sixteen times daily.

According to ISKCON, the word *hare* actually means *hara,* and it refers to the energy of the Lord. The words "Krishna" and "Rama" are forms of addressing the Lord himself. According to Prabhupada, they mean

the supreme pleasure; and Hara is supreme pleasure energy of the Lord.[26]

The chanting of this mantra makes one feel at once "a transcendental ecstasy coming through from the spiritual stratum."[27] Swami Prabhupada describes many transcendental ecstasies that occur, such as being struck dumb, perspiring, the hair standing up on the body, trembling, and falling into a trance.

Through chanting this mantra one can associate personally with Krishna, because there is no difference between the name and form of Krishna; and through constant spiritual association one becomes spiritually self-realized.[28] The chanting of the mantra removes one's consciousness from material desires and anxieties and fixes it on Krishna. This slowly enlightens and helps one realize one's true nature and identity—as an eternal servant of the supreme personality of the Godhead.

When one attains this self-realization and Krishna consciousness, one is delivered from the bondage of births and deaths and is transported to the spiritual world called Goloka-Vrindavan. There Krishna lives eternally in the highest love relationship with Radha. There are millions of wish-fulfilling trees and Surabhi cows in Goloka. One can take as much milk as one likes from a Surabhi cow, have all one's desires carried out by the wish-fulfilling trees, and live happily forever as a servant of Krishna.

That Swami Prabhupada gave meaning, purpose, discipline, and ethical standards to many disillusioned young people is indisputable. And that he saved many from ruining their lives through abuse of drugs and sex is also commendable.

The depth of devotion in the Western devotees can't fail to impress an outsider. The implicit faith, total abandonment, and loving devotion of the devotees produces in them not only contentment but a thrilling ecstasy as well. That the movement as a whole is satisfying to them is obvious from the fact that they sacrifice much for the glory of Krishna—their liberty, time, body, mind, and wealth. Ex-Beatle George Harrison donated $19,000 to meet the entire cost of publishing two volumes on Krishna by Swami Prabhupada.

However, even though the movement seems to meet some of the emotional and sociological needs of its followers, it is utterly unsatisfying in regard to the intellect. On the surface, Swami Prabhupada didn't seem to view the intellect as necessarily evil. ISKCON claims that it has the highest philosophical basis for its faith and that it can be defended. Yet the devotees are not allowed to "waste time" in intellectual discussions or theological disputes, even though their magazines are full of polemic against other faiths. The devotees are discouraged from reading books other than ISKCON's own. The movement confesses that its teachings are justified purely on the authority of the Hindu scriptures, though no attempt is made to establish the authenticity of scriptures on reasonable grounds. Most devotees don't even read the scriptures for themselves. They simply accept Prabhupada's interpretation of them as pure and authoritative.

If the devotees read the scriptures, they would know that the stories of Krishna and Radha are not based on authoritative scriptures, much less on facts. No Radha is mentioned in the *Vedas, Upanishads, Bhagavad Gita, Harivamsha, Vishnu Purana,* or even the *Bhagavad Purana*—the movement's chief scripture. D. S. Sharma writes:

> All that the *Bhagavad Purana* states is that among the Gopis who lavished their affections on Krishna, there was a favorite Gopi with whom Krishna is said to have wandered in the forests and caused jealousy in the minds of the other Gopis. Out of this shadowy figure arose Radha, who became in later literature the symbol of the most passionate love which the human heart is capable of.[29]

Radha, with whom Krishna is said to have enjoyed so many "pastimes," doesn't appear in Hindu literature until about the tenth century A.D. Stories of the love of Radha and Krishna become prominent only in the twelfth century through Jayadeva's *Gita Govinda*.

Main Philosophical Weaknesses

Hare Krishna teachings spring from their inadequate view of God. They ascribe personality to the supreme God but deny definite moral character to Him. Consequently, the whole system becomes amoral. To bring in morality, they have to assume an independent moral law—the law of karma—but it results in various inconsistencies. God is supreme in everything—the supreme cheater as well. He's not always honest and reliable. He can take incarnation as Buddha and deceive people. Prabhupada writes:

> In transcendence notoriousness had the same absolute connotation as eminence.[30]

ISKCON believes that "the yogi should be able, when the occasion arises, to reject even moral behavior and do what is necessary to serve Krishna."[31] It is suggested that "to improve spiritually you must rise above even the mode of goodness."[32] A devotee can commit any evil because no action done for Krishna has any bad reaction. Krishna says

> anyone whose full consciousness is always absorbed in Me, even in lust, is elevated. As a fried seed cannot fructify, so any desire in connection with My loving service cannot produce any fruitive result, as in ordinary Karma.[33]

What this means is that because Krishna is independent of the law of Karma, anybody who is in Krishna consciousness is also free from the law. The religious can afford to be immoral whereas the irreligious, who are not in Krishna consciousness, should be moral.

But their view of how souls get into the bondage of births and deaths remains a mystery which is both insoluble and unacceptable. If no actions or desires have any consequences when one is in Krishna consciousness, and if souls in their original state are God, then how can their desire to enjoy material pleasures be considered bad karma that brings them into bondage? And if Krishna sends souls into bondage without any fault of their own, as Prabhupada sometimes suggests, then how can we escape the conclusion that Krishna is cruel and unworthy of loving service?

Their views of an amoral God and of the independent moral law of karma also weaken their view of salvation. If the law of karma is an eternal law of morals, then how can a guru set it aside during initiation? Much of recent guruism has adopted the Christian teaching that Jesus took the punishment of humanity's sin upon Himself on the cross, but this teaching doesn't square with guruism. In Christianity, God's moral law is absolute, and violation of it must be punished. The holy God can't overlook sin. On the cross, God, out of love, takes the punishment due to humanity upon Himself. But in ISKCON, when the guru initiates a disciple, the guru is said to simply take the bad karma upon himself.

The reason for this is that ISKCON doesn't really believe in an absolute law of karma—which they only assume to fill the moral vacuum created by the amoral character of God. They conveniently ignore or set aside the law of karma whenever necessary. Their argument for vegetarianism is that killing animals results in bad karma which takes us lower in the next birth, that even "killing a potato or hurting an apple tree" results in bad karma. But if vegetables and fruit are offered to the Lord before eating them, then murdering them has no consequences. Why doesn't this same principle apply to non-vegetarian food? Can't a devotee offer meat to Krishna and eat it in order to gain strength to serve him? No adequate argument is given against non-vegetarianism.

All their morality is arbitrary, reflecting more the cultural prejudices of Swami Prabhupada than the moral demands of the law of karma. Prabhupada discourages devotees from getting married. But if they are married, they are allowed sexual intercourse only once a month, on a night designated in the *Vedas* for fertility, and only after chanting for five or six hours. This becomes hard to understand when one contrasts it with the pastimes of Krishna himself. Prabhupada teaches that it is a literal fact that when Krishna walked in human shape on the earth five thousand years ago, he danced with about a hundred gopis at one time, all of them lost in orgiastic bliss, each convinced that he was making love to her alone.

Faye Levine, who lived in the New York ISKCON center for a long time, writes:

> The Hare Krishna ideology both denies sexuality to its adherents and tantalizes them with the tales and images of a sexy God.[34]

From all reports, the growth rate of the Hare Krishna movement in the West has already become very slow. It doesn't seem to have a great future. The strongest opposition has come from feminist movements because of the low position it gives to women. Prabhupada regards women "as prone to degradation, of little intelligence, and untrustworthy."[35] He advises devotees to

> never put [their] trust in a diplomat or a woman.[36]

However, the International Society for Krishna Consciousness does represent a deep-seated human need—the need to love, worship, and serve God—which must be met.

PART III

THE MODERNISTIC GURUS

No TRADITION CAN easily remain purely orthodox in a pluralistic society where many faiths and ideologies constantly interact and challenge each other. Some thinkers are bound to attempt new syntheses.

Mahesh Yogi is working hard trying to synthesize orthodox monistic Hinduism with current scientific thinking. He is willing to go so far as to deny that his is a religion at all. He sells his metaphysical concepts and religious practices as scientific facts and discoveries, hoping to win recognition from secular governments.

Bhagavan Rajneesh, who comes from a Jain family, is trying a synthesis of elements of monistic Hinduism, Tantra, Jainism, and Zen Buddhism, with insights drawn from Freudian psychology and other academic disciplines.

Brahma Kumari Ishwariya Vishv Vidhyalaya, perhaps the most heterodox sect, is outrightly theistic, pluralistic, and deterministic. Because of its cutting polemic against orthodox Hinduism, it is not even considered Hindu by many otherwise quite syncretistic Hindus. A chapter on this sect hasn't been included, because it neither has a living guru nor encourages worship of its human founder, Dada Lekhraj. It doesn't quite fall within the periphery of guruism.

Chapter Six

Transcendental Meditation

MAHARISHI MAHESH YOGI, the man behind TM, was born around 1918. in central India in a nonpriestly caste. Not much is known about his past because he refuses to talk about it. In 1940, he took a bachelor's degree in physics from Allahabad University. Then until 1953, he sought enlightenment under his guru Swami Brahmananda Saraswati, who was then Sankaracharya of Jyotirmath in the Himalayas. It is said that just before the Swami died, he commissioned Mahesh Yogi to evolve a simple form of meditation which anyone could learn and practice. In obedience to this directive, Mahesh hid away in the Himalayas for two years. When he emerged, he started the TM movement, and in 1956 he took the title "Maharishi," meaning "Great Seer."

In 1958, after he found the South Indians reluctant to accept him and his technique of Transcendental Meditation because he was a non-Brahmin, he decided to take it to the West—to the people "who are in the habit of receiving things quickly." He first went to England and then, in 1961, to America.

Because of historical and intellectual factors, Mahesh Yogi became more popular in the West than any other contemporary Hindu guru. The conversion of the Beatles to TM was a major factor. They soon gave it up, however, with John Lennon describing it as "just a waste of time." But while they were with the guru, he made headlines. Another factor was the apt time of Mahesh Yogi's arrival in California, a state known for its fertile climate for cults. When he got there in 1965, he found the youth revolution in full swing, although the students were beginning to get disillusioned with the political alternatives offered by the

73

New Left. In the autumn of 1965 about forty students from the University of California enrolled in a course on the principles and practice of Transcendental Meditation. By 1971 the number had risen to seventy-three thousand, recording a growth of 300 percent a year.

The momentum of this incredible growth rate has been sustained by the strong support which the Maharishi has received from the academic and professional world because of his ability to dovetail and continually modify his teachings to fit in with modern "scientific" thinking as popularized by current science fiction.

The popular movie *Star Trek* suggests that the universe may be a projection of a spiritual-electrical consciousness which is identical to the essence of humanity. If so, then through exerting the will of consciousness, effects can be achieved which are infinitely greater than what present methods of science can hope to match in foreseeable centuries. In this worldview the distinction between science, magic, and religion collapses. Even though the learned realize that this science fiction is not merely unscientific but also antiscientific, yet millions who have rejected the worldview of naturalistic science as unsatisfactory are now inclined to accept science fiction as true. Many are willing to examine the possibility of its truth.

The Maharishi speaks in this intellectual climate, to people who are willing to test the possibility that the consciousness within us may be the ultimate reality of the universe. If our inner power, which projected the universe in the first place, can be tapped, then we may have a power infinitely greater than the power of the atom. This power—if it really exists and is achievable—could enable us to create a utopia, whereas modern technological power is likely to end up destroying us.

Defining Terms

"Creative intelligence" is the Maharishi's term for the ultimate reality and being which is God.[1] It is defined as

> the impelling life force which manifests itself in the evolutionary process through creation of new forms and new relationships in the universe. The science of creative intelligence is a systematic study of its nature, origin, and development.[2]

So the term "creative intelligence" is the Maharishi's counterpart for the word "God," and the "science of creative intelligence" equals "theology."

Transcendental Meditation is that contemplation in which a person surpasses thought, reason, and the consciousness of his individuality to become aware of the creative intelligence. One isn't aware of anything except for the pure consciousness which is God.

The Maharishi points out that the physical universe is made up of energy in various forms. The Maharishi assumes that beneath these ever-changing forms of energy there exists a fundamental form of energy which is absolutely stable and so subtle that we can perceive it neither with our senses nor our latest technological devices. This form of energy he calls God or creative intelligence. "This is the source of all matter and energy." He calls this form of energy "pure existence" and asserts that it is "pure consciousness." The Maharishi believes that as physics goes on refining its methods of studying energy, one day

> it is bound to strike against [this] unmanifested aspect of existence, [and will] declare Being a scientific reality. It is just a matter of time.[3]

Even though physics has not yet developed a method of reaching this pure energy, the Maharishi has found "a direct and practical way in which everyone can experience it."[4] This way is, of course, Transcendental Meditation. From his experience of Being, the Maharishi knows that "it" is "without attributes and therefore unable to create."[5] However, he calls it "almighty, creative intelligence,"[6] which is "omnipresent."[7]

The material universe and its inhabitants are temporary expressions of the eternal Being. The Maharishi accepts Hindu monistic philosophy and believes that reality is only one. Plurality is only the temporary expression of the one, like the waves of an ocean.

The Maharishi doesn't use the traditional monistic doctrine of maya to explain the existence of the world and its individuals. Instead he modifies the doctrine of karma and ascribes creation to it:

> That which acts like the force of wind to produce a wave, on the ocean of unmanifested Being is Karma. . . . [There are] two realities at the root of Creation. One is the eternal reality of absolute being, and the other is the reality of Karma.[8]

Being has an inherent tendency or impulse to vibrate and become manifest. This tendency is called prana. "Reflected upon by karma, prana gains individuality and appears as individual mind." Simultaneously, the senses are also materialized:

> Matter comes into being to form the physical machinery through which the five senses of perception find their expression and to justify the validity of their creation to exist and act as the agents of mind.[9]

According to the Maharishi, due to the influence of karma upon Being, the mind evolves first and then the senses, the nervous system, the body, and finally matter.

Matter and our individuality are not illusory in the Maharishi's thought, but he doesn't call them real either. The eternal, changeless Being alone is real. The material universe is neither real nor unreal. It is mithya; that is, it has a phenomenal existence only. Usually we consider the world and our individuality to be real. This is ignorance and bondage. When in our consciousness,

> the object predominates and the subject (Self or Being) is as if lost in the object, the subject is said to be in bondage.[10]

Becoming aware of the subject or the self is liberation. Until one attains liberation, one is repeatedly reborn in various bodies. To be liberated, one has to transcend individuality and merge into the cosmic mind. One has to come

> out of what one is not. To be is to enter the realm of impersonal nature; to come out of the field of doing and thinking and to be established in the field of Being.[11]

Forms of Consciousness

Liberation, according to traditional monistic Hindu thought, is attaining an altered state of one's consciousness called turya. This is usually considered to be the fourth state, the first three being dreamless sleep consciousness, dream consciousness, and waking consciousness. But the Maharishi, following some neo-orthodox Hindu thinkers such as Aurobindo Ghosh, believes in seven states of consciousness: dreamless sleep consciousness, dream consciousness, waking consciousness, transcendental consciousness, cosmic consciousness, God consciousness, and unity consciousness.

In dreamless sleep, we are aware of neither the objective world, nor subjective consciousness. In the dream state, we have hallucinatory awareness of the outer world but not of self. In the normal waking state, we are aware of the outer world, but not of self. In transcendental consciousness, we become aware of the self within and lose awareness of the outer world. In the remaining three states—cosmic, God, and unity consciousness—we are simultaneously aware of both the self and the outer world. The difference is that we progressively come to perceive the subtler aspects of the objective world until we see that the objective world that appears as material to us is really pure consciousness.

Specifically, in cosmic consciousness, one is simultaneously aware both of the material world and of pure self. In God consciousness, the devotee begins to see the subtler levels of the material world. The Maharishi's concept of the God consciousness state is rather vague. He believes that when one reaches this state of consciousness one becomes God—one perfects all one's senses and abilities and becomes an "almighty supreme Being as the head of creation."[12] Dr. Anthony Campbell, who expounds the Maharishi's thought in *Seven States of Consciousness*, writes:

> For the people at this level of awareness the world is suffused with the light of Being, which in this state is seen to be personal. This is not a question of belief, but simply of perception. It depends, in fact, upon the physiological condition of one's nervous system.[13]

It is called God consciousness because in this state reality is perceived and experienced as personal consciousness, bliss, and peace. Feelings of holiness and sacredness are aroused. God consciousness is not the highest state, because even in this the duality of self and the outer world persist. But in unity consciousness, the apparent paradox of the absolute and the relative world is fully resolved. One perceives their essential identity. In other words, one sees that there is no difference between myself, other selves, and the material world. It is all one. This liberation, this oneness, isn't seen intellectually but intuitively or mystically. After attaining this state, one is not reborn; one merges into the universal consciousness.

Paths to Liberation

The Maharishi describes five paths to liberation: the psychological or intellectual approach, the emotional approach, the physiological approach, the psychophysiological approach, and the mechanical approach. He considers the first four to be very difficult for ordinary people and the fifth, the mechanical path of Transcendental Meditation, to be the easiest and best.

The intellectual path is what has been called jnana marg or raja yoga. The Maharishi says that this path to enlightenment is "a path of Self-hypnotism."[14] It consists of three steps. First, you discriminate between the real and the unreal and contemplate on the "transient, futile, ever-changing, perishable nature of the world."[15] The second step is to contemplate the oneness and the eternal features of Being. The third step is to live Being in practical life through the practice of establishing in the depth of consciousness the oneness of eternal life: I am that, thou art that, and all this is that.

The emotional path is the path of devotion or bhakti marga. The devotee cultivates the love of God in his or her heart.

As love increases, in his heart the devotee gains a greater degree of happiness. His heart finds its goal when his love rests in the eternal existence of God. The devotee and God become one. The drop of water finds itself in the fullness of the ocean and the two unite. The unity is complete . . . [and] unity alone is. Here is the one leaving no trace of the other.[16]

The psychological path of God-realization is the same as the hatha yoga. It is possible to experience self through physical exercises because all experience depends upon a specific condition of the nervous system. For example, hearing a sound is a result of some specific activity in the nervous system. This activity is responsible for providing the experience of the sound. Likewise, by physically stimulating the nervous system we can create transcendental consciousness.

The psychophysiological path to God realization consists of a combination of the physiological approach with the intellectual or emotional. This simultaneous use of both the body and the mind (or heart) can help us to arrive at the goal with "greater ease in the shortest time."

However, Mahesh Yogi feels that these four techniques, though possible and legitimate, are difficult for ordinary people. He advocates the mechanical path, or Transcendental Meditation, as the most natural, the easiest, and the best. He says that this is what the *Bhagavad Gita* calls the path of action or karma yoga. He writes:

> God-realization is possible in a mechanical way, because it is a matter of perception. And perception is a mechanical process. To see an object we have only to open our eyes and sight of the object comes automatically without the use of intellect or emotions.[17]

Likewise, to perceive our internal self, we have to let consciousness travel inward. The natural tendency of the mind is to travel in the direction of greater bliss. If it is directed towards pure consciousness, it automatically and mechanically gets there:

> Perception in the outward direction is the result of a progressive increase of activity in the nervous system; perception in the inward direction is the result of diminishing activity until the nervous system ceases to function and reaches a state of stillness, a state of restful alertness.[18]

The technique of Transcendental Meditation is usually not advertised as a path to God-realization because that would brand it as a religion and make it unacceptable to secular governments and institutions. It is described instead as a "simple technique for realizing your full mental potential and attaining a deep sense of rest." One is shown impressive scientific charts and graphs "proving" that TM has many physiological, psychological, and sociological advantages, such as better skin resistance, decreased cardiac output, decreased concentration of blood lactate, faster reaction time, increased perceptual ability, fewer spontaneous galvanic skin responses, effective interaction with the environment, superior perceptual motor performance, increased learning ability, reduced use of tranquilizers, developed and peaceful personality, better social relationships, and more.

Initiation

Potential devotees are assured that they don't have to change their religious beliefs in order to practice TM. Bob Jono and I were impressed by these "scientific proofs" for the validity of TM, so we decided to take a four-day course at the beautiful Academy of Meditation at Shankaracharya Nagar, Rishikesh. We had to offer fresh flowers, fruit, sweets, camphor, a white handkerchief, and a small fee of Rs. 11/- each.

A worship ceremony was arranged in which the picture of Mahesh Yogi's guru was worshiped. The initiator recited Sanskrit prayer, including one the Maharishi has written at the end of his commentary on the *Bhagavad Gita*. This prayer offers worship to the main gurus who stand in the tradition of Advaita Vedanta. The last half of it says:

> To Shankaracharya, the redeemer, hailed as Krishna and Badarayana, to the commentator of the Brahma Sutras, I bow down again and again. At whose door the whole galaxy of gods pray for perfection day and night, adorned with

immeasurable glory, preceptor of the whole world, having bowed down to him, we gain fulfillment.[19]

The recitation of the prayers had a soothing effect. They were intended to make us passive and receptive so that the initiator could plant the mantra (bij, or seed) deep in our subconscious mind with the help of psychic forces generated by his worship of these deities.

Bob and I were given our mantras separately because they are supposed to be kept secret. We were asked to recite them slowly in our minds, with our eyes closed. We were told that as we meditated, we would at first be conscious of the mantra and also of other things; that is, our consciousness would be at a grosser level. But slowly as we moved to the subtler levels of consciousness, we would lose awareness of all thoughts and then of the mantra also. We would eventually transcend thinking and experience transcendental consciousness itself. In a twenty-minute period, we would be likely to transcend four to five times.

Bob felt that he transcended. I wasn't sure if I did, though for a short time my chin shivered strangely and my face became tense. That evening during meditation I got a slight headache, and I slept poorly. The teacher explained it as either a result of not meditating properly or as a natural result of the release of pent-up tensions. Sometimes I felt relaxed after meditation but because my sleeplessness continued, I had to give it up altogether. Bob didn't have any such trouble. He gave it up later simply because he didn't notice any significant improvement.

After initiation, one is supposed to have two hours of personal instruction daily for three successive days. Then for the next month there are "checking sessions" once a week. The teacher asks questions to determine how well meditation is going. Then for the first year there are tune-up sessions once a month. Those with special interest can take advanced courses in subsequent years.

The Maharishi and his followers are convinced that Transcendental Meditation "deals with the fundamentals of all problems in life and suggests one solution to eradicate all suffering."[20]

It is claimed that because the individual establishes contact with pure consciousness or the almighty creative intelligence during meditation, the devotee increases his or her consciousness, creativity, and intelligence. And because pure consciousness is bliss, the individual is relieved of tensions and attains peace, which in turn results in harmonious relationships with others and nature. When the individual becomes good, the problems of the world are solved. Individuals develop their full potential and fulfill their philosophical aspirations to know the ultimate reality and the religious aspiration to merge in it.

Transcendental Meditation has undoubtedly attained unparalleled success. It has given peace, rest, and meaning to many individuals. The great vision of the Maharishi to solve all the problems of the world—as seen in his world plan—is certainly commendable; with thirty thousand people signing up every month for TM, one can be excused for making utopian claims and predictions. However, the flaws in Maharishi's teachings should become apparent even to a casual observer.

Problems in Consistency

The Maharishi believes that ultimately all duality or plurality is mithya; unity or pure consciousness alone is real. He says the universe and human beings are the waves on the ocean of being. But when he begins to describe the process by which the waves come into existence, he talks of two realities—the ocean of Being and the wind of karma. Usually, karma is considered to be the action of an individual. How can someone's karma come before existence? Failing to find an exit from this dilemma, the Maharishi asserts that the individual comes before karma and karma precedes the individual. There really is no beginning:

The cycle of creation and dissolution is the eternal cycle in the eternity of being.[21]

The world never got started. It has always been. But if individuals and the universe have always existed, then the talk of monism is nonsense. Here is absolute pluralism indeed!

Moreover, if the cycle of individuality and karma is eternal, then how can it come to an end? How can one transcend one's individuality? Liberation becomes a logical impossibility.

Within this philosophy, liberation would also be impossible on another ground: if karma is an eternal moral law, then how can it be simply set aside by the practice of TM? Where do the good and bad consequences of my bad karma go? How can alteration of my consciousness remove my karma?

Besides the fact that Maharishi has to give up his monism in order to explain the emergence of personality and the universe, he doesn't give a plausible explanation of how personality can emerge out of impersonal being. Can stones and oxygen molecules also come into existence because of the karma of their previous lives? Will they have to be reborn as humans and practice TM in order to merge back into unity consciousness?

Can we live with the Maharishi's answers? If personality is ultimately mithya and the cycle of karma producing individuals and individuals producing karma is eternal, then human life and history are meaningless and insignificant. In his commentary on the *Bhagavad Gita*, the Maharishi does see the logical implication of his view:

The present phenomenal phase of existence is seen to have no permanent significance.[22]

If this is so, why bother improving the world and helping individuals reach the full potential of their insignificant lives? Neither the Maharishi nor his followers can live consistently with their philosophy. Their world plan shows that they take "the present phenomenal phase of existence" to be significant, though their whole philosophy argues against it.

Benefits and Scientific Proofs

The best bait the Maharishi has used so far to draw converts is the array of scientific "proofs" to show that TM results in unique physical, emotional, intellectual, and social advancements—including the 1972 publication of *Scientific Research into Transcendental Meditation,* containing sixteen plates which show—through scientific graphs and charts—the unique results of TM. Most of these studies were conducted by the meditators themselves, and many by Dr. Keith Wallace, president of the Maharishi International University. Dr. Herbert Benson, an associate professor at Harvard Medical School, cooperated in many of these studies, though he pointed out that some of the research was inadequate because it didn't take into account those who stopped meditating and continued using drugs or those who would have stopped drug use anyway.[23] The Maharishi's movement, however, has continued to use the results of these studies for propaganda purposes.

After further investigations into the positive benefits of TM, Dr. Benson developed a simple method—relaxing and silently repeating the word "one"—which he claims gives the same results as TM. Anyone can learn it in a minute, without a fee and without going to TM classes. Dr. Benson's book *Relaxation Response* became a best seller and is demystifying TM as well as giving a cheap alternative to those looking for an exercise for relaxation. Transcendental Meditation does relax many people, but as Dr. John Laragh, perhaps the leading expert on hypertension in the U.S., says:

> I'm not sure that meditating has had any different effect on blood pressure than relaxing and sitting on a couch and reading a book.[24]

Psychology Today in April 1974 published a three-part article evaluating TM. The writers concluded that TM helps some people relax, is valueless to others, and is harmful to a few. Researcher Gary Schwartz warned that too much meditation may interfere with logical thought process because the whole technique is geared to take one beyond reason and thinking.[25]

Dr. Leon S. Otis, a scientist at the Stanford Research Institute International, Menlo Park, California, has done extensive scientific research on the effects of TM. This research has been published by Deane H. Shapiro and Roger N. Walsh in *Meditation: Classical and Contemporary Perspectives.* Dr. Otis said that he found "no differences in EEG, alpha frequency, heart rate, blood pressure, peripheral blood pulse volume, respiration rate, skin temperature, or personality measures between the TM and non-TM meditators." On the other hand, he found that the "TM subjects showed significantly more sleep stage I than control subjects." More shocking was Otis's discovery that TM causes many adverse behavioral effects on those who practice it for long periods. He circulated a thirty-item checklist to TM practitioners and teachers concerning such things as ability to relax, awareness, creativity, and emotional stability.

For analyzing the results of his research, Dr. Otis divided the TM practitioners who responded to his questionnaire into three groups: those who had dropped out of TM, short-term participants (three to six months), and long-term participants (over eighteen months). Before starting his investigations, Dr. Otis said that his "original expectations were that the number of adverse effects reported would be negatively correlated with the length of time in meditation and that dropouts would report the greatest number of adverse effects." The results turned out to be the opposite. "The number and severity of complaints," Dr. Otis said, "were positively related to the duration of meditation. That is, people who had been meditating for the longest period of time reported the most adverse effects."

The list of adverse effects, such as anxiety, confusion, and frustration, that have been admitted to by a significant percentage of meditators is enough to caution any curious person. But that is not all. TM empties the mind, and the mantra is often the name of a demon. Thus TM opens up the possibility of demon possession. Many ex-meditators have testified to this effect. No doubt some people dismiss the phenomenon of spirit possession as being sheer superstition, but the Maharishi himself believes in it and warns against it.[26] An ex-TM teacher described her experience of the demonic:

> I attended a training course in Fiuggi, Italy, where I learned from Maharishi how to be a TM instructor. Along with about a thousand others from all over the United States and the world, I spent three months meditating from three to ten hours a day. I had a vivid experience of demonic oppression while there, when in the night during sleep I woke with a sense of fear and apprehension, as pressure was being put all over my head and body by a spirit who was trying to enter my body. I commanded it to leave and resisted it until it left.[27]

Such experiences show that TM is by no means good or helpful for everyone. It does help some people physiologically, but it is not without dangers. Stanley Dean, a famous psychiatrist, sums up the chief scientific complaint against TM:

> Anyone who claims exclusivity is immediately suspect. The TM people's claim that theirs is the best of all possible worlds is nonsense. It is a sales gimmick. Meditation has been a way of achieving mental serenity through the ages, and they have no patent on it.[28]

Lord Tennyson used to experience mystic "ecstasy," "transcendent wonder," and "clearness of mind" by using the same technique which the Maharishi has mystified with monistic philosophy and secret initiation. Tennyson wrote:

I have . . . had . . . a kind of waking trance. . . . This has come upon me through repeating my own name to myself silently, till all at once, as it were out of the intensity of the consciousness of individuality, individuality itself seemed to dissolve and fade away into boundless being, and this not a confused state but the clearest.[29]

From the experience of Tennyson and the findings of Dr. Herbert Benson, it is obvious that the essential technique that TM uses for relaxation is quite simple. It gives rest and peace, but these benefits have been blown up and presented as the panacea for all the world's ills. An impression is created that these claims are based on scientific evidence, whereas there really is no such evidence.

The Maharishi has taken a simple technique which relaxes people—and in some cases alters one's consciousness—and has mystified it, yet he claims that it is not a religion. This is his second deception.

TM has succeeded in gaining recognition and support from secular governments, educational institutions, and even from Christian churches because the Maharishi constantly claims that "we are not a religion."[30] His followers urge non-meditators to become meditators by asserting that

TM is a natural, easy, systematic and scientifically verifiable technique. It is not a religion or philosophy.[31]

The Maharishi claims that TM is compatible with all religions. The Westerners accept this assertion uncritically because they usually equate religion with a set of dogmas, but the acceptance of the Maharishi's philosophy is not a prerequisite in order to practice TM. They often don't know that the practice of TM is meant to lead them to the monistic philosophy of the Maharishi. In his commentary on the *Bhagavad Gita,* he writes:

Meditation is a process which provides increasing charm at every step on the way to the Transcendent. The experience of this charm causes faith to grow. . . . The practice of transcendental meditation is such that it can be started from whatever level of faith a person may have, for it brings faith to the faithless and dispels the doubts in the mind of the skeptic by providing direct experience of Reality.[32]

The practice of TM is a bait to hook people into the Maharishi's religion, but the bait has been well camouflaged as a "simple, natural, scientific technique for peace and happiness." The Maharishi says, "Today we have to sell TM in secular terms through the agency of governments, because politics and secularism dominate people's minds." But in another moment "when religion dominates mass consciousness," he advises his followers that "transcendental meditation should be taught in terms of religion."[33]

Maharishi, who has tried to sell "instant nirvana" to humanity and "instant utopia" to world governments, has achieved an instant popularity around the world. One of the basic secrets of his phenomenal success can be summed up in a single word—deception. He succeeded in misleading millions of people, including governmental agencies, into believing that TM was a scientific and not a religious technique. This gave him respectability and entrance into thousands of government institutions and access to taxpayers' funds in many countries.

In the Appellate Court

Controversy over whether the Maharishi's philosophy was "pure science" or religion led the debate into the U.S. court system. Defeated in the district court, he proceeded to take his case to the U.S. court of appeals in Philadelphia. The counsel for TM argued that TM and SCI should be permitted entrance into the public schools as a true science. Oral arguments were heard on December 11, 1978. The presiding judge quoted the following from TM's initiation ceremony:

Guru in the glory of Brahma,
Guru in the glory of Vishnu,
Guru in the glory of the great Lord Shiva,
Guru in the glory of the personified transcendented
fullness of Brahman, to Him,
to Shri Guru Dev adorned with glory,
I bow down.

Then the judge asked, "What's scientific about that?" Instead of responding directly, the Maharishi's lawyer referred to an affidavit which stated that such ceremonies were sometimes used for secular occasions in India. The court remarked that the effect of that affidavit was to "take a cow and put a sign on it that says 'horse.'"

On February 2, 1978, the panel of the Appellate Court, consisting of three judges, gave its ruling upholding the lower court's decision against TM. A thirty-four page concurring opinion was given by one of the judges, which discussed the legal question involved in the case regarding the definition of religion and declared that TM was religion and not merely religious in nature.

The Maharishi could have gone on to the Supreme Court to challenge this ruling and try to preserve the right to teach TM in schools as a true science. Instead, he tried another deception.

TM as Medicine

The Maharishi decided to sell TM as an established treatment for many ailments and a panacea for public health care. From 1979 onwards this became the chief strategy of the movement. The first attempts were made in America, the United Kingdom, West Germany, and Denmark.

A "society promoting the medical use of TM" was established in Denmark, claiming a membership of forty doctors whose names were not made known to the public. The society proposed that

> TM be seen as a valuable supplement to existing medical treatment and an effective prophylactic means to avoid resource-wasting institutional treatment. Clinical research has shown that the method has been useful as a part of a treatment of various diseases, e.g., high blood pressure, asthmatic diseases, [and] overweight and sleeping problems.

The doctors proposed that similar research be done in public health programs to show the good effects of TM and urged that TM treatment be subsidized by public health insurance.

This triggered off a national debate. The question was raised in parliament, and the Minister for the Interior, Knud Enggard, presented a report from the health department. They found it strange that a group of medical doctors should recommend one particular system of meditation, TM, which used rituals related to Hindu gods when the same effect could be obtained through the use of neutral systems of meditation.

The proposal was given its death blow by the ethical committee of the Danish Medical Society. A woman who had been prescribed the practice of TM as a medical treatment asked the Committee whether this was correct. The ethical committee said:

> It is inconceivable that any doctor would require a patient to receive such treatment. . . .
> Even if there are very few who will understand the words of the ritual or the mantra, subsequent explanation of the meaning can undoubtedly cause discomfort or indeed give rise to serious inner conflicts, especially for religious individuals who have been through the process on the assumption that the words used were of a neutral character with no religious associations.

TM couldn't accept the advice of the ethical committee, because that would have meant eliminating the distinction between the esoteric and exoteric teachings of TM. If they explained to their "patients" that the mantra was the name of a deity and that puja was idol worship of it, then it would be established that TM was a religion and not a medical treatment. This would imply that TM ought to be sold as a religion, not as a science or as a medical treatment. If sold as a religion, it could claim neither easy acceptance nor state funding.

Is TM a Religion?

A Philadelphia judge ruled that it was. However, a religion which uses deception as its basic strategy for self propagation is an irreligious religion. Far from being a religion that can provide utopia, it is a mercenary religion and a mockery of all that is genuine in Hinduism.

Maharishi Mahesh Yogi has been appealing to all the world governments through full-page advertisements in magazines to allow him to solve all their problems through TM. He is prepared to work for the governments to be paid on the basis of results. He claims that "the discovery of the Unified Field of all the laws of Nature . . . has raised us to the doorstep of Utopia." Therefore, all problems can be solved through his technology. The simple problem with this claim, though, is that in many of the countries the government itself is the biggest socioeconomic problem. In the Philippines, then-President Marcos gave a formal invitation to the Maharishi to help solve his problems. Yet popular movements described as law-and-order problems by the rulers are not the ones that need solution; societies such as the Philippines need to be saved from oppressive, tyrannical, exploitative governments. But Maharishi is on the side of the governments—whatever their nature—because they have the kind of money that can pay his fee. The poor—oppressed by their governments—can't pay even the initiation fee, let alone the fee he demands for solving their problems.

How can a religious leader build the edifice of his movement on such deceptions? The Maharishi finds justification for such deception in the *Bhagavad Gita:*

> Those deluded by the gunas of Nature are attached to the actions of the gunas. Let not him who knows the whole disturb the ignorant who knows only the part.

Commenting on this verse, the Maharishi writes:

> If the enlightened man wants to bless one who is ignorant, he should meet him on the level of his ignorance and try to lift him up from there by giving him the key to transcending, so that he may gain bliss-consciousness and experience the Reality of life. He should not tell him about the level of the realized, because it would only confuse him.[34]

That the Maharishi would ask a person to start meditating before understanding the whole religious philosophy is understandable. But to assure a would-be meditator that "we are not a religion" is a definite lie. Such lying and deception are permissible in the Maharishi's religion because ultimately his monistic philosophy doesn't admit the duality of good and evil. Nothing can be ultimately evil in his system.

Chapter Seven

Acharya Rajneesh

FEW OTHER RELIGIOUS personalities of India possess a more brilliant intellect than does Rajneesh, and yet no one is more militantly anti-intellectual than he is. With his superb oratory, penetrating parables, and courageous critique of our cultural and religious traditions, Rajneesh (wrote one of his earlier biographers in 1970) "has begun to hold a commanding historical significance in India."[1] His daring denunciations of traditional philosophy, religion, scriptures, morality, values, and ideals, his outspoken criticisms of men like Gandhi and Vinoba, and his bold advocacy of sex as a legitimate means of salvation have no doubt won him many enemies, yet already there are tens of thousands who have accepted him as Bhagavan (God). They claim:

> Acharya Rajneesh is an Enlightened One, who has become one with Infinity, the Totality. He is not—but the Infinity breathes through him. He is not a person but the Divinity personified. Transcendental Truth shines every moment through him. He . . . is not living in Cosmic Consciousness, but has become the Cosmic Consciousness. Even further, he lives beyond Cosmos, beyond Being—in No-Being, in No-thingness, in the Great Void—Nirvana.[2]

Through discourses, radio-talks, interviews, magazines, books, and meditation camps, Rajneesh claims to enlighten and awaken people to freedom and authentic individuality. To the materialists who seek pleasure outside of themselves is shown the way to turn in and establish union with the inner bliss. The ascetics who have excessive attachment to detachment are invited to attain fulfillment, naturalness, and spontaneity. The passion of his soul is to make people free and genuine.

Rajneesh Chandra Mohan was born on December 11, 1931, at Kuchwada, in district Raisen, Madhya Pradesh. His father Shri Babulall was a businessman who had to move to Gadarwara, Narsimhapur, in 1934 because of financial problems. It was here that Rajneesh studied at Jabalpur and obtained a Bachelor of Arts degree. In 1957 he completed his postgraduate work in philosophy as a top student at the University of Saugar. Rajneesh was a versatile student, "an exquisite painter, a voracious reader, a poet and an amateur photographer." Because of poor economic conditions at home, he had to suspend studies for a while and work as an assistant editor in the daily newspaper *Navabharat*.

From 1957–1967, he taught philosophy in two colleges. Then he resigned from his job to consecrate his life to "the spiritual regeneration of humanity, to spread practical spirituality for every man." Though not as boldly utopian as Mahesh Yogi, he too gave the impression that the spiritual regeneration of humanity was nearly upon them:

> I see that a spiritual regeneration in the whole world is in the offing, and a new man is about to be born. We are passing through the birth-pangs.[3]

For some time, after resigning from his service, he lived at Jabalpur and traveled widely, lecturing at cultural and religious centers throughout India. Then he made his headquarters at Bombay. His early morning meditations at the seashore became notorious for their noise and crudity. In 1974 he was forced to move to Pune, where he bought a huge bungalow in a rich residential area. In six years he won many followers, earned great amounts of money, but also made many enemies so that he was forced to flee India on June 1, 1981. That same year he bought a 64,229 acre ranch near Antelope, Oregon, and set out to build a utopian commune of sannyasins.

Though Rajneesh intended to be a champion of the commoner and wanted to "spread practical spirituality," his followers, even in the 1970s, were mostly drawn from the affluent class. The entrance fee for each of his religious discourses was often Rs. 10. And he taught that only the rich could become spiritual, "that the materially poor can ever be spiritual is out-and-out absurd."[4]

Rajneesh—one-time owner of an estate worth seven million dollars and a fleet of seventy-four Rolls-Royces, protected by a private security force called "peace force," equipped with semiautomatic weapons—is as far removed from the common person as any guru can be. In fact, it has become hard to conceive how a guru can be reincarnated after seven hundred years to awaken mankind and yet be unavailable to the common person.

Having been a student and teacher of philosophy, Rajneesh is one of the most widely-read gurus. His authorized biographer, Dr. Ramachandra Prasad, points out the various sources of Rajneesh's thoughts. Even though born as a Jain, Rajneesh says outright that he is neither a Jain nor a Hindu. He doesn't like old labels. His rejection of the intellect as a valid source of knowledge and his acceptance of mysticism and silence smack simultaneously of contemporary Western philosophy and of Buddhism.[5]

His initial assumption that reality is ultimately one and that all diversity is illusory comes from the *Upanishads*. He agrees that "this soul of mine within the heart, this is 'Brahman'. " His view that the average person is ignorant, unawakened, and unenlightened comes from Gurdjieff's view of humanity as machine.

Rajneesh takes his doctrine of inner void (shoonya) and sudden enlightenment from his studies in Zen Buddhism, particularly from the writings of D. T. Suzuki. Zen Buddhism also is the "inexhaustible quarry from which the Acharya has drawn some of his stories and parables."[6]

The hatred of conventionalism and orthodoxy, the passionate plea for spontaneity and freedom come from Krishnamurti. Dr. Prasad maintains that:

> Rajneesh's message in a majority of his discourses is permeated through and through with ideas that remind us of Krishnamurti. His words for many are but a modern Hindi adaptation of Buddhist, and more especially of Krishnamurti's teaching.[7]

Rajneesh's view of sex and mysticism is a deliberate combination of tantrism and modern psychology. P. D. Ouspensky's emphasis on the kinship between sexual and mystical states was of the greatest influences on Rajneesh, even though the influences of Colin Wilson, Kenneth Walker, D. H. Lawrence, and Nietzsche are also apparent.[8] Also, Rajneesh's critique of the contemporary politico-economic situation in India is largely based on the writings of Arthur Koestler.[9]

There is much as well that Rajneesh has learned from religious leaders such as Mahavir, Buddha, and Christ. He is familiar with their teachings and freely quotes and misquotes them wherever he agrees or disagrees with them. At times he just puts his ideas into their mouths to exploit their influence—in spite of all his hatred of authority!

However, Rajneesh is not merely a mixture of various trends. He does have great contradictions—he glories in them—yet he has great ability to synthesize different ideas in his own framework.

His philosophy is, strictly speaking, an anti-philosophy because of his avowed anti-intellectualism. Rajneesh is not a philosopher proper but a mystic of feeling. He is dogmatic on the point that reason can't know the truth and words can't express it. He says:

> Dharma [religion] has nothing to do with thoughts or thinking. It has to do with not-thinking. Thinking is philosophy. It does give you results or conclusions but does not give you satisfaction.[10]

Truth or God—in fact, everything—is rationally unknown and unknowable according to Rajneesh. Religions have claimed that they know about God, the universe, and humanity. Science claims that it knows. But Rajneesh asserts that this is all "fiction" born of pride, an unwillingness to confess that we don't know. The husband thinks he knows the wife. The wife thinks she knows her husband or her child, but in reality she doesn't. We don't even know ourselves. "Do you know what is beauty?" asks Rajneesh. "Do you know what is truth? Do you know what is good? We do not know anything. But because nobody knows anything, and yet everybody claims that he knows, therefore no human being can lift up a finger and say, You are lying."[11]

Because reason doesn't know the truth, it can't be communicated in words, neither the words of the scriptures nor of the gurus. Rajneesh keeps asking us not to believe his own words. Ultimately, the truth can only be known in silence. "All who have known so far, have known through silence, not knowledge."[12] Rajneesh is out to show us the ways of "killing the mind, transcending the mind."[13] According to him truth appears in a state of thoughtlessness; it can't be tied down to a thought. Rajneesh doesn't attach much importance to words, misusing the Bible in his defense: "The letter killeth, but the spirit giveth life."

In fact, according to Rajneesh, the intellect is the "chief villain," Satan within us. Just as a prism divides one ray into seven, so the mind divides one reality into many. Because most people live at the level of the mind, they continue in ignorance, considering plurality and duality to be real:

> If you want to know and realize that which is undivided, go beyond mind. Do not use your mind as the instrument. . . . There is no problem in the reality and there is no need of any answer. But when you think, there are problems; when you do not think and realize, there are no problems. So, religion is a process to go beyond thinking, to achieve a point in your mind where there is no thinking at all.[14]

Even though Rajneesh is against philosophy, against thinking, he does have definite philosophical assumptions on which his mysticism rests.

Regarding the ultimate reality, Rajneesh thinks that we can never know how or why this universe came about. Like Buddha, he prefers to be silent on the ultimate metaphysical questions.

His basic assumption is that behind all the multiplicity in the world there is one reality: void, emptiness (shoonya). He calls this God or Brahman. This same reality manifests itself as the world. There is no transcendent creator, who creates the world outside of himself or as distinct from himself. The creation or the creative process itself is God. Rajneesh rejects the duality of creator and creation.

> The world and God are not two things. The creation is the Creator. It is not like a painter. A painter creates a painting. The moment the painting is created there are two things, the painter and the painting. The Creation is like a dancer, where the dance and the dancer are one.[15]

According to Rajneesh, the universe's impersonality has neither a cause nor a purpose. "If God is a person then we can ask, why have you created the world? But God is not a person. God is the process. . . . Existence is without any cause. . . . In the beginning there is no cause, so in the end there can be no purpose."[16] If we questioned Rajneesh, he would ask us to look around:

> A bullock cart is going. I see its wheels. The wheels revolve round the axis. The wheels go round and round on what is fixed and motionless. In the background of motion there is inactivity behind activity. Void resides behind existence.
>
> Similarly one day I saw a violent dust-storm. A big ball of dust was rising up in circular motion but in the middle there was a point where everything was quiet and steady. Is not the radical truth of the world manifest through those symbols?
>
> Is not voidness seated behind entire existence? Is there no inactivity behind all actions?[17]

Of course you can argue that the two analogies given above prove nothing. In the first, it is not the inactivity of the axis that is the background of the motion of the wheels but the activity of the oxen. Even the axis is not motionless; it is moving forward and thereby causing the motion in the wheels. Likewise, in the second, it can be argued that the quiet point at the center of the dust storm is not the cause of the motion. In fact, the reverse is more true. However, Rajneesh is not trying to prove voidness by the intellect. He knows that it cannot be proven. He has accepted it on the authority of the scriptures, even though he keeps denouncing them, and is only trying to illustrate his belief by analogies.

In one of his earliest meditation camps held near Ranakpur in June 1964, Rajneesh declared, "You have assembled here in this solitary place to realize God, truth, your own self. But may I ask you a question? He whom you are seeking, is He away from you? The one that is away can be sought, but how can that be sought which is your own self?[18] Rajneesh intimates that we are God. Somehow or other, the void begins to think of itself as an individual. How or why this happens Rajneesh does not know. He usually refuses to take shelter in the doctrine of maya; such speculations to him are useless. His burden is that we should become enlightened and see that our bondage is illusory. Yet he seems to accept some of the basic Hindu concepts such as transmigration and karma. Once God somehow becomes individualized, "It" remains an individual soul until it attains self-realization. These souls keep "floating in the sky." Husband and wife during coitus create circumstances in which a soul can descend into a body. "When the condition which is necessary, useful and appropriate for a particular soul is fulfilled, that soul gets born."[19] Does this imply dualism of soul and body? Or plurality of souls? Rajneesh doesn't want us to be bothered with such idle speculations. However, he does think a great deal on the nature of human bondage.

All individuals acknowledge that there is something fundamentally wrong with humanity. But they differ in their interpretation of what is wrong. The religious diagnosis of man's problem falls in two categories. Some religions, especially those in the Judeo-Christian tradition, consider our problem to be moral. That is, we are guilty of having broken God's moral law. We are sinners and need to be saved from our sin. This implies forgiveness for sins committed, deliverance from sinful habits, power to live above sin, and reestablishment of fellowship with God, which sin has severed.

But most Indian religions don't view our ultimate problem as moral. They consider it to be metaphysical—that is, our problem is that we are human. As long as we remain human, we are in bondage. Salvation lies in becoming void. Though this view sometimes incorporates sinfulness as a secondary problem, it doesn't ultimately consider us to be sinful, because we are God. The problem is that we are ignorant of our divinity. Our consciousness has become individual. It needs to be universal. Rajneesh makes it plain that in his view we are not sinners, though he isn't clear as to what our fundamental problem is. At times he suggests that we are in a mess because of the manner in which our parents conceived us. At other times he blames traditional religions and cultures for all of our problems. Just as when a seed fails to germinate in a certain soil we blame the soil, so also when "flowers do not bloom in man's life we ought to hold his religion and culture responsible for it, not him."[20]

In his *From Sex to Super Consciousness*, Rajneesh argues—rather, asserts without arguing—that religions have so far condemned sex as sin. This, he concludes, has made humanity more sexual. Sex is indeed divine, but sexuality is evil. Because children are born through sexuality, they are weak and sick, frustrated and degraded. We should instead accept sex as a door to divinity. Then children will be born through celibacy. They will be the supermen, as contemplated by Nietzsche and Aurobindo, and all the problems of the world will be resolved.

Sometimes Rajneesh also suggests that our problem is that we are ignorant of our true nature. We are void but think of ourselves as human. This is imaginary or pseudo-bondage. Rajneesh illustrates this bondage through parables:

> A huge caravan reached an inn in a desert. The owner of the camels ordered that the pegs be driven in the ground and the camels be tied to them with ropes so that they may rest. It was found that the peg and the rope of one of the camels was lost. They could not leave the camel untied, because they feared it may wander off. So they requested the proprietor of the inn for a peg and a rope.
>
> The proprietor replied, "We do not have any peg or rope, but why don't you drive the peg in the ground, tie a rope and tell the camel to sleep?"
>
> The owner of the caravan was amazed: "Wouldn't we have done it if we had a peg and a rope? Which peg shall we drive and what rope shall we tie?"
>
> The innkeeper laughed at this: "You don't have to tie the camel with a real rope and peg; camels can be tied with imaginary pegs and ropes, too. Drive an imaginary peg in the ground and tie a pseudo-rope around its neck and tell it to sleep."

There was no other way. They didn't believe it would work, but nevertheless they drove the imaginary peg into the ground. They hammered on the peg which was not. The camel heard the hammering and thought that the peg was being driven. The rope that was not was tied to its neck. The camel thought that it was being tied. As they had asked the other camels to sleep, so they asked this one. The camel sat down and slept.

When the caravan was getting ready to move next morning, they pulled out the pegs of the 99 camels and untied the ropes. But because the 100th had none, they didn't bother to pull out the peg or the untie the rope. The 99 camels got up but the 100th refused to get up. They were worried. They asked the old innkeeper what magic he had done that the camel had been stuck on the ground and was not standing up.

The old man replied, "First pull out the peg and untie the rope."

"But there is no peg and there is no rope," they protested.

"They may not be there for you, but they are there for the camel. Pull it out, untie it. As you had driven the imaginary peg in the ground and tied the false rope, you will have to take them off too."

They went. They pulled out the peg which wasn't there and untied the rope that didn't exist. The camel stood up and got ready to move with the others. They were all amazed and asked the innkeeper, "What's the secret?"

He replied, "Not only camels but men are tied to the peg which doesn't exist and imprisoned by ropes that are not. I have no experience of the camel, but advised you according to my experience of men."[21]

Rajneesh says that he agrees with the old innkeeper:

Having seen men I have also reached this conclusion. Man's slavery is also dependent on totally untrue and imaginary prisons. Man can be liberated if he can only see that his needs are false. The slavery is not real, it needs to be broken. It is imaginary. Therefore, its realization alone is its destruction. We don't have to do anything to liberate ourselves, because we are not really tied at all.[22]

How does this pseudo-bondage affect us? Rajneesh says it turns us into machines. We imagine that we act and think. In reality, like a machine we only react. We are not free to have our own thoughts and actions. "A man insults you and you start boiling with anger. Isn't this boiling purely mechanical? But you will say, I made myself angry. Did you make yourself angry or just become angry?" All the actions of an unenlightened person are sheer reactions according to Rajneesh. Only someone enlightened is capable of action:

Buddha was passing through a village. Some men threw stones at him, abused him and insulted him. Buddha said to these friends: "I have to go quickly to another village. If your conversation is over then may I go? But if you still have some stones left to throw, should I wait a little longer? But I can't wait for too long. I have to reach the other village early."

Those men replied, "Do you call this conversation? We have clearly insulted you, abused you and thrown stones. But can't you see that these are abuses, this is an insult? But there does not even seem to be any anger in your eyes."

Buddha said, "If you had come ten years ago you would have succeeded in making me angry. Then I was not my own master. All my actions were mechanical. If someone respected me I was pleased and if someone abused me I felt insulted. All these actions were purely mechanical; at that time I was not their master. But you have come a little late. Now I am my own master. Now nothing is mechanical in me. What I do not want to do does not happen. Only that happens which I want to do."[23]

Rajneesh at times asserts that all problems and suffering come from the fact that we live a mechanical life, a life in ignorance of our eternal freedom. We aren't free to do what we want because we don't know that we're free. We don't want war. Yet in five thousand years we have fought hundreds of wars. And now we are getting ready perhaps for a final war. The solution to all our problems lies in self-realization. We need to realize that we are free, that we are not the little ego that we ignorantly think we are but the universal self.

Rajneesh says that for thousands of years religions, scriptures, and gurus have been cruel to humanity. They have led us to search for God outside of ourselves, whereas religion is not about temples, scriptures, morality, contemplation, concentration, or saint adoration. It is going within ourselves. It is meditation.

Our problem is that we live at the level of intellect; we ignorantly take duality to be real. We take self and not-self as two opposing things, good and bad as different, body and soul as opposed. Salvation lies in going beyond mind and perceiving the oneness of reality in meditation. But meditation is not action. It's not even thinking or contemplating. It is just "being." This is shoonya:

> It would be wrong for me to say that I was practicing meditation; it would be correct to say I was in meditation. This is just like love. I am in love; love cannot be made.[24]

Even though meditation ultimately is not action, Rajneesh teaches many artificial devices to help us take our mind beyond thinking. These devices may be psychological exercises of autosuggestion or exhausting physical exercises which release us from thinking for some time. The following is a psychological meditation suggested for the night:

> Spread your body with ease on the floor and relax all the limbs completely, close your eyes and for about two minutes pass on the suggestion to yourself that the whole body is relaxing. The body will gradually be relaxed. Then for about two minutes visualize that your breathing is becoming gentle. Breathing will become gentle. Finally, visualize for about two minutes that thoughts are coming to a stop. Such willed auto-suggestion leads to complete relaxation, and contentlessness (shoonya); when the mind becomes perfectly calm, be thoroughly awake in your inner being (antas) and be a witness to that calm. This being a witness (saakshi bhava) will take you to yourself.[25]

One of the physical techniques is called "whirling meditation," supposedly an ancient Sufi technique. The meditators often practice it together in the after-noons during Rajneesh's camps. It requires you to make your whole being as receptive and unconscious as possible.

No food or drink should be taken for sometime before the meditation. Loose clothing and bare feet are best. The meditation takes two hours, and it is essential that the whole programme is completed.

The whirling is done on the spot; it is not a dance. You should move in a clockwise direction, and only if you find that impossible, do it anti-clockwise.

Let your body and arms be soft and for the first 15 minutes rotate slowly. Keep your eyes open all the time, but de-focus as soon as you can so that images become unformed and endlessly flowing. If it helps, imagine yourself pivoting around your navel. Should someone whirl into you, feel his energy and absorb it—and make a little room.

After 15 minutes the music will become progressively faster. Attune yourself to the rhythm and increase your speed with the music. The whirling lasts for one and a half hours. The final half hour of this is the fastest, and it is marked by the introduction of clashing cymbals. During this period you should spin so fast that you cannot remain upright and your body topples involuntarily.

If your body is soft you will land softly: the earth will absorb your energy. Do not allow your mind to arrange your fall prematurely. If you are still whirling when the music stops, simply let yourself drop to the ground.

Once you have fallen, the second part of the meditation starts, lasting for half an hour. Roll onto your stomach immediately so that your bare navel touches the earth. Only if this causes great discomfort should you lie on your back. Then press your body close to the earth, blend into it and recapture the moment of childhood when you pressed yourself on to your mother's breast. Keep your eyes closed and remain passive and dreamy.[26]

This may seem to be a gross and crazy meditation to those who associate spirituality with quiet, serene, and moral contemplation. The sight of the nude or seminude meditators may be repelling to others. Rajneesh, however, doesn't care for what those bound by meaningless tradition may think. Truth is to be found in spontaneity, naturalness, and freedom.

Lest anyone wonder about references to the navel, it should be explained that according to Rajneesh the soul resides in the region of the navel of the human body, not in the forehead as has been traditionally thought. In his book *Antaryatra,* he suggests that the reason why science and religion haven't been able to destroy ignorance and why our history is full of wars, crimes, hatred, conflicts, and social struggles is that so far we have only cultivated our head and ignored the navel region, which is the "root" of our existence. Education will continue to drive people mad until the emphasis is shifted from head to navel.

When through these meditations we "transcend thinking" and "kill our mind," then Rajneesh believes enlightenment, or Zen Satori, will dawn upon us. In a state of nonthinking or speechlessness we shall realize the truth, the self, the oneness, or reality. Besides these meditations, Rajneesh also advocates sexual or tantric meditation as a means of attaining superconsciousness.

His outspoken teachings on sex perhaps account more for the popularity of Rajneesh than anything else. When most of those interested in Hinduism seemed to be preferring yoga, Rajneesh revived tantra. Both yoga and tantra aim at union with the divine, he admits, but yoga is a path of struggle, tantra a path of surrender. Yoga produces pride. Tantra makes us humble, gentle, and loving.

> Yoga says bring your will to absolute perfection and you will be liberated. Tantra says dissolve your will completely. Become totally emptied of it, and that will be your liberation. And both are right.[27]

He acknowledges the danger that people could be drawn to tantra not to experience God but only to indulge in sex and says these are wrong reasons. Yet he vehemently criticizes all religions—often unjustly—for having regarded sex as something sinful. Sex is good. It is divine.

> If a seeker is not interested in sex, he is not a seeker at all. He may be a philosopher, but he is not a seeker. And philosophy is more or less non-sense—thinking about things which are of no use.[28]

Tantra is not concerned about the philosophical questions. Is there a God or moksha or heaven or hell? It is not concerned with such things but with life. Sex is the very presupposition of life. "Sexuality and spirituality are two ends of one energy."

> How can we "make the sex act a meditation"? By surrender!
> Anything becomes a god if you can surrender. So your surrender creates Divinity. There is nothing Divine; there is only a surrendering mind which creates Divinity.
> Surrender to a wife and she becomes Divine. Surrender to a husband and he becomes Divine. The Divinity is revealed through surrender. Surrender to a stone and there is no stone now. That stone has become a statue, a person—alive.[29]

In order to turn sex play into meditation there should be a total letting go. It is during the sexual act that we are most insulated from the outside world and are able to descend to the innermost depths of our being. Rarely, if ever, do we lose ourself to become completely artistic, completely tender and kind, completely free from our sense of the individual self. For a moment at least we leave our separateness behind and the "two become one flesh." For a moment we become nonexistent and attain timelessness. This is the state of samadhi (superconsciousness) where time, thoughts, and ego are transcended. Only love remains, and love is God.

Though Rajneesh advocates free sex in tantra—premarital or extramarital sex allowed—he insists that tantra is not sexual. Sexuality is mental and is thinking about sex, of which religious ascetics are most guilty. Tantra, on the other hand, not only leads to samadhi, but also to celibacy (brahmacharya). It treats sex as

> simply a door; while making love to a woman, you are really making love to Existence itself. The woman is just a door; the man is just a door.[30]

Once you learn to reach samadhi through sex you don't need to have intercourse with a member of the opposite sex. You can then have it with the whole universe—"with a tree, with the moon, with anything." Or you can just shut yourself alone in a room and have sex and experience samadhi, provided you know how to.

Traditionalists may feel this is immoral. But Rajneesh declares tantra is amoral. It is a science. He hates morality because it "creates hypocrisy"; it makes you "feel guilt and self-condemnation." He hates nothing more than hypocrisy and argues that it "cannot disappear from the earth unless morality disappears."[31] Because hypocrisy is the shadow of morality, they coexist.

Rajneesh realizes that society will find his teachings on sex hard to take, so he freely—and unfairly—puts his ideas into the mouths of other recognized religious authorities. In a lecture on Jesus Christ, Rajneesh said that when Jesus taught "you must be born again" in order to enter the kingdom of heaven, He meant that you must have sexual meditation. The argument was simple: reality is one. God, self, or heaven is consciousness within us. Duality is evil. The ultimate duality is sexual—duality of man and woman. In sexual intercourse you transcend this duality and the two become one flesh. Rajneesh maintains this is experiencing heaven. In his book *The Mustard Seed,* Rajneesh quotes Christ as saying, "When you make the male and female into a single one . . . then you shall enter the kingdom."[32] Anyone who has read the New Testament with some objectivity even once will realize how fantastic this interpretation is. The Christ of the New Testament is not a monist but a dualist in the sense that He believes that God is distinct from humanity. We are not divine but sinners. The new birth is the experience of forgiveness of sin and receiving the divine nature through the agency of the Holy Spirit. A person is born again by repenting for his or her sins and accepting Christ as Savior and Lord. No such quotation of Christ's exists in the Bible.

It would be an insult to Rajneesh's brilliant intellect to say that he has misunderstood Christ. We can only hold that this is a deliberate, dishonest interpretation of Christ in order to exploit his authority in favor of Rajneeshism. "Dishonesty is immoral and Bhagavan can't do anything evil," someone may argue. Not really. Rajneesh doesn't believe anything is immoral or evil in this universe.

> We have divided the world into the good and the evil. The world is not so divided.

The good and evil are our valuations. If there is no man on the Earth there will neither be good nor bad. Things will exist. Things will be, but there will be no valuation. Valuation is human. It is our imposition, it is our projection.[33]

So Rajneesh's monistic philosophy would not allow us to call anything evil— neither his advocacy of nudity, nor his allowance of extramarital sex, nor his dishonest use of the authority of Christ. According to his philosophy, there is no evil in this world, yet he himself is the fiercest critic of all that is bad and evil in our society. He condemns religious leaders for making the world poisonous, sexy, ugly, and debaucherous.[34] He condemns men like Gandhi and Vinoba for the mess in our politics.[35] Rajneesh doesn't worry about contradictions:

So what? Being inconsistent is a virtue, a sign of being progressive. It is the traditionalist who is tied to a dead orthodoxy and is consistent. If we want to say one thing about the progressive man, then we can say he is consistently inconsistent.[36]

As a progressive, Rajneesh believes in being inconsistent, but he doesn't allow others to do the same. Like Koestler, he criticizes Gandhi because his "methods of using nonviolence had their Himalayan inconsistencies."[37] And Rajneesh strongly chastises Indians for the same infraction:

We are very contradictory people. On the one hand we say politics is getting corrupt . . . and on the other hand we say good people should not enter into politics.[38]

Mystic Experience

Is the emptiness of shoonya, advocated by Rajneesh, an experience of God? Rajneesh, after all, has no basis whatsoever for calling shoonya or silence "God." Why not consider sound to be God as does Balyogeshwar?

Once reason and scriptures have been rejected as valid means to attain knowledge, all one is left with is experience. Then why is experience of silence more divine than experience of noise? Jan van Ruysbroeck, the famous medieval mystic, experienced the void or emptiness. Professor Zaehner sums up Ruysbroeck's findings:

Emptiness is the prelude to Holiness. To rest in this emptiness is dangerous for this is a "house swept and garnished," and though it is possible that God may enter in if the furniture is fair, it is equally likely that the proverbial seven devils will rush in if either the remaining furniture is foul or if there is no furniture at all; for "when men wish to exercise and possess this rest without the works of virtue, then they fall into spiritual pride, and into a self-complacency from which they seldom recover. And at such times they believe themselves to have and to be that which they never achieve."[39]

Spiritual Regeneration

Can the philosophy of amoral monism bring about significant moral change?

The best way to answer this question is to examine Rajneesh's unsuccessful attempts to build utopias in his own small communes in Pune and, later, in Antelope, Oregon. Rajneesh had to flee from Pune secretly without even informing most of his followers about the move. This was because his movement had bred enormous hostility against itself, and even though the ashram had become grossly overcrowded, it had been impossible to obtain another site in India to build his utopian commune because of governmental opposition.

The hostility was a predictable backlash from the conservative Hindu community of Pune. Rajneesh had gone on condemning the evils of established religion for a long time, but then the reports of nudity, rapes, sex orgies, and violence in his own meditation camps reached alarming proportions. His meditation camps included no-holds-barred encounter groups. In the padded, windowless basement rooms of Krishna House at Koregoan Park, the encounter could include punching, kicking, screaming, or engaging in sex. The participants have alleged that frustrations were allowed to be worked out by beating each other bloody. There were reports of broken bones. The ashram officials themselves acknowledged the violence when they announced it had been stopped following an indication from Bhagawan Shree Rajneesh that it had "fulfilled its function within the overall context of the ashram as an evolving spiritual commune."[40]

The rumors of gross sexuality were confirmed by the BBC when it screened a documentary which had been filmed secretly in one of Rajneesh's closed-door meditation camps. Rajneesh himself is said to have had many girlfriends. In the early years there was Kranti, a widowed cousin, who trailed him like a shadow. In 1969, a young woman from Britain, Christine Woolf (renamed Yoga Vivek) replaced Kranti. Rajneesh considered Woolf to be a reincarnation of his childhood girlfriend Shashi. Kranti couldn't tolerate another young female around the guru and therefore left.

Rajneesh often favored some women disciples with private darshans or audiences. One ex-sannyasin said that some women regarded sex with Rajneesh as "the ultimate darshan . . . . The girls enjoyed it and he enjoyed it, and why not? There's no law that says the guru doesn't sleep with his disciples. It's always happened."[41]

Troubles

Rajneesh's problems with the officials in Pune started because of violations of visa regulations by the sannyasins; tax evasion by his organizations; the smuggling of drugs, cash, and gold by the sannyasins; and false police reports and court cases started by his followers against citizens and officials.

Between 1976 and 1980, at least twenty-six foreign sannyasins lived in the Pune ashram without valid visas. At least six of them were convicted and fined. But the officials stopped pursuing the cases when the Rajneesh Foundation agreed that these sannyasins would leave the country. However, instead of making them leave, the movement started arranging marriages between non-Commonwealth citizens and Commonwealth citizens. This was done so that the non-Commonwealth citizens might obtain Commonwealth passports and thus continue in India without visas.

Many people believed that unpaid taxes was one of the main reasons behind Rajneesh's secretive exit from Pune. Even after all plans for the move to the United States had been finalized and an advance party had been dispatched on May 14, 1981, the movement still kept both insiders and outsiders in the dark about the move. It also deliberately misled the followers who were to be left behind. On May 15, Ma Anand Sheela, who had by then taken over the leadership of the movement from Ma Yoga Laxmi, formally announced that Pune would remain the "centre of our activities," even though an international commune would be set up in Gujarat, and a health resort in the Himalayas. Sheela reassured the disciples—who had donated most of their time, talent, and money in building the ashram and who felt insecure because of the rumors that the ashram was about to be closed—by pledging that she wouldn't leave Pune until the last sannyasin was provided for.

On the night of May 31, however, about forty selected sannyasins gathered to say goodbye to the guru. The other sannyasins only saw the guru and Sheela leave with a convoy of cars. He was gone before most of them even knew what was happening. Many started crying, and several important leaders came and consoled them by saying "that he had not left." The convoy drove all night, straight to the Bombay International Airport, where a Pan American Boeing 747 was waiting. Before dawn, the guru had flown off to the United States, leaving behind a legacy of an estimated Rs. 72 million in unpaid taxes.

In December 1984, Chandra Singh, the Income Tax Commissioner of Appeals, Pune, ruled assessments worth Rs. 3,908,690 for 1978-79, Rs. 7,925,892 for 1979-80, and Rs. 11,784,422 for 1980-81 alone. Besides this, he also made the foundation liable for a wealth tax of Rs. 5,839,269 for 1977-78 and Rs. 3,642,032 for 1978-79. It is unnecessary to multiply examples.

The smuggling of currency, drugs, and gold is also established fact. Former sannyasins have disclosed that black market currency transactions were routine in the Pune ashram. On June 25, 1983, the Bombay police arrested three leading Rajneesh men—Laherchand B. Shah, Chandrakant B. Desai, and Sudhir K. Khona—on charges of unauthorized acquisition and transfer of $100,000 and of $28,160. The three spent three days in jail and were then released on bail.

According to ex-sannyasins, the drug smuggling started as a means for penniless disciples to make money to pay for their stay in Pune. But it soon became an indirect, yet important, source of donations to the movement. Three

British sannyasins, Judith Ashton, Anne Curland, and Margot Gordon, were arrested on smuggling charges in Paris in 1979. The most ambitious known smuggling attempt was made in 1979 when fifty kilograms of marijuana were packed into the frame and furnishings of a hippie-style bus traveling from Pune to Europe. About twenty disciples had invested in the deal and another twenty had worked on the bus. The contraband, however, was discovered in Yugoslavia, and three sannyasins were put in jail for a year. Other sannyasin drug couriers have also been caught in different countries.

Maria Grazia Mori, who was once known as Deeksha in Rajneesh's inner circle, admitted that several top leaders, including Sheela, discussed ways of smuggling raw gold coins out of the country. They decided to turn the gold into jewelry, some of it made to look like cheap brass bangles. Stephanie J. Gilbert, a London jewelry maker whose sannyasin name was Magyan Bhakti, admitted to having made two dozen heavy gold bangles in the weeks before the guru left India.

Another major problem that preceded Rajneesh's exit from Pune was a series of criminal charges that were hurled by the citizens against the ashramites and vice-versa. Among the well-known cases is the entrapment of Shri Amarsingh Jadhavrao, which is said to have been planned by Sheela herself. Jadhavrao, a businessman from Pune, had rented his three-hundred-year-old fortress at Saswad to the movement. When a dispute broke out between him and the ashram, Sheela proceeded to send a young sannyasin girl to his home to trap him in a molestation case. A police officer, Bhosle, attached to the foreigner's registration office, who was dealing with the sannyasins' visa problems, found himself in a similar case. Still another involved a brother of the charity commissioner. The police have written off these cases as false complaints; a senior official has said that they "were simple cases of entrapment. Whenever they found anybody stepping out of line in his dealings with them, they would set him up and trap him in a molestation case." The police officials, however, were not able to prosecute the foundation or its members for lodging false and malicious complaints since the people responsible had already left.

Another fraud was the famous fire insurance case which took place a few weeks before Rajneesh flew off to the United States. The ashram had insured its godown against fire some years previous. It then took a fresh insurance policy of Rs. 25 lakhs on the contents of the godown. Two months later, homemade bombs went off in the godown. The ashramites tried to implicate Shri Jadhavrao in the case and called in the police and the CID. They declared their loss to be over Rs. 1.5 crores and filed insurance claims. A year later both the police and the CID officials were unanimous in their charge that the incidents were rigged by Rajneesh's followers. Additional Inspector General of the CID, Mr. Ramakant Kulkarni, has stated that the circumstances ruled out the possibility of involvement of outside persons: no outsider had access to the godown, which was manned round the clock. Besides, they had their own security guards.

As the investigation progressed, the ashram officials themselves lowered their declaration of losses from Rs. 1.5 crores to Rs. 5 lakhs. The interesting fact about the case was that only the books written in Hindi and some regional languages, which had not sold and were useless for the movement which was shifting to the U.S., were burnt. Books written in English remained untouched by the fire.

The cumulative effect of these and many other factors was that all attempts by the movement to secure a larger space in India for building a dream city were foiled by both the Janata and the Congress governments during 1977-79 and 1980-81 respectively. The ex-prime minister, Shri Morarji Desai, whom Rajneesh called "a cunning fascist," was especially opposed to his expansion moves. Mrs. Indira Gandhi, who encouraged Rajneesh while she was out of power, grew cold towards him after she came back to power in 1980 in order to please the conservative Hindu lobby of Pune.

Rajneeshpuram, the utopian dream city of Rajneesh, began with a bang in 1981 at Antelope, Oregon. Rajneesh predicted in *The Book of Books*, vol. 6: "This commune is going to be the source, but it will have branches all over the world. It will be the root, but it is going to become a big tree. It is going to reach every country, every potential person."

After four years, the signs of disintegration and retrenchment were more than visible. Ma Anand Sheela had masterminded the move to Oregon, partly to snatch away the leadership from Ma Yoga Laxmi, and had boasted to a lawyer in a court deposition, "I am the head of the religion. And I request you to respect that and address me in the same fashion." She was later dismissed from the movement along with most of the other top leaders, including Rajneesh's reincarnated girlfriend Yoga Viveka, for alleged charges of corruption. Yet corruption existed right from the start of the movement. Sheela's brother Bipin is said to have made a commission of $250,000 on the sale of the ranch itself. The commission dispute is still continuing among the brokers.

In 1981, the movement claimed 575 meditation centers in thirty-two countries. In 1985, they listed only 19 centers in ten countries. The dream city, which had claimed to be the only city in the world without crime, violence, and unemployment, had turned into an armed enclave, with Rajneesh himself driving around in an armored Rolls-Royce.

In 1984, Rajneesh spent $100,000 on contracts for security alone. This was apart from the $25,000 spent on his private peace force. By contrast, the police bureau in the capital city of Portland, with its 745-member force charged with the protection of a population of 371,500, had budgeted only $45,000 for 1984-85.

The following is the list of known weapons which Rajneesh's peace force owned to keep his tiny city free from crime: six SGW CAR-15 assault rifles; fifteen Galil assault rifles; seven Springfield M-1 A-1 assault rifles; three Ruger Mini-14 rifles; sixteen Uzi carbines; three Remington model 870 riot guns; twenty-two Smith and Wesson revolvers, 38.357 Magnum; two Smith and Wesson revolvers, .38 Special; one telescopic rifle, Ruger Model 77; two Detonics semiautomatic pistols, 9 mm; and one Detonics semiautomatic pistol, 145 mm.

The ashram owned 125,000 known rounds of ammunition as well as 26 magazines for the AR-15's, 71 magazines for the Uzis and 90 magazines for the Galils. They made at least three unsuccessful attempts to get fully automatic weapons.

The headquarters of the movement became so deeply entangled in over thirty active court cases that they had to set up the full-time Rajneesh Legal Services Corporation with eight employees and a host of volunteer paralegals. They won some cases but lost others. In May 1985, a U.S. District Court jury awarded $1.7 million to a former sannyasin after it found out that Sheela had deceived her into lending more than $300,000 to the movement in 1980.

The most crucial legal battle, however, was the case regarding the criminal and civil investigations made by the Immigration and Naturalization Services into allegations of immigration fraud involving Rajneesh himself, more than forty of his disciples, and assorted Rajneesh organizations. A prima facie case claimed that Rajneesh had entered the U.S. on the fake grounds of "necessary medical treatment" and had stayed on to propagate his religion.

Meanwhile, the Attorney General Dave Frohn Mayer gave his opinion in late 1983 that incorporation of Rajneeshpuram into the state was unconstitutional. His opinion was followed by a federal court law suit contending that the Rajneesh church controlled the city, which violated constitutional provisions assuring the separation of church and state.

Legal opinion was that these two cases would drive Rajneesh to exit into oblivion. However, Rajneesh tried to fight back, because he had little respect for the institutions of civilization. "Who makes your laws? asked Rajneesh. "Who makes your constitution? Who is responsible for running your society and arranging and managing the society? Just people as blind as you, maybe more learned, maybe more informed. But it makes no difference whether a blind man is more informed about the light or less informed about light—a blind man is a blind man."[42]

In conclusion we ask, What kind of spiritual regeneration can the amoral monism of Rajneesh bring to this world? A moment's thought will lead to the inevitable answer—anarchy. An ex-disciple said "Rajneesh allows his disciples to sin as they have never sinned before, only he does not call it sin."

Rajneesh Arrested While Fleeing U.S.

The "sins" of the Bhagwan finally caught up with him when he was arrested in a Hollywood-style drama at Charlotte-Douglass International Airport on the night of October 28, 1985. Rajneesh was attempting to fly out of the U.S. under cover of darkness after a federal grand jury had indicted him in an immigration case. Rajneesh was taken in handcuffs at 1:00 A.M. after his plane landed to refuel at the airport. His pilot was unaware that the authorities had been tipped off regarding their plans to charter two planes and fly off to Bermuda. The officials surrounded the plane secretly at night, and after the engines were cut off, they sprang the surprise. Rajneesh was later denied bail by the U.S. magistrate Barbara Delaney because he had already demonstrated his desire and ability to flee the country.

Simultaneously, Ma Anand Sheela, who had been hiding in West Germany since September 1985, was also arrested on an attempted-murder warrant from the United States. Rajneesh blamed Sheela, the ex-head of his religion, for attempting to murder him as well as for poisoning Michael Sullivan, the Oregon district attorney. Rajneesh held her responsible for fifty-five million dollars missing from his commune.

Anand Sheela, on the other hand, described Rajneesh as "a con." She charged him with exploiting people's emotions and taking all kinds of drugs. The Godman "is a spoilt little boy," she said. "I never went to him because he was a holy man, but because he was a man of my eyes."

The authorities felt relieved that Rajneesh had attempted to fly out of Rajneeshpuram and thus made his own arrest easy. Otherwise, to arrest him in his own city might have meant a fierce and bloody battle. Rajneesh, who had all along condemned governments for piling up arms and fighting wars, had well fortified his own city against an invasion from law-enforcing authorities in the U.S.

On November 14, 1985, Rajneesh struck a plea bargain with the U.S. District Court according to a well-established custom of jurisprudence in the U.S. According to the bargain, Rajneesh pleaded guilty to two federal immigration crimes: arranging sham marriages among his followers to violate visa regulations and making false statements to immigration officials to conceal his intention to remain permanently in the Unites States when he entered on a temporary visitor's visa in June 1981.

Under the agreement, Rajneesh paid $400,000 in fines and prosecution costs, received a suspended prison sentence of ten years, agreed to leave the U.S. in five days, and was placed on probation for five years. He agreed not to return to the United States during his term of probation without written permission from the U.S. attorney general.

PART IV

THE THAUMATURGIC GURUS

INDIA HAS ALWAYS had men and women with siddhies (supernormal powers). The masses have feared and worshiped them, yet miracles haven't held a high place of honor in the history of Hinduism. The people who did have siddhies were often looked down upon by the religious leaders because these powers were usually obtained through "the way of perversion"—indulgence in sex, wine, demon worship, and black magic. The phenomenon of spirit-possession, which is usually associated with the manifestation of the supernatural, has also been considered evil. But this was inconsistent with general Hindu monism, according to which there is only one spirit—God, who is both good and evil and beyond them. Now monism has worked itself out more logically, and all supernormal power is accepted as divine.

Sathya Sai Baba, who claims to have the spirit of Sai Baba of Shirdi, declares himself to be God. One hears incredible stories of his miracles from respectable witnesses.

Swami Muktananda of Ganeshpuri, Bombay, didn't claim to have performed many miracles, but he had the kundalini power to give various psychic experiences to his devotees.

Chapter Eight

Sathya Sai Baba

No Other Religious leader in India has so much charisma and so many converts as does Sri Sathya Sai Baba. "Baba is indeed God with the three qualities of omnipotence, omniscience, and omnipresence," claim hundreds of thousands of devotees. Khushwant Singh, former editor of the *Illustrated Weekly of India,* has reported that "next to Indira Gandhi, he is the biggest draw."

The Original Sai Baba

Sri Sathya Sai Baba claims to be the reincarnation of the Sai Baba of Shirdi (Maharashtra), who died on October 15, 1918, eight years before the birth of the more recent Sai Baba. No one knows the real name, the parents, or the birthplace of the original Sai Baba. He came to Shirdi at about the age of sixteen. His austerities greatly impressed the local people. Later he began to perform miracles as well.

For over a hundred years, no one has claimed to know the early history of the Shirdi Baba. Sri Sathya Sai Baba has recently begun to tell the story of his predecessor's birth, according to which the Shirdi Baba was an incarnation of Shiva.[1]

Shirdi Sai, who was declared mad by many contemporaries due to his erratic behavior and was reported to be homosexual by others, proclaimed one day, "Main Allah hun" (I am Allah—God). From about 1910 to 1918, he was actually worshiped as God by many. After his death, Sai Baba supposedly continued to appear to his devotees in their dreams to help them physically, materially, and spiritually. Shirdi became famous as a place where God lived and therefore was an important pilgrimage center.

There have been at least three other spiritual preceptors in Shirdi Sai's tradition: Upasani Baba, Meher Baba, and Sati Godavari Mataji. These three have claimed to be God, and Mataji has even claimed to be one with the Shirdi Sai. But only Sathya Sai Baba has claimed to be the reincarnation of the earlier Baba. And he was the first in claiming that the earlier Baba was an incarnation of Shiva.

Not all followers of the Shirdi Sai have accepted Sathya Sai as their guru's reincarnation. Many have tried to prove that Sathya Sai Baba is a fraud. However, he has slowly won over the masses. His fame and following has much surpassed that of his predecessor.

Sathya Sai Baba

Sathyanarayan Raju was born in Puttaparthi, in the Ananthpur district of Andhra Pradesh. He received his initial religious education from his grandfather Kondama Raju. His formal education began in his own village, but later he moved to the high school at Uravakonda. A bright student, he was especially interested in drama, music, poetry, and acting. At the age of eight, he is said to have written songs for the village opera. At ten, he organized a Bhajan group to sing the praises of Sai Baba of Shirdi. At twelve, he wrote a drama under the guidance of his teacher Sri Thimma Raju.

A strange experience apparently transformed Sai Baba in Uravakonda on March 8, 1940. At about 7:00 P.M., Sathya leaped into the air with a loud shriek, holding one toe of his right foot. For several years, the story was that he "was stung by a big black scorpion." Now Baba denies that there was any scorpion there. In any case, he writhed in pain for some time but had a sound sleep during the night. The next evening he fell unconscious, and his breathing became difficult. When he regained consciousness the following morning, he changed in his behavior. His Australian devotee and biographer, Howard Murphet, writes:

> The boy was by no means normal in behavior. He seemed at times to be a different person. He seldom answered when spoken to, he had little interest in food, he would suddenly burst into song or poetry, sometimes quoting long Sanskrit passages far beyond anything learned in his formal education and training. Off and on he would become stiff, appearing to leave his body and go somewhere else. At times he would have strength of ten; at other times he was weak as a lotus stalk. There was much alternate laughter and weeping but occasionally he would become very serious and give a discourse on the highest Vedanta philosophy.[2]

This abnormal behavior convinced his parents that some evil spirit had possessed him. Professor Gokak, his well-known Indian follower, writes:

> He was subjected to great suffering by the family because they called in exorcists

to treat him, believing that he was possessed by the devil.[3]

The torture inflicted by one of the exorcists was so horrible that the parents decided that it was better for the boy to live and be possessed by these evil spirits than for him to die at the hands of the exorcists. So they took him home.

On the morning of May 23, 1940, Sathya gathered around him some of his family members and with a wave of his hand "took from the air sugar candy and flowers" and distributed them to those present. Soon the neighbors began to crowd in. In a jovial mood, Sathya "produced" more candy, flowers, and payasam (milk with rice) for each person. The news that his son was performing siddhies reached his father. The father had had enough worries and strain for the last two months due to the boy. Angrily he walked home and shouted at him, "This is too much! It must stop! What are you? Tell me—a ghost, or a god, or a madcap?" Sathya replied calmly, "I am Sai Baba. . . . I have come to ward off your troubles, keep your houses clean and pure."

During the following weeks, Sathyanarayan made more claims. He also gave more "evidence" that the spirit of Sai Baba of Shirdi had come into him by producing with a wave of his hands items which linked him with the old Baba— photographs, dates and flowers from the Shirdi Shrine, and the sacred ash (vibhuti), which the Shirdi Sai also used to distribute.

Sathyanarayan didn't fit into school life again, and so on October 20, 1940, he threw away his books and announced that he was leaving. "My devotees are calling me, I have my work."

At first his miracles drew a few devotees; now they number in the millions. He has a magnificent ashram at Puttaparthi called Prashanthi Nilayam (abode of great peace). It too has become a holy place of pilgrimage. Three famous festivals are celebrated every year at the Prashanthi Nilayam—Dussehra, Baba's birthday, and Mahasivaratri. On a hill behind Prashanthi Nilayam, he has established a hospital, and in the ashram itself there is an academy for Vedic and Sanskrit study. In August 1966, Prashanthi Nilayam was separated from the village Puttaparthi and constituted into an administrative unit named Prasanthi Nilayam Township.

As Sri Sathya Sai Baba's popularity and influence have grown, he has made greater claims about his person and mission. At first it was believed that the spirit of the Shirdi Sai had come into him. Soon the phenomenon was interpreted as the reincarnation of the Sai Baba. Later he began claiming to be an avatar (incarnation). During the Dussehra Festival in 1961, he claimed that he was an avatar greater than Rama and Krishna:

> Rama was the embodiment of Sathya [truth] and Dharma [righteousness]; Krishna of Shanthi [peace] and Prem [love] . . . I have come embodying all the four.[4]

Also, one of Baba's famous sayings is:

> Krishna was busy with love or war
> The *gopis* or the *Kshatriyas*.
> Rama's time was taken up
> With family affairs.
> Sathya Sai has come for all humanity.[5]

By 1963 Baba had begun to claim that he was the incarnation of Shiva and Shakti. This last claim is significant because so far Hinduism has believed that Vishnu—the god responsible for sustaining the world—is the only one who takes incarnation; not Shiva or his consort Shakti, who are in charge of the destruction of the world. Not only does Baba claim to be a Hindu avatar. Since the Westerners have begun to follow him, he has also declared that he is Jesus Christ who has come again.

Baba's initial claim about his mission was, "I have come to ward off your troubles." Now his claim is that he has come for "the establishment of Dharma [righteousness] in the world."[6] In 1968, he declared that "it was his mission to restore India to her former spiritual glory . . . [and] that he would not rest from his labors till this had been achieved."[7] In a speech at Delhi, he proclaimed that the nations of the world were a railway train: India, the engine, drew it on the spiritual path, and the Bhagavan himself was the engine driver. He says that he has come for the spiritual regeneration of humanity through the all-around regeneration of India and has pronounced in unequivocal terms that he would leave the world only after completing his mission.[8]

There are about two thousand Sathya Sai samitis (committees) in India actively seeking to fulfill his mission. Similar committees have been formed to pioneer his work in many other countries. The United States, where Baba has never been, is said to have about one hundred Sathya Sai samitis preparing the country for his visit. These samitis meet once a week and seek to organize nagar sankirtan (itinerary singing) in their locality once a month. The samitis organize Sai seva dals (Sai service groups) for men and Sai mahila mandals (ladies' fellowships) for women. Men usually serve the poor and sick, whereas women conduct Sai balmandirs, where children are taught spirituality. The followers of Sathya Sai Baba, many of whom come from affluent homes, have started five colleges in his name. Their desire is to have at least one Sai College in every state of India.

The movement's monthly magazine, *Sanathan Sarathi* (Eternal Charioteer), is published in many languages. Books in many languages are constantly coming out of their printing press at Whitefield.

Judging from the number of houses and shops that have his photograph in a central place, it would seem that Sathya Sai Baba is becoming the deity of an ever-increasing number of Indians. Irrespective of whether or not he is an avatar greater than Rama or Krishna, it will not surprise me if Baba soon has more worshipers than either Rama or Krishna. And the new and subtle form of Shaivism that he represents overshadows the Vaishnavism of millions who have hitherto worshiped incarnations of Vishnu.

Philosophy

The fundamental philosophy of Sri Sathya Sai Baba is the same as that of other monistic gurus. He accepts the value of Hindu scriptures but emphasizes that reading them is not enough: "Scanning a map or turning over a guidebook will not give you the thrill of the actual visit."[9] At times he goes so far as to say, "You need not even read the scriptures, the *Gita* or the *Upanishads*. You will hear a gita [divine song] specially designed for you if only you call upon the Lord in your heart."[10]

Baba teaches that God is ultimately nirguna (without attributes) but also has a saguna (attributed) aspect for the spiritually immature. Baba basically regards the world as an illusion caused by maya—"The world is an illusion; do not put your trust in it."[11] But because he realizes that this view of the world doesn't encourage involvement in its problems, he also says that this world is divine.[12]

People, according to Baba, are atman (self or God), but under the influence of maya we forget that we are God. The easiest way to liberation—to a realization of our true self—is through devotion.

Bhakti cleanses the heart, uplifts the desires and gives a comprehensive outlook. It brings down the grace of God, just as the clouds descend and bring rains upon the field. Plants cannot rise up to get their life-juice. The mother has to bow down in order to rock the cradle. Devotion has the power which brings God down.[13]

Sai Baba's teachings regarding bhakti marga can be summed up:

1. Realize the absolute triviality and unimportance of the things, honors, and emoluments of this world and of the next.
2. Realize that you are in bondage to the lower worlds and aspire to get free.
3. Realize that our senses naturally gaze outwards, but an aspirant for self-realization must look inward.
4. Turn away from wrongdoing and compose yourself so that your mind is at rest.
5. Lead a life of truth, penance, insight, and right conduct.
6. Choose the good, not the pleasant.
7. Control your mind and senses; don't let them run around like wild and vicious horses.
8. Purify your mind by getting rid of the illusion, "I am the body" or "I am the mind." Discharge the duties of your station in life satisfactorily.
9. Find a guru. The knowledge of the self is so subtle that no one by their own effort can ever hope to attain it. The help of a great teacher, who has walked the path himself and attained self-realization, is absolutely necessary.

10. *Realize your utter helplessness and surrender to the guru. Then the divine grace will come. The light will shine. The joy will flow through you.*[14]

The popularity of Sathya Sai Baba essentially rests on his miracles. These are taken as the proof that he is an avatar. His miracles include materialization of objects by the waving of his hands, healing of the sick, knowing the thoughts of devotees—whatever the distance between them—and multiplying food. A long list of miracles has been catalogued by Mr. Murphet in his book *Sai Baba: Man of Miracles.*

A prominent devotee, Dr. S. Bhagvantham, M.Sc., Ph.D., D.Sc., a former director of the All India Institute of Science, Bangalore, and former scientific advisor to the Ministry of Defense in New Delhi, wrote the article "Baba Transcends Laws of Science" in the *Bhavan's Journal* of November 28, 1971. Many of his experiences with Baba are recorded as well by Mr. Murphet.

In 1959, Dr. Bhagvantham went with Sai Baba for a walk on the sands of the river Chitravati. After a while, Baba asked him to select a place on the sands to sit down. When the doctor hesitated, the Baba insisted, explaining that only in this way could Bhagvantham's scientific mind be quite sure that Baba had not led him to a spot where an object had been "planted" in the sands.

After the scientist had chosen a place and seated himself on the sands, Baba began to tease the doctor a little. He made fun of the complacent, "all-knowing" attitude of many scientists and deplored their ignorance of or indifference to the ancient wisdom to be found in Hindu scriptures.

The doctor's pride was stung. He retorted that not all scientists were of this materialistic outlook. He himself had a family tradition of Sanskrit learning and a deep interest in the spiritual classics of India. Then, to defend his fellow scientists, Dr. Bhagvantham told how the great scientist Oppenheimer had been a student of the *Bhagavad Gita.* "Would you like a copy of it?" Baba asked him suddenly, scooping up a handful of sand as he spoke. "Here it is," he continued. "Hold out your hands."

Bhagvantham cupped his hands to catch the sand as Baba dropped it. But when it reached the scientist's waiting palms, it was no longer the golden sand of the Chitravati. It was a red covered *Bhagavad Gita* printed in the Telugu script. It seemed quite new to Dr. Bhagvantham and didn't have the name of printer or publisher!

Other miracles give evidence of Sai Baba's healing powers. One day in 1960, Sai Baba was visiting the scientist's home in Bangalore. Dr. Bhagvantham, who was then the director of All India Institute of Science, had known Baba for about a year and was struggling to make the incredible phenomena he had witnessed fit into his scientific framework. One of his sons was mentally retarded. Some doctors had advised piercing the lumbar region of his spine to remove cerebrospinal fluid to relieve the pressure on the brain. Other experts had been against such treatment, fearing that it might only make the matter worse. Bhagvantham had decided not to have it done.

Baba saw the boy and asked about him. The scientist began to talk about his son's case and then Baba took over the narration and himself narrated all that had happened, including the medical debate about the advisability of a lumbar puncture. He went on to say that this would do no harm, but would in fact help the boy. Baba added that he himself would do the puncture.

Dr. Bhagvantham was startled. Doubt and fear agitated his mind. He wondered about things like professional qualifications for such an operation. But before he could utter a word, Baba waved his hand and materialized some vibhuti (ash). Uncovering the boy's back, he rubbed this ash on the lumbar region. Next, with another wave of the hand, he took from the air a hollow surgical needle, about four inches long.

The father felt himself in the presence of a power so beyond his understanding that he could say nothing; he just waited, watched, and hoped for the best. The boy, apparently anesthetized by Baba's vibhuti, seemed semiconscious. Baba inserted the needle, without any hesitation, on precisely the right spot. The needle seemed to go right in out of sight. The father began to worry about how it would be recovered.

Meanwhile, Baba was massaging the back and removing the fluid that came out through the needle. Altogether, about one cubic centimeter of the fluid came out. Then, massaging more strongly, or in a different way, Baba brought the needle out of the boy's back. He held it in the air as if handing it to some invisible nurse. Immediately it vanished away.

"Have you a surgical dressing?" the Baba then asked the watching, spellbound people in the room. Another of the doctor's sons, Ramakrishna, replied that he could get a dressing in ten minutes by telephoning the Institute.

"Too long!" Baba laughed, waving his hand again and receiving a dressing of the right type, as if from a trained assistant in another dimension. Carefully he arranged it on the boy's back and then brought him around to full consciousness. The patient seemed to suffer no pain or discomfort either during or after the operation. On being asked a few years later whether the boy was any better, the doctor replied cautiously, "Yes, his condition has improved, though not remarkably, but who knows what he would have been like without the operation? Swami says he will go on improving as he grows older."

This case of healing doesn't sound as fantastic, instantaneous, and complete as many other stories. But it is interesting because, if true, it shows that Baba's healings are not merely the psychosomatic healings of gurus like Rajneesh or Dattabal. Secondly, it is interesting because it concerns the son of a man whose testimony can't be lightly ignored. Sai Baba has, however, performed other types of miracles.

When Bhagvantham's son, Dr. S. Balakrishna, was moving into a new house in Hyderabad, he asked Baba to perform the house blessing ceremony. Baba himself named the auspicious day and promised to come. Dr. Bhagvantham was away on a government mission to Moscow but was scheduled to be back in Hyderabad on the morning of that day.

However, engine trouble in the plane compelled him to spend the night at Tashkent. Baba, who had arrived in Hyderabad that night before the ceremony, informed the family of the plane trouble and that the father was staying in Tashkent overnight but would be flying to Delhi the following day.

Next day Baba carried out the ceremony as prearranged. In his usual miraculous manner, he "produced" a beautiful statue of Shirdi Baba, three inches high and made of solid gold, for the shrine room of the house.

All were sorry that Dr. Bhagvantham could not come. They asked Baba whether he was back in Delhi. He told them that he was in the office of the minister of defense at that moment. Baba then booked a call to the minister's office, making it a personal call to Dr. Bhagvantham. The call came through in a few minutes. All were surprised to know that Dr. Bhagvantham was indeed there discussing the country's defense problems with Mr. V. K. Krishna Menon, then the defense minister.

These experiences have transformed Dr. Bhagvantham from a near-agnostic to a full-fledged believer. Hundreds of such testimonies given by high and low are convincing millions that Baba indeed is omnipotent, omniscient, and omnipresent God. However, there is also a growing number of disillusioned devotees—some through intimate experiences with Baba—who have become convinced that he is the very antithesis of God.

It is easy to find admiring devotees of a guru or ample literature in his favor; you just have to go to the ashram. But for a researcher like myself, who in a limited period wanted to study all the outstanding gurus, it was not always easy to hunt for devotees who had been disillusioned. However, in the case of Sri Sathya Sai Baba, Bob Jono and I were fortunate to find Mr. and Mrs. Carroll, a godly couple who lived not far from Baba's college and residence, Brindavan. They graciously welcomed us to stay with them, because visitors aren't allowed to stay in Brindavan when Baba isn't there in Whitefield.

Being very hospitable, the Carrolls have had many foreign devotees in need of accommodation stay at their home. They have seen many ardent devotees get disillusioned for various reasons. Through the Carrolls, I have been able to procure interesting and revealing documents from two people and will limit myself to them, an Indian and an American.

The Indian gentleman, N. C. Gunpuley, is a great patriot, a Hindu, and an intimate friend of our late President Zakir Hussain. He has spent most of his working years in the foreign service in European countries. After his retirement, his only desire was to serve the poor and the sick in his motherland. In 1970, he donated seven acres of his beautiful land to Sathya Sai Baba for the building of a thirty-bed hospital. Baba also took over the charitable dispensary which Mr. Gunpuley was running and promised to pay for it. However, Gunpuley's experiences from 1970-75 form one long story of disappointment and frustration. Baba neither kept his promises nor showed any concern for the sick and the poor. At one time he completely ignored the deed and decided to build huts for his foreign devotees instead of a hospital for the poor—an idea which had to be given up at the protests of Mr. Gunpuley.

Mr. Gunpuley narrated his experiences with Baba in his *Brief Synopsis of Sathya Sai Health and Education Trust* (August 1974), of which he kindly lent me a copy. This was his conclusion:

> I have passed through the most ugly experiences with the politics and politicians of the country, and also . . . through spirituality and religion about which we Indians are so very proud. . . . I had hoped that the latter would save me from my predicament and turned my attention wholly and solely to Sri Sathya Sai Baba, the great religious savant of this place, and have been waiting for the great solution for the last four and a quarter years.

The American Tal Brooke is a genuine spiritual seeker who lived with Baba for nineteen months. He really believed that Baba was an avatar and Jesus Christ come again. He was so trusted that Baba had him give discourses before large audiences. During this time, Tal also wrote a two-hundred page book on the Baba which was just about ready to be published in Calcutta when he saw the inner life of the Baba and turned away from him, consequently scrapping the book. On September 8, 1971, Brooke wrote a general letter explaining in detail to his friends the reasons for his turning away. Over a period of time, he had begun to dislike Baba's "self-glorification," which was so unlike Christ. One day Mrs. Carroll challenged Tal about the credibility of Baba's claims and powers. Baba claimed that he was God and could turn the whole earth into air if he wanted to. She asked Brooke, "If it is really so, why doesn't Baba put some water in those two bore wells that were drilled on the land donated to Baba for the hospital?" These questions began to create doubts in Brooke's mind.

In the religious psychology of India, it is believed that there are six psychic centers, called chakras, in the human body which give us various religious experiences when the serpent power called kundalini shakti passes through them. Various means are used in different sects to arouse this power in order to purify the chakras. Sai Baba uses secret sessions with his intimate followers in which he helps purify their lower chakras by handling their sexual organs.

At first when Sai Baba had his private session with Tal Brooke, the latter accepted this sexual encounter as a token of Baba's grace. If a medical doctor can handle your sexual organs to help you physically, what is wrong with a spiritual preceptor handling them to help you spiritually? Gradually, Tal came to know that Baba had similar sessions with many of his fellow devotees and some of the young schoolboys. Most of Baba's followers didn't see anything wrong with this because Baba taught that all morality is relative. What is wrong in one situation may be right in another. What is wrong for you and me may be good for a higher being. Tal's conscience, however, began to trouble him over this issue. Finally, one day he ran into a young Indian man in Whitefield, and a debate with him destroyed all of Tal's rationalizations. He felt he could no longer accept this practice as a spiritual exercise.

In Tal's letter, circulated to friends of his who were still following Baba, he wrote that the first reason that made him turn against Baba was:

> Baba's sexual encounters with a number people. . . . Who were those people? First of all there was me. Then there was Alpine Squartz, and the kid from UCLA, and the disciple of Yogi Bhajan, and two other members of the "Seven Rockets" if they will have the honesty to confess, and then there were some of the young school boys, and then I ran into a guy who blew my mind (yes, Baba could be purifying your chakras . . . but you can only stretch this thing for so long and justify it for so long . . . and if he is God he can do the job without handling your genitalia). As I have said, talking to the guy in Whitefield blew my mind, because something was coming through on a level of truth that I simply could no longer shut out or deny. I had to face it. . . . It was fortunate that I had had my own personal direct encounter with Baba, for to have listened to [this guy] otherwise would not have been possible. I would have physically mauled him. The truth in his account chipped away [at me] for a long time. I knew my time with the Baba was almost definitely up. . . . I was revulsed, felt nauseous, in a state of shock that lasted at least two weeks.

Tal Brooke has published the account of his day with Sai Baba in a book, *Avatar of Night: The Hidden Side of Sai Baba* (Vikas Publishing House, New Delhi). In this book, Tal tells us that the young man referred to earlier was Patrick, an Anglo-Indian from Whitefield itself, whom Baba—in spite of claiming omniscience—mistook to be an American. After a few group interviews, Baba called Patrick to his chambers for a private interview. At the end of the "interview," Sai Baba collected Patrick's semen in a little white handkerchief, and then told him that the whole "world lay in the palm of his hand, and that anything Patrick wanted he could have" (330).

Phil, a friend of Tal and an ex-follower of Sai Baba who delved into astrology for ten years and then taught it at the six-day school at Frisco, said "semen is the most potent thing used in heavy occult. . . . That is why there's such a heavy emphasis on sex in covens." When Phil and his wife decided to have their second child, they took a vow of celibacy for a year because they believed the occult teaching that if you store up your semen for a solar year, you can pull into this world the highest soul imaginable to incarnate into the body of your child, something on the level of a rishi or a master. Phil, with his theoretical and practical knowledge of the occult and close associations with Baba, believed that semen was the source of Baba's occult powers.

Sai Baba hasn't sued Tal Brooke for charges of defamation. Tal claims that in three countries of the world, as well as in the offices of the Vikas Publishing House, there is enough collected documentary evidence to fight out any court case.

Brooke's second blow was an encounter with God himself. He had been praying earnestly for a long time that God would reveal Himself as well as show him who Baba was. This in fact occurred while he was praying to God in a hotel in Bangalore: "God intervened and made His presence known to me in a way that made me shudder with tears for two full hours." Brooke had a vision of Christ, and he remembered the following words of Jesus Christ which explained to him who Baba was:

> For there shall arise false Christs and false prophets who shall show great signs and miracles so as to lead astray, if possible, even the elect (Matt. 24:24).

During the nineteen months, Tal had seen many things in Baba's life that didn't seem right, but he had always—as he says—put them in a little hole in his mind. He writes:

> As I sobbed, the hole burst and about a thousand things concerning Baba that never clicked came exploding out in a continuous stream. . . . I have rarely experienced such clarity of mind, such clarity and freedom of spirit. There it was for me to see; these bits of information took shape and formed a mosaic, and the evidence was undeniable against Baba. When compared to the living force of the truth of Christ, a perfect standard with which to measure, Baba became a shadow.

Of course, the testimonies of Baba's ardent devotees can't be accepted blindly, nor can those of his disillusioned devotees. But when a person claims to be God or an avatar, he is either telling the truth or deceiving us. If the latter is the case, then it must be exposed. Indifference to such a claim is not to be permitted. The crucial question remains: Is Sathya Sai Baba an avatar?

Miracles

The followers of Sathya Sai Baba usually argue that Baba's miracles prove that he is an avatar. But do they? The Baba himself says, "So called 'miracles' are not miracles, nor do they prove Divinity."[15]

There are many miracle-doers in India today, as there have always been. Bhagavan Neel Kanth Thataji, Amiya Roy Chowdhury (known as Dadaji), and Dattabal Desai are well-known gurus who claim to perform miracles of materialization and healing. Then there are many not-so-well-known figures: the author has himself seen many paralytics, polio patients, and the deaf, dumb, and blind healed through prayers by Mrs. Rajamma Devanandan—a Christian from Hyderabad. Then there are any number of magicians in India who can produce vibhuti, sweets, rings, statues, and watches from "nowhere." If miracles prove avatarhood, then all these would be avatars. Some of them, such as Bhagavan Neel Kanth Thataji, do claim to be God. But Baba says he alone is the avatar in this age.

> The Avatar is one only, and only this one body is taken by the Avatar.[16]

He claims to be the only avatar today and also the only true guru.[17] If miracles don't prove divinity, as Baba himself acknowledges, then what proofs are there of his avatarhood? None at all! We merely have his claim—against the weight of the entire Hindu tradition and the Christian Scriptures.

Hinduism has traditionally believed—Bhagavata being an exception—that Vishnu, never Shiva, takes ten avatars: the Matsya or fish incarnation; the Koorma or tortoise; the Varaha or boar; Narasimha or man-lion; Vamana; Parasurama; Rama; Balrama (some say Buddha instead of Balrama); Sri Krishna; and Kalki. Of these, nine have already come; only Kalki is yet to come. *Bhagavata Purana*, which mentions twenty-two avatars, also says that only Kalki is left to come at the end of the Kaliyuga. It is believed that Kalki will come when evil becomes so predominant that people eat even the flesh of saints. Obviously such a situation doesn't exist yet. Therefore, Sai Baba's claim to be an incarnation of Shiva-Shakti has no support in Hindu scriptures or traditions. The idea that any god, including Vishnu, will take three consecutive incarnations within a century or two has no parallel in Hindu history or mythology. To believe that Sai Baba is an avatar greater than Rama and Krishna goes directly against classical Hinduism.

Also, to believe that Sai Baba is Jesus Christ come again is to reject Christ's own words in the Bible:

> If they say to you, "Behold, he is in the wilderness," do not go forth, or "Behold, He is in the inner rooms," do not believe them. For just as the lightning comes from the east, and flashes even to the west, so shall the coming of the Son of Man be.[18]

The Bible makes plain that when Jesus comes again, He will come directly from heaven, in the clouds, and everyone will see Him coming—just as everyone sees and hears lightning. No one will need to tell anyone else. Jesus said that the second time He comes, His purpose will be to judge the world, not to restore the former spiritual glory of India.[19]

Philosophical Inconsistencies

The concepts of the grace of God, Ishwara, and guru or avatar don't make sense in Advaitic (non-dualistic) philosophy. To believe in avatarhood, the Advaitin has to believe that God is pure consciousness. Under the influence of "Its" own power of maya, It forgets that It is God and thinks Itself to be human.

Then, to liberate Itself from this ignorance, It sends Itself to the world as avatar.

The monistic sects in Hinduism have borrowed the idea of avatar from the theistic sects, but the belief in incarnation can't fit logically into monistic philosophy. One can accept Sathya Sai Baba as avatar only at the cost of intellectual suicide.

If Sathya Sai Baba isn't an avatar, can he possibly be a reincarnation of the Sai Baba of Shirdi? This too is logically impossible. For liberation, according to Sathya Sai Baba, means merging of our soul in Brahman, just as a river merges into the ocean. If the Sai Baba of Shirdi had attained liberation, how could he be reincarnated? Can a river come back after merging into the ocean?

If he is not an avatar or a reincarnation of Sai Baba of Shirdi, then who is he? Could it be that the initial diagnosis of his parents was right? Could it be that the spirit that had possessed Sai Baba of Shirdi came into him on March 8, 1940, and that, as he says, it wasn't a scorpion that bit him? Symptoms that he exhibited that day and on the following days would certainly indicate an experience of possession by a spirit. Many other things in his life since then, such as his frequent bouts of unconsciousness, his frequent attacks of deadly sickness and sudden recovery, and his supernatural powers, can be so understood. This would also allow for various charges that have been made against his character and integrity from time to time. The *Illustrated Weekly of India* published a letter to the editor, according to which

> a suit was filed in 1973 in the Civil Judge's Court, Bangalore district, against Sathya Sai Baba for recovering from him a sum of Rs. 94,800. After one year's litigation the case was withdrawn in September 1974.
>
> It is to be noted that Sathya Sai Baba talks of *Dharma* and nonattachment but owns extensive immovable properties in many parts of India, owns posh cars, lives in style and, as the said court proceedings have revealed, indulges in business dealings amounting to lakhs of rupees.[20]

Why is the possession of one person by another spirit considered evil in most cultures? The answer would seem to be that it destroys the selfhood of the one possessed. In the preface to his famous *Screwtape Letters*, C. S. Lewis suggests that one of the motives behind the activities of the devil is a kind of hunger, something similar to our perverted human passion to dominate—almost to digest our fellow beings—to make their whole intellectual and emotional life merely an extension of our own:

> On earth this desire is often called "Love." In Hell I feign they recognize it as hunger. But there the hunger is more ravenous, and a fuller satisfaction is possible. There, I suggest, the stronger spirit . . . can really and irrevocably suck the weaker into itself and permanently gorge its own being on the weaker's outraged individuality. It is (I feign) for this that devils desire human souls and the souls of one another.[21]

Shouldn't the parents of Sathyanarayan Raju consider it evil that the personality of their son is forcefully enslaved by another spirit?

Spiritual Degeneration

Leaving aside the question as to who Sathya Sai Baba really is, can he really bring about an all-around regeneration of Indian society? No one can deny that many followers of Sathya Sai Baba are genuinely seeking to solve India's problems, even though the majority follow him for selfish reasons. However, it seems absurd to believe that Sai Baba will regenerate India for two simple reasons: Baba says the kaliyuga or dark age is going to continue for another five thousand years.[22] If this is true, then the dream of a golden era around the corner is purely utopian, and the genuine efforts of his followers to bring about the golden age are doomed to failure. The second reason is that even though the Sathya Sai movement is trying to solve the socioeconomic problems of the world, the impulse for such activity comes not from Baba's own philosophy but from outside criticism of Hindu philosophy.

The Hindu concept of spirituality makes a person selfish or at best otherworldly. It provides no motivation for social action. It is only to answer these criticisms that Baba asks his followers to be involved in social service, for his own views of human life and body-consciousness as bondage and of the world as an illusion can never provide a basis for improvement of the world, body, or mind. Consider this famous saying of Baba:

Rebuked by his wife
For not shedding even a tear
Over the death of their only child,
The Man explains
I dreamed last night
That I was blessed with seven sons.
They all vanished when I woke up.
Who shall I weep for?
The seven that are vapor
Or the one that is dust?
The seven are a dream
And the one a daydream.
Though the soul may be born or die
As son or father,
It is immortal in itself.[23]

If humanity is simply dust or daydream, then we are certainly not worth weeping for, nor are we worth caring for. That Baba's philosophy logically leads his followers away from involvement with social problems is obvious. If the goal of one's philosophy is to seek moksha or deliverance from the world, then one can only become interested in life by being inconsistent with one's philosophy. If one is consistent, one can't say that the goal is to regenerate the world.

The growing popularity of Sri Sathya Sai Baba met with a setback when the seven-year-old "miracle" boy, Sai Krishna, was exposed as a fraud by the committee which Bangalore University set up to investigate superstitions and miracles.

Hundreds of people became followers of Sri Sathya Sai Baba because Sai Krishna started "miraculously" producing sacred ash and other objects out of the air. He and his parents claimed that these were given to him by Sai Baba. Thousands flocked to see the boy at Pandavpura. An Australian devotee of Sai Baba apparently made a movie on the boy to be shown abroad.

For a long time the twelve-member committee of Bangalore University tried to obtain permission from the boy's parents to investigate the authenticity of his miracles. Finally they were invited to attend the weekly bhajans as ordinary devotees but were prohibited from touching the boy. No miracles took place on July 8, 1976, when three of the team members went officially. On July 15, three other members attended the bhajans incognito and exposed the origin of the sacred ash. They found that the ash was hidden in the boy's vest and came out when he pulled a string hidden in his clothes! This naturally brought great embarrassment to the followers of Sathya Sai Baba. Ardent followers made loud but fruitless attempts to dissociate Sathya Sai Baba from Sai Krishna, but no reasonable explanation was possible. Why did "God" allow a family to fool the world for eight months and to bring hundreds into his fold by deception? Didn't he know that this was all a fraud?

The *Current* weekly (September 11, 1976), in their cover story, featured professional magician Niranjan Mathur and a renowned Hatha Yogi named L. S. Rao, both of whom claimed that the miracles of Sathya Sai Baba were only sleight of hand. Niranjan Mathur, who performs more impressive "miracles" of materialization, claimed that he was willing to serve Sai Baba as a slave for the rest of his life if the Baba could prove to him that his "miracles" were supernatural. His standing challenge is: "I can trap them [Godmen] while they perform their tricks if I can examine their hands just before they perform their so called miracles. But they won't be able to catch me, when I perform them."

The Bangalore University committee has repeatedly requested Sathya Sai Baba to permit them to examine the authenticity of his miracles, but he has refused their request.

Chapter Nine

Swami Muktananda Paramahansa

THE TERM "GOD" refers to that reality which is ultimate in the universe, that which has existed forever and caused everything to exist, that which is the absolute, the universal, which gives final meaning to every particular thing.

Humanity has conceived of God in different ways. Some say that God has revealed Himself to be an infinite-personal spirit, absolutely good and holy. These people say that God has created the universe outside of Himself or distinct from Himself. Humans, being part of the created universe, are not God. Others conceive of God as an infinite-impersonal existence. They consider its essential nature to be consciousness, light, sound, or silence. They usually consider the universe to be indistinct from God, a manifestation of Him. The mainstream of Hinduism, at least since Shankara, has thought that the world is an unreal, illusory manifestation of God. It is a superimposition of God just as a snake could be superimposed on a rope through ignorance. To these people all that is, is God—this is known as pantheism. Many pantheists today, though, do not consider the world to be unreal. They take it as real, but only as a manifestation of God, not something distinct from God. Everything including mankind is God, but our problem is that we don't realize it. Salvation lies in self-realization. The guru is self-realized; therefore, he is God.

Swami Muktananda of Ganeshpuri, near Bombay, claims to be God—the ultimate reality of the universe. He was an ascetic for many years, wandering all over India seeking God. Then after a series of strange experiences, he came to feel that he was God. He could help his devotees realize that they were God, he said, if they would surrender to him.

The story of Muktananda's birth is very interesting. His mother, wife of a rich landlord, prayed daily for the gift of a son at the temple of Lord Manjunath in Dharmsthala (Karnataka). One day a sadhu advised her to repeat the mantra "om namah shivaya" and said that God would soon bless her with a son. The prophecy was fulfilled on May 16, 1908, when the young Krishna was born in most unusual circumstances. The mother was conducting her daily morning ablution under a coconut tree. The child came without warning, with a suddenness and agility that have been characteristic of him ever since, and fell into the water basin under the tree.

The little Krishna was welcomed as a gift from heaven and was weighed in gold and silver, which were then offered to Lord Manjunath in return for his gift.

Krishna grew to be a well-built, agile, intelligent, clever, and mischievous boy. He was an imaginative leader and a ruthless fighter but was uninterested in academic education at school.

Krishna's father was also a deeply religious man. Each night he would gather the family and read portions from the *Ramayana* or *Mahabharata*. During festivals he would invite saints and sadhus for religious discourses at his home. At times he would arrange for yakshaya nas (dramas) which portrayed the story of the *Mahabharata*. The character of sages and yogis appealed most to the boy in these mythological shows. He admired their wisdom and power and desired their command even over the rulers and kings. He had always wanted to be a hero, a sadhu, without even "knowing the exact meaning of the word. To his simple mind it meant going from place to place."[1]

A small event at the age of fifteen set the course of his life. Swami Nityananda, who had already earned fame and following as an avadhoot (mystic), was invited by a Muslim mill owner for a bhandara on Kadri Hill, near Mangalore. The boy by chance ran into Swami Nityananda who at once embraced him, stroked him on the cheeks, and then suddenly walked away. The boy "felt a strange magnetic spell," and the impact of this encounter has remained with him ever since.

Krishna's spirit grew restless and impatient after this incident. His aversion to studies increased, and within six months he left home to become a sadhu. Krishna walked away penniless from home but had no worries. First he went to Mysore and then to Hubli. There he was guided to the math of Sidharudha Swami, where he began to learn Sanskrit, Vedanta, and yoga. He took sannyasa (renunciation) in this math and became Swami Muktananda.

In 1929, Muktananda left Hubli shortly after the death of Sri Sidharudha Swami. This was the beginning of his lone wanderings, which brought him in touch with about sixty Hindu saints. In the later part of this period, he received special attention from Ziprauanna and Harigiri Baba, both of whom noted his impending realization. The former was a naked ascetic who spent his days sitting on a refuse heap. He healed Muktananda's incessant headaches by making him sit on his lap and licking his head. He blessed Muktananda, saying, "Your fame will reach the highest heaven." Through water that had been poured on Ziprauanna's foot, Muktananda cured a woman in an advanced state of tuberculosis.

Harigiri Baba himself was very strange. At times he would dress up like a king; on other occasions he would be almost naked. He told Muktananda that he was no longer a swami but was now a maharaja (king).

> You need no longer live in a hut at Yeola. You have now to live in a palatial building. Cast away your ochre clothes and wear silken garments instead. You are no longer a sannyasin, but a maharaja. You shall not ask but only give.[2]

Muktananda indeed lived like a maharaja in his ashram during his lifetime. Peter Brent writes:

> Near him, you can only surrender to his force or leave. He is absolute monarch in his domain and expects from all who stay in it their taxes of devotion.[3]

Within two months of this meeting with Harigiri Baba, Muktananda again met Swami Nityananda. It was he who led Muktananda to the "ultimate divine goal and through whose grace he merged into the all pervading reality."

In July 1947, Muktananda came to Ganeshpuri intending to stay for a few days with Nityananda. Finding a guru to whom he could surrender himself, he stayed on. He lived there in a hut near the temple of the goddess Vajreshwari. One night, he saw a beautiful young woman coming out of the temple. He followed her with curiosity, but she disappeared in the nearby river. Next morning, Bhagavan Nityananda assured him that he had had a vision of the goddess herself.

On August 15, 1947, when Muktananda went for Bhagavan Nityananda's darshan, the latter came out wearing his wooden sandals. He smiled at Muktananda and said, "Will you take these sandals? Will you wear them?"

Muktananda replied, "I would certainly take the sandals but would not wear them. I shall worship them."[4]

He accepted the sandals in the hem of his garment. Nityananda then sat down and described the significance of the panchakshari mantra (om namah shivaya) at great length. While listening to this discourse, Muktananda "felt intoxicated and fell into a trance." Later,

> still in the trance-like state, [he] placed the sandals on his head and started to return to his hut at Vajreshwari. On the way he perforce stopped under a tree. There he had a unique experience. He saw divine light on all sides. Slowly he merged with the light and felt that he was everywhere. He felt blissful. He experienced that all-pervading Infinite Principle of Brahman . . . as his own Self."[5]

He remained in a trance-like, ecstatic state for some days, and after two months he returned to Yeola. He continued his sadhana (spiritual practices) there and also kept visiting other places. Of particular significance were his visits to

Chalisgaon, where he lived in a bhootkhana (a haunted place where nobody dared to live). It is said that "whoever tried to live in the house was thrown out and . . . four persons had lost their lives in that manner."[6]

During these eight years of intense sadhana, Muktananda had amazing spiritual experiences which he describes as the awakening of kundalini, supposedly the divine power that lies coiled at the base of the spine in human beings. Muktananda says it is our "innermost reality, which we call the inner Self, the true Self, because That is perfect, self-propelling, and self-luminous."[7]

In tantric yoga it has been maintained that once kundalini shakti (or serpent power) has been aroused it rises up and travels from the base of the spinal column to the head. During this time it passes through six psychic centers or chakras in the body. This rising of power gives many different experiences. Describing his own, Swami Muktananda said:

> Once Nityananda gave me a fruit and asked me to go to Yeola and continue my sadhana there. I carried the fruit with me to Yeola. On reaching my destination, I ate it and then sat for meditation. . . . I started feeling restless and uneasy. Within moments things were happening to me. I could not understand it. I was perturbed mentally and emotionally. My mind seemed deluded. By the time evening came this delusion became worse. . . . I felt I would soon become insane. . . .
>
> As I again sat for meditation, I felt there was great commotion around. My entire body started aching and automatically assumed padmasana, the lotus posture. . . . I felt severe pain in the knot below the navel. I tried to shout but could not even articulate. . . . Next I saw ugly and dreadful demon-like figures. I thought them to be evil spirits.
>
> I then saw blazes of fire on all sides and felt that I too was burning. After a while I felt a little better. Suddenly I saw a large ball of light approaching me from the front; as it approached, its light grew brighter and brighter. It then entered unobstructed through the closed doors of my *kutir* and merged into my head. My eyes were forcibly closed and I felt a fainting sensation. I was terrified by the powerfully dazzling light.
>
> Finally I saw a blue flame of light which first grew larger and then diminished to the size of a small pearl.[8]

Swami Muktananda was greatly perturbed by this, but Harigiri Baba came to him the next day and assured him, "Good times have come for you, not bad. You are going to be better off soon. You will attain the Godhead."[9]

So Muktananda sat again for meditation, and the experiences of "divinity" began again. He says, "I felt the same pain in the chakra below the navel, and a variety of visions appeared before me. I even saw naked men and women."[10] These made him wonder if he had strayed from his vows of sannyasa or had made some mistake. But later, on reading a book, he came to know that what had happened to him was that his kundalini had been awakened by the grace of the siddha guru, and all his experiences were the "reward of virtuous actions, not the bitter fruit of sinful deeds."[11]

As his sadhana progressed, the frightful visions ceased. But he continued to have visions. He heard "very sweet and melodious divine music" and saw different kinds of light—red, white, gold, or black. "After the vision of black light came a blue light. It was very enchanting and about the size of a small pearl."[12] Gradually, "a feeling that [he] was different from [his] body now began to develop in [him]."[13] The vision of a blue pearl is the final experience of God, according to Muktananda. He said that "the final attainment comes only when the neel bindu [the blue, pearl-like spot of light] remains steady in the vision of sadhana."[14] Once the neel bindu has become fixed and steady, "the realization dawns that God, guru, and he himself are one in Essence."[15] This, according to Muktananda, is "real Advaita or nonduality." Now the sadhaka can see "clearly that this world is only a dream or an illusion. He also realizes that he is different from the world and yet one with it at the same time."[16] Having reached this state, he becomes jivan mukta—one liberated in this life itself.

It is obvious that Swami Muktananda, who died in 1982, shared the traditional monistic or pantheistic worldview. He did not ask people to study the scriptures, nor did he give lectures because he had little use for "hair-splitting metaphysics."[17] He believed we are divine and could realize our divinity by the awakening of kundalini power. One doesn't need elaborate austerities, yoga, or spiritual practices in order to awaken the kundalini; guru kripa (guru's grace) is enough. One can obtain the grace by surrender and devotion to the guru. He said:

> Do not do anything. Do not use any methods or techniques. Just sit down and meditate. How does the guru's grace reach one? Well, gurudev's shakti catches them [devotees] like a strong infection. [He] either touches them on the face or eyes, or gives a mantra or raises his glasses and scrutinizes them, making them feel uncomfortable, or just tells them, "Go inside and meditate," and it happens. They begin to float, transported into another world of divine lights of different colours; they see the Blue Pearl of dazzling blue light or begin to see a mental movie or different scenes of past or future events, or hear celestial melodies, have visions of divine beings. Sometimes the body starts to do strange movements automatically.[18]

Swami Muktananda acknowledged that there were many different forms of yogas or paths of attaining liberation. But the path he advocated is called the perfect yoga (siddha yoga) or great yoga (maha yoga). "This yoga encompasses all other forms of yoga." It is simple. You just have to surrender to the guru; he does everything. "He may use, abuse, or anger but his methods prove effective."[19]

Because Swami Muktananda didn't believe in theories or metaphysics, he was thoroughly inconsistent in his statements. In one breath he could say that "the world is not an illusion but a manifestation of the Divine Consciousness."[20] And in the next: "The world was never created but is only an illusion. Just as in the dark, a rope may be mistaken for a snake, so also the world is an illusion created by the mind and superimposed on Parabrahman."[21]

With regard to morals, he said that "Divine Reality pervades everything. Even what appear to be opposites are in fact expressions of the same Reality."[22] In other words, nothing is ultimately good or evil because both are expressions of the divine. Therefore "a jnani is beyond do's and don'ts."[23] So his followers try "to give up . . . even praiseworthy desires for purity, will and discipline."[24] However, drugs, meat, drink, sex, playing cards, gambling, club life, parties, and movies are considered to be bad by his followers.[25]

His followers don't bother about these intellectual inconsistencies because the intellect is looked down upon as a hindrance in religious matters. "Instead of thinking about how, when and why the world was created, seek the Truth; try to liberate yourself from bondage."[26] His followers seek to be delivered from the "impossible webs of intellect."[27]

It is interesting that even though Swami Muktananda was a monist and believed that God alone is, he still believed in the existence of evil spirits, demons, and haunted houses. Could his experiences actually have been demonic, inspired by the evil spirits whom he saw during his experiences? Or were they just abnormal mental experiences brought about by excessive meditation, austerities, fastings, and wishful thinking? Naturally, the interpretations will differ depending on one's worldview. If one takes a completely naturalistic perspective, then, like Charles S. J. White, one can legitimately ask "whether they [the experiences] are not hysterical or other types of psychologically abnormal states."[28] This interpretation is supported by Muktananda's own confession that "he frequently found himself in a condition bordering on madness or complete physical breakdown."[29]

This interpretation also finds support from the classic experience of John Custance. Custance often suffered from acute mania, during which he thought himself to be God. In his book, he narrates the symptoms that often preceded attacks of mania:

> At the onset of phases of manic excitement, I have sometimes noticed the typical symptoms, the pleasurable tingling of the spinal cord and warm sense of well-being in the solar plexus, long before any reaction in the mental sphere occurred. I had the excited shivers in the spinal column and tingling of the nerves that always herald my manic phases.[30]

Physiologically, one can't distinguish the experiences of Muktananda from John Custance's experience of madness. However, the weakness of this interpretation is that it doesn't account for the hundreds, if not thousands, of devotees who have experienced similar things without undergoing such intense sadhana.

The alternative interpretation, especially if one believes that there are evil spiritual forces (as Muktananda did)—call them bhoot, brahamarakshasa, or demons—would be that these experiences are not divine but demonic. Meditating in haunted homes, sitting in the lap of a naked sadhu who sits on a refuse heap, seeing evil spirits, getting pain and fever, having visions of naked men and women, and becoming almost mad don't sound like very "divine" experiences. Muktananda said that the "supreme goal is the same for the followers of all religions." In his own case, the supreme attainment was seeing the blue light. According to some religious traditions, Satan himself appears as an angel of light.[31] Could it be that when the "large ball of light" merged into Muktananda's head, it was a demon and not God that came into him and that the mystic experiences that Muktananda gave to his disciples were given through the power of demons? This is what William James has called "diabolical mysticism":

> Religious mysticism is only one half of mysticism. The other half has no accumulated traditions except those which the textbooks on insanity supply. Open any one of these, and you will find abundant cases in which "mystical ideas" are cited as characteristic symptoms of enfeebled or deluded states of mind. In delusional insanity, paranoia, as they sometimes call it, we may have diabolical mysticism, a sort of religious mysticism turned upside down. The same sense of ineffable importance in the smallest events, the same texts and words coming with new meanings, the same voices and visions and leadings and missions, the same controlling by extraneous powers; only this time the emotion is pessimistic: instead of consolations we have desolations; the meanings are dreadful; and the powers are enemies of life. It is evident from the point of view of their psychological mechanism, that classic mysticism and these lower mysticisms spring from the same mental level, from that great subliminal or transmarginal region of which science is beginning to admit the existence, but of which so little is really known. That region contains every kind of matter: "seraph and snake" abide there side by side. To come from thence is no infallible credential. What comes must be sifted and tested.[32]

How can we determine whether the mystic experiences of Muktananda and his disciples are divine or purely psychological or demonic? The old religious dictum could be of help: "Watch out for false prophets . . . by their fruits you shall know them" (Matt. 8:15-16). William Rodarmor, a lawyer turned journalist, spent months investigating every aspect of Muktananda's life, teaching, and movement. One of his articles, "The Secret Life of Swami Muktananda," was published by *Co-Evolution Quarterly* in the winter of 1983. He narrates in detail the criminal acts of violence and corruption of Swami Muktananda, which are not really "secret."

Most of the disciples of the inner circle of Muktananda didn't object to the fact that he regularly had sex with the female devotees.

Mrs. Chandra Dinga, an American devotee who was head of the food services put up with Muktananda's sexual perversion for a long time, until she became upset that he was molesting a thirteen-year-old girl who had been entrusted to the ashram by her parents.

Stan Trout, formerly Swami Abhayananda, served Muktananda for ten years as teacher and ashram director. He says he left his service because the guru "sent two of his bodyguards to deliver threats to two young married women who had been speaking to others of Muktananda's sexual liaison with a number of young girls in his ashram. It was immediately clear to me that I could not represent a guru who was not only taking sexual advantages of his female devotees but was threatening with bodily harm those who revealed the truth about him."

The facts of financial corruption in Muktananda's establishment are yet to be fully uncovered. One of his successors, Swami Chidvilasananda, denied in her interview with William Rodarmor that they had a secret account in a Swiss Bank. But Ed Oliver, chief of their foundation, conceded in an October 1, 1983, interview with the *Los Angeles Times* that there was a Swiss account with $1.5 million in it. According to some ex-followers, Swami Muktananda had himself said that the account had more than five million dollars. Amma, a lady who was Muktananda's companion for twenty years, has disclosed that the account has always been operated by Chidvilasananda herself. Why does she then deny having this account?

A devotee argued that it was not for him, a seeker after truth, to be bothered with these matters. It was for the income tax department to unearth the tax evasion and black money.

Scandal of the "Perfect Way"

Between October 1985 and January 1986, Muktananda's movement both split and got entangled in a scandal which has had consequences as far-reaching as the scandals in Rajneeshism and the Divine Light Mission.

In 1982, Swami Muktananda appointed Swami Nityananda and his older sister Swami Chidvilasananda to head the Gurudev Siddha Peeth as his joint successors. Lust for power led to the rivalry for total control. According to the reports, Swami Nityananda was forced to abdicate his throne on October 24, 1985. He was kept a prisoner and forced to give up his throne in favor of becoming a disciple of his sister, who had the support of the automatic-gun-wielding foreign sannyasins.

Ilayas Khan, a handyman at the Ganeshpuri ashram, confessed that he was offered Rs. 5 lakhs and a revolver to murder his guru. Later, instead of murdering him, captors succeeded in smuggling the guru out of the country on December 2, 1985, in a state of drugged semiconsciousness. The story that "leaked out" was that he had renounced his position to marry his American secretary, Devyani.

Three trustees resigned in protest of the murky goings-on in the movement at the top level. Others fought to keep or gain control over the empire worth

Rs. 300 crore. Meanwhile, the funds at Ganeshpuri were fast depleting. In two years, 50 percent of Rs. 40 million was used to spread the spirituality of the "Perfect Way."

PART V

THE AUDIO-LUMINOUS GURUS

GOD IS INFINITE, almost blinding, light. He is the primordial sound—the word—that reverberates throughout the universe. He is also within us. Until we come to the lotus feet of the sadguru (true guru), we will remain unhappy, seeking peace, enslaved in the cycle of birth and death. But if we come to the living master, receive the true knowledge, and practice true meditation, we will see the light and hear the sound. We will merge into God and obtain liberation.

Many sects, mainly in North India, believe God to be sound and light. For them, surat-shabd yoga (union of soul with word) is the only means of realizing God. While each group claims the authenticity of their guru, they also assert that their teachings have been universally taught by all true saints always.

In recent years, Radha Soami Satsang (Beas), Jai Gurudev Dharam Pracharak Sangh, and the Divine Light Mission have been the most influential of these sects. The Radha Soamis derive their inspiration more from Sikhism; the other two favor Hinduism. But they belong to neither and prefer to be called sant mat—the path of saints. Historically, Sant Kabir and Guru Nanak were the forerunners of sant mat, but the present sects claim that the sant mat has existed since the dawn of civilization.

Though initially included in the research, the Jai Gurudev Dharam Pracharak Sang (JGDPS) need no longer be discussed at length. It started as a religious sect; later it was turned into a political weapon by certain political parties. Its founder, Sri Tulsidas Ji Maharaj, overstepped himself at Kanput on January 23, 1975 when he tried to declare that he was Netaji Subhash Chandra Bose (whose death is controversial). It now seems unlikely that his movement will draw much attention.

Chapter Ten

The Divine Light Mission

THE SPECTACULAR RISE and the scandalous fall of the Divine Light Mission has made it the most publicized sect of our day. Its recently dethroned leader, Balyogeshwar, alias Guru Maharaj Ji, was claimed to be "the brightest event in the history of the planet." Balyogeshwar's father, the founder of the Mission, had declared him to be be the "born saint"; his mother, the patron of the Mission, and Bal Bhagavan, his oldest brother and the new leader of the Mission, called him the "perfect master." Like Sai Baba, Balyogeshwar claimed the he was Jesus Christ come again and Krishna reincarnated. Millions believed him and surrendered their minds to him. They testified that he had given them the experience of divinity. This brilliant star has turned out to be a meteor that flashed across gurudom only to sputter out into darkness.

The founder of the Divine Light Mission, Shri Hans Ji Maharaj, was born in Badrinath, UP. He was drawn to the Arya Samaj at an early age because of his religious inclinations. Later, by sheer coincidence, he met a saint known as Dada Guru and became his disciple. He entered samadhi while meditating, only the day after his initiation. He lost his body consciousness and realized the divinity within.

Dada Guru had appointed Shri Hans Ji to be his successor, but after the guru's death a small band of disciples refused to acknowledge Hans Ji's leadership. Therefore, he left for Sindh and Lahore and started disseminating the knowledge of Divine Light and Holy Name. From 1930 onwards he visited Delhi frequently, preaching to the laborers of the Delhi Cloth Mills.

His simple, practical, well-illustrated lectures, with a strong moral tone backed by his magnetic personality, attracted many followers. By 1960, it is claimed that "tens of thousands" had taken initiation, and subsequently the Divine Light Mission was founded. (The Mission is not always honest in giving statistics; a book published by the Mission in 1970 claims that there were approximately a hundred thousand members at that time.[1] But a book published in 1973 claims that in 1966 they had several million followers.[2])

Generally, in the tradition of sant mat, guruship is hereditary or at least confined to the family. Shri Hans Ji Maharaj married Rajeshwari Devi because his first wife did not bear him a son. Mataji and he had four sons; all were claimed to be divine, but the youngest was the "born saint," the "perfect master." Rajeshwari Devi became the "divine mother," but the first wife, who lived in Dehra Dun, had no place in the Mission. Balyogeshwar became the leader of the sect after his father's death on July 19, 1966.

Balyogeshwar was born on December 10, 1957, at Hardwar. He had his schooling at St. Joseph's Academy, Dehra Dun. His father initiated him when he was six years old, but it took about a month of meditation before he realized his divinity.

On August 1, 1966, when he was eight years old, he declared himself to be the "perfect master." To the thousands of devotees present at his father's funeral, he said, "Why are you weeping? Haven't you learned the lesson that your master taught you? The perfect master never dies. Maharaj Ji is here, among you now." Awed at this declaration, his mother, brother, and mahatmas (apostles) prostrated themselves at his feet and received his blessing.

At a mammoth gathering in Delhi in November 1970, Balyogeshwar said, "I declare that I will establish peace in this world." Six months later he went on his first tour to Great Britain, Canada, and the United States. His mission had phenomenal success in the West. By 1972, the DLM (Divine Light Mission) claimed 45 centers in the U.S. with fifteen thousand members. By June 1973, they claimed to have 480 centers in 38 countries.

The Mission launched a popular paper called *The Divine Times* and a magazine, *And It Is Divine*. Their movies, *Lord of the Universe* and *Satguru Has Come* attracted many viewers.

Balyogeshwar reached the zenith of his popularity during the Millennium Festival, 1973, in Houston. There his devotees declared him to be the savior of the world who was ushering in the thousand years of utopia. It wouldn't perhaps be an exaggeration to say that at that time his popularity overshadowed that of all the gurus and religious leaders in the world. But it didn't take very long for it to dwindle to almost nothing.

The descent began in late 1973 when the sixteen-year-old god married his twenty-four-year-old American secretary, Marylin Louise Johnson. By the middle of 1974, he had reached the point of no return on the road described as "unspiritual" by his mother, brother, and C. L. Tandon, the secretary general of the Mission in India. The "divine mother" spent virtually the whole of 1974 trying to get her son back on the proper path. Mr. Tandon made two visits to the U.S. to persuade the "perfect master" to mend his ways but was appalled to see that "night clubs," "illicit relations," and liquor were part of the routine of the young guru. Also, the four taboos of the mission—"no sex, no alcohol, no consumption of non-vegetarian food, and complete celibacy"—had been broken within the ashram in the U.S.[3]

The cracks within the "divine family" became impossible to cement after Balyogeshwar issued directives that the photographs of his mother were to be removed from all the centers, since she was no longer divine, and in their place were to be put photographs of his wife who was "the incarnation of the goddess Durga." This precipitated a situation in which his mother, the patron of the Mission, had to remove him from leadership and enthrone his eldest brother, Bal Bhagavan, in his place.

Balyogeshwar and his Western followers, however, described his mother's step as "ridiculous," since he had taken over the complete management of the Mission on his sixteenth birthday in December 1973 in accordance with the will of his divine father. Joe Anctil, Balyogeshwar's press secretary, defended the perfect master on the grounds that he wasn't following any traditions or Indian concepts and so couldn't be bound by Indian social taboos. Mr. Anctil argued that "Maharaj Ji doesn't say what to eat, drink or smoke. He wants to change the hearts of men and not their habits." Besides, he argued, when Balyogeshwar's mother was in the U.S., "she lived exactly the [same] lifestyle,"[4] and Balyogeshwar had to remove her from the Mission because she "had mismanaged the Mission which caused [them] to be in debt at the time."

After Bal Bhagavan was declared to be the leader of the Mission, Balyogeshwar levelled serious charges against his brother's character as well, for which they went to court. The particular case was withdrawn because this "battle of bhagavans" made the entire "divine family" a laughingstock to the world. But the legal battle for ownership of the property in the West continued. The Western followers have generally sided with the "perfect master," whereas the Indians have generally accepted the leadership of Bal Bhagavan. The average Indian devotee is in fact little bothered with these details. In talking to some, I found that they still consider Balyogeshwar to be God. One of them said to me, "Lord Krishna also lived this kind of life and we worship him as God; why hold Balyogeshwar guilty?"

The Divine Light Mission has not been interested in teachings and philosophies. Balyogeshwar and his brother have consistently rejected "theoretical" knowledge as "useless." I found the DLM devotees most difficult to talk to, because they neither wanted to teach their philosophy to me nor answer philosophical questions and objections. Their one comment was, "Take the practical knowledge of the experience of Sound and Light and all your doubts and questions will be answered."

"Practical knowledge" or simply "knowledge" is a term used to describe meditation. DLM claims that the knowledge has been handed down through the ages from one realized person to another. It was there when the world began, and it is with us now. In times of greater darkness, great saints are sent to disseminate this knowledge. The knowledge or meditation consists of four techniques; namely, the techniques of seeing the divine light, hearing the divine sound, tasting the divine nectar, and hearing the divine word. These techniques are taught by the guru or by the mahatmas authorized by him in a secret initiation ceremony which includes meditation.[5]

A person is initiated only after a mahatma can see that he is spiritually prepared. There is no definite criterion for judging whether or not a person is ready. You can go to a mahatma today and be declared unprepared. But go to another and you may be told that you have been ready for a long time. The main thing a mahatma generally looks for is the intensity of one's desire to receive the knowledge. Often people fall on their hands and knees before the mahatmas to beg for knowledge. They may be refused even after such prayers.

After some people have been selected for initiation, they are taken into a closed room where the mahatma explains to them the importance of the knowledge, satsang, and the sadguru. The would-be initiates make an open profession that they will follow no other guru or saint except their own and that they will worship and serve the sadguru with all their hearts, strength, wealth, and talents. Serving the sadguru in practice means obeying the orders of the mahatma and propagating the knowledge.

After making the vows, one by one the initiates bow before the picture of the sadguru and worship it. Then the mahatma gives the knowledge or the techniques of meditation.

In order to show the divine light, the mahatma asks the initiates to close their eyes. Then he places his middle finger and thumb on their eyes and starting from the corner of the eyeballs he presses the eyeballs up from the bottom so that if the eyelids were open the center of the pupils would be looking at the "third eye."[6] If the initiate concentrates on this point, he may see a light; some others see a psychedelic movie of moving patterns and brilliant colors, while some don't see anything at all.

The technique of hearing the music or the sound is simple. The initiate is asked to block his ears with his thumbs so that he does not hear any external sounds. When he listens long enough to his inner silence, he can eventually hear some noises. To some people this sounds like celestial music, while others think they are hearing their favorite tune played on some heavenly instrument.

The technique of tasting nectar is a very difficult yogic exercise. Usually it is experienced after much practice. The initiate has to try and curl his tongue to come up to the back of the throat and then has to swallow the tongue in such a way that it points upwards. Here the tongue is supposed to hit a point and make contact with the nectar that is constantly flowing through one's body. It is claimed that this nectar is indescribably tasty and that it is the "living water" of which Jesus spoke. Some of the devotees also describe it as the "bread of life" and claim that after making contact with the ever-flowing stream of nectar you can live without food or water—but no one has as yet come forward to demonstrate these claims.

Hearing the word is the main meditation. In fact, it is often regarded as the knowledge. It is simply a breathing exercise in which one sits in a lotus position, if possible, with both hands on the knees, and concentrates on breathing in and out, in and out. Through concentrating on this, one supposedly tunes into that "primordial vibration," the word or logos which has created the universe and sustains it. By constant meditation, one is supposed to reach samadhi or the expanded state of consciousness, which according to the DLM is the purpose of life. You know that you have reached samadhi by the light. At the initiation, the light seen may be only a small point. But as you meditate the light gets brighter. Eventually the light overtakes you, and you become literally full of this light. Once you feel or perceive that you have become the light, you are assured that you have reached samadhi, or have merged into God. You will never be reborn.

The monistic presuppositions of the Divine Light Mission and those aspects of its teachings which it shares with the Radha Soami Satsang will be touched on later. Here we need only say of Sri Balyogeshwar that his life—which has been described by his mother and brother as immoral—is quite consistent with his philosophy. If God is impersonal sound, light, nectar, word, or consciousness without any specific moral qualities; if liberation is merging into this impersonal, amoral God; and if the way to liberation is through autosuggestion and physical manipulation of certain nerves; then there is no need for anyone to be moral. Balyogeshwar's so-called "immoral" life in no way disproves his claim to divinity and guruship.

I have seen slogans and posters put up in many of our cities by the Vishwa Shanti Dal (World Peace Corps), asking us to receive knowledge from Balyogeshwar the avatar!

To those who can't accept an immoral man as an incarnation of God, this must seem to be the height of religious deception. If the Vishwa Shanti Dal succeeds in putting Balyogeshwar back on the religious map of the world, it will become a classic example of the gullibility of humanity. This must cause us all to reexamine our beliefs and deities. Do we also believe blindly? If we do, then our beliefs are no better than those of DLM's followers.

Chapter Eleven

Radha Soami Satsang (Beas)

IT WAS A Hindu banker in Agra who started the Radha Soami Satsang in the middle of the last century. The original center is still at Agra, though the breakaway group at Beas (Punjab) has more dynamic leadership and a larger following. The early history of the movement has been a subject of controversy.[1]

The sect at Beas was founded by Baba Jaimal Singh. It spread rapidly between the years 1903 and 1948 under the leadership of Huzur Sawan Singh Ji Maharaj. The present guru, Maharaj Charan Singh, the grandson of Sawan Singh Ji Maharaj, is a graduate in law and arts. His intelligent mind, handsome looks, and sophisticated graciousness make him so winsome that it is little wonder that he has attracted many foreigners and upper-class Indians to the sect.

The Radha Soami Satsang perhaps commands a greater following, but is less well known, than Jai Gurudev or the Divine Light Mission because Maharaj Charan Singh does not go in for propaganda or proselytization. Charan Singh does not even want his birthday to be celebrated, a practice which is very popular with all the other gurus. His followers are not encouraged to preach. Outsiders are usually drawn to him by the fervent devotion of the devotees for their guru. It is striking that Charan Singh does not even initiate everybody who seeks initiation. One really has to be spiritually prepared, because the guru "can by a mere look know one's past, present and future lives and thus determine whether one is ready for initiation or not!"

Their ashram impressed me as a well-built university. It is a beautiful little colony on the banks of the river Beas. Over 150 people live there permanently.

On weekends the number may swell to a couple thousand because of those who come to attend the religious gathering known as satsang. During their special gatherings, called bhandaras, as many as 200,000 people gather there to hear the satsang and receive initiation. They are all welcome to join in the free meals called langar, though some prefer to eat in the little canteen and pay for it. The devotees freely render their joyful service on these occasions. The great organization and faith required to feed 200,000 people free of charge for a couple of days is adequate evidence for many that this movement is of God.

During the satsang, bhajans are sung and the teachings of sant mat are expounded by the master. They use simple Punjabi for the main satsang but also have an English satsang for foreigners and others. The satsang may be followed by a secret initiation ceremony.

Those who renounce non-vegetarian food and the use of intoxicants, if selected, have a special session with the master. He gives them the nam (Name of God). They are taught the technique of meditating on this name by concentrating on the "third eye" together with recitation of "the name." The "third eye" is supposed to be in the forehead above the nose, between the eyebrows. Nam, or "the name," is the technical title given to the five mantras which the guru gives at initiation to be used at progressive stages in meditation. When the initiates concentrate on the third-eye region and recite "the name," they find their third eye slowly opening and body consciousness being lost. The devotees begin to see visions and hear the word. This word is the divine sound current which is vibrating within us. It emanates from God, permeates the entire universe, and goes back to God. When the soul contacts the word, it merges into it and begins to travel Godwards with it. When the soul rises upward on it journey towards God, it passes through many worlds, meeting different people and enjoying various experiences. After rising up to a certain level, it meets with the sadguru in his radiant form, who then takes it up to its highest goal—God.

During initiation, devotees are told about the kinds of experiences they will have, the worlds they will pass through, and the persons they will meet. They are also told of the persons with whom they may talk and those they should avoid during their soul's journey. Before initiation, devotees vow that they will not divulge the nam to anyone, nor will they talk of their experiences to anyone, not even to their fellow devotees.

Both JGDPS and DLM have similar secret initiation ceremonies. In Radha Soami Satsang, the sadguru usually gives initiation, while in DLM mahatmas are also appointed for this purpose. Both groups use techniques to show the light and to hear the sound. Tulsidas Ji, the leader of JGDPS, also shows light to initiates. Two of his devotees confidentially reported that the guru took them to a dark room and asked them to concentrate on the shining stone in his ring. They were told that if they were spiritually ready they would see divine visions—

and sure enough they did! I haven't been able to find out the techniques used to show the "light" or hear the "sound" during initiation by the Radha Soami, but I assume that it resembles those used by the other two sects because both the DLM and JGDPS derive much from the theoretical aspects of the teachings of the Radha Soami.

Unlike the DLM, the Radha Soami Satsang puts great emphasis on theoretical teaching. The books of the sect contain quite elaborate theology, cosmology, anthropology, and soteriology. Being an eclectic faith, it draws its philosophy from Hindu, Muslim, Sikh, and Christian traditions. It seeks to transcend them all and encompass them within its own system. But it becomes confused at many points, and its exponents contradict each other.

God, according to sant mat, is one (ekankar) and formless (nirankar). He is without personality, without name. He can't be said to be anywhere, as he is everywhere. He does assume many forms, but none of them embrace his entire being. He is called by many names such as "anami purush" (nameless being) and "dayal" (implying that he is gracious). When he limits himself a little, he is called "agam purush" (inaccessible being); when limited a little more, he is known as "alkah purush" (invisible being). When he takes a definite form for the purpose of administrating the affairs of the universe, he then becomes "sat purush" or "sat nam."

Monotheism or Pantheism?

Radha Soamis assert that God is attributeless and impersonal, yet they attribute to "him" the qualities of love, grace, wisdom, and power. Julian P. Johnson, a Western expounder and defender of the sant mat, asserts that "monotheism is an established and concrete fact"[2] and that monism, "which goes so far as to identify spirit and matter and make all of these identical with God, is not accepted by the masters."[3] Yet he also rejects all dualism—"the moment we introduce anything into the world which is not a part of God, we introduce a bewildering duality into the scheme of things, landing ourselves in a maze of philosophical difficulties."[4]

He also writes that "there is absolute unity in this universe, organic unity and oneness throughout, and there is but one universal Force, creative and all-sustaining, which is never separated from it, nor can it be separated."[5] Maharaj Charan Singh also says that "everything that has been created is nothing but His own projection."[6] I know some devotees who virtually accept Shankara's monism in toto. Radha Soamis and Jai Gurudev also incorporate Hindu polytheism into their system by asserting that there are countless gods and goddesses, lords, rulers, and governors in the universe. These also have creative powers; according to them, "Kal Niranjan is the creator of the physical universe."[7]

Sant mat also postulates a negative power in the cosmos called "kal niranjan." He is the universal mind, the devil. He has created this physical universe, but most religions mistake him for the supreme God. This is because they don't know the supreme God, nor the existence of higher worlds.

Kal, according to Maharaj Charan Singh, "is a power. It is our mind. Universal mind is kal. The Lord actually is shabd (word), and shabd emanates from the Lord. Similarly, the mind emanates from kal, and the mind ultimately is kal."[8] Balyogeshwar also teaches this: "the devil is the son of man that comes to mind, through mind, from mind."[9]

But according to sant mat, the devil comes from God. Maharaj Charan Singh writes that kal "has come from the Supreme Father," and "whatever he is doing, he is doing by the orders of the Supreme Being."[10] "It is his duty to try to hold us here, in the bondage of mind and matter."[11]

Traditionally, sant mat has conceived the cosmos as consisting of four grand divisions. But Maharaj Charan Singh says that because the knowledge of the cosmos is gained through mystic experience, it is difficult to describe it by mere words. He says some mystics "have described just two regions; some have classified the two regions into four, some into five and some into eight regions."[12] Therefore, one can't be dogmatic. However, the following are the four grand divisions—from the highest downwards—of the universe which the soul sees as it rises up to merge into God. The first is sat desh. This is the highest region, made purely of spirit substance and inhabited by pure spirits—pure because they are uncontaminated by matter or mind. There are countless spirits, and they enjoy the greatest conceivable happiness. This region, which is almost infinitely vast, is all light, life, and power. It is the grand capital or the center of the entire creation. From here the great creative sound current emanates, goes to the farthest corner of the universe, and returns to this sat desh.

Sat desh is the realm of immortality. It is the highest heaven, though not the heaven of other religions. According to Radha Soami and Jai Gurudev, the heaven of all other religions is a much lower region. The founders of other religions "had never reached that exalted region."[13] Only the masters of sant mat know of this sat desh and can take us there because they have come from there.

The second level is brahmanda (the egg of Brahm). The ancient Hindu rishis considered Brahm to be the supreme being "because they knew of no one higher. But the saints know that there is not only one Brahm but countless numbers of brahms, who are governors over so many brahmandas."[14] These countless brahmandas circle around the supreme region in their own orbits. Each of them has its own governor or ruler.

The brahmanda is lower than the sat desh because it isn't pure spirit. It is lightly tinted with mind. It is spirit-realized matter. Though the brahmanda is also a region of light and bliss, it is somewhat smaller and darker than the sat desh, but it is incomparably vaster than our material universe. The lowest section of brahmanda is the home of the universal mind. When a soul descends from sat desh, it passes through these "exquisitely beautiful regions of Mind and . . . associates with the Mind and puts on the coverings of causal and astral bodies."[15] During surat-shabd yoga when the soul rises up on its way to sat desh it passes again through brahmanda and discards the attributes of mind there.

The third region is called the anda. This is the lowest of the heavens and lies nearest to the material universe. It is commonly called the astral plane. Anda has many subdivisions. At its center lies the most gorgeous cluster of lights— called "sahasra dal kanwal" by the saints. The soul is always thrilled when it passes through this "magnificent city of light." Millions of the great souls of history, including the founders of many religions, live here in bliss. They often think that they are in immortal heaven, but it is not so. After millions of years, this region of anda also gets destroyed during dissolution. The sahasra dal kanwal is the actual powerhouse of our material universe. The power that creates and sustains our universe flows out of it.

The last is pinda, the "gross material" universe. It embraces all the galaxies known and unknown to astronomy. In it, matter predominates over mind and spirit. Our earth is a small and insignificant part of it. Though there seems to be beauty and light in pinda, it is in pitch darkness when compared to sat desh. In this region, "the spirit is untraceable, the mind is perturbed and restless and, being confined within the limits of physical functioning, [it] creates an illusory individuality which causes us to forget that we all are 'one' with the Supreme Creator."[16]

This is bondage—when the soul is so bound up with mind and matter that it considers itself distinct from God. The sadgurus are sent by God into this world to show the path of liberation to the souls in bondage.

Sant mat believes that we are a soul which is held in bondage by four layers—three bodies and one mind. First is the physical body, called "asthul sharir." Inside it is the astral body called "shuksham sharir," or the subtle body. The astral body represents the physical body, though it is much finer. When the physical body dies, the soul is transported in its astral body to the higher planes of existence. Within the astral body is the causal body, the karan sharir. This extremely subtle body keeps a perfect record and impression of all our actions and experiences. These past records determine our present character and our future lives. The causal body is also called the mental body because it receives and transmits impressions between the soul and mind as well as between the mind and the astral body.

The mind is the fourth unit. It is closely connected with the karan sharir. According to the psychology of the masters, the mind is not the part which knows or thinks. It is neither self-conscious nor self-acting. It is the soul that is conscious and knows. God doesn't have a mind because mind is "only an instrument which encumbers the soul, obscures its light and impedes its progress."[17] Only the negative power and its subordinates have minds. Mind is the cause of imperfections which we call evils. It is the bondage from which the soul needs to be liberated with the sadguru's help.

How did the soul get into this bondage? Sant mat teaches that God created kal, the negative power, whose authorities for 134 ages pleased God. God then permitted him to ask for a boon. He requested a kingdom like God's with souls in it. He was given the power to create the material universe to which souls were sent from sat desh. While the souls were descending they passed through the regions of mind and matter and became associated with them. Because the mind and matter obstructed the true light and wisdom, the souls forgot that they were really God and that their true home was sat desh. They then began to enjoy sensual and material pleasures, including meat and intoxicants.

The sadgurus have an indispensable position in sant mat. Without a living sadguru, no one can attain liberation. The sadgurus are far superior to the gods ruling in the brahmandas and pindas. They are also more powerful than the negative power, kal. They dwell in the sat desh and are the chief executives of the supreme sat purush himself. They come from him to take the souls back to sat desh. The supreme, gracious God has two liberating powers—the word and the sadgurus. The divine word or sound is within all of us, but our associations with mind and matter have made us oblivious to it. The master comes invisibly in a human body. Though he has great power, he is not allowed to perform miracles. If we accept him as our guru, he then through initiation cuts off our relationship with kal, so that we are no longer under this negative power and don't have to pay for our karma. Our accounts are transferred from kal to sadguru. The sadguru also puts the soul back into contact with the sound current. Constant contact with the current helps to "nullify the reserve karma." This enables our souls to proceed on their homeward journey. Later, when the soul gets out of the body during meditation and rises upwards to the sat desh, it is met by the master himself in his radiant form and is guided through the vast expanses of the cosmos.

Radha Soami Satsang teaches the surat-shabd yoga (union of soul with word), which it claims is the simplest, the most original, and the only way of attaining liberation. This yoga involves neither physical exercises nor the rising of kundalini. It consists in connecting the soul (surat) with the sound current (shabd).

The shabd is the most emphasized feature in sant mat, along with the need for a living master. The shabd is called the word, the sound current, or the audible life stream. It is divine and within us. It takes the soul back to God.

A secret initiation from a living sadguru is the first step in surat-shabd yoga. Then the initiates are required to practice meditation for two and a half hours daily, preferably in the morning. In order to meditate, the devotee should sit in a comfortable but alert position and fix attention on the third eye. Then he should begin simran, or the repetition of the nam given by the master. This helps concentration and closes the nine doors of the outer world: the two eyes, two ears, two nostrils, the mouth, the sex organ, and the rectum. When the entire attention is fixed inside on the third eye, the devotee will begin to see flashes of light and hear sounds.

> When this concentration has reached its maximum within the ability of the individual, the soul has sufficient force to penetrate the tenth door. That is an opening in the subtle body near the middle of the forehead. At first, one only looks out through this door. But by and by he goes out through it and leaves the body completely. He then steps out into a new world which he never saw before.[18]

This is the astral world. The soul proceeds upwards, and when it reaches the zone called ashta dal kanwal, it meets its master in his radiant form. The soul is taken further. At this stage simran is stopped, and meditators fix their gaze on the beautiful form of the master. This is called dhyan. Simran and dhyan are the two essential exercises in this yoga. Once individuals are initiated, their deliverance from the cycle of births and deaths is certain. If they stray from the path, they are sure to be delivered within a maximum of four more lives.

"Scriptural Proof"

The Radha Soami and the Divine Light Mission are fond of quoting the scriptures of other religions, especially the Bible, to substantiate their beliefs. But the passages are almost always interpreted completely out of context. They only use two exegetical principles for other scriptures: (1) The teachings of the sant mat are true; therefore, those like Christ, Krishna, Rama, and Buddha "must have taught the same things."[19] Whatever in the Bible, *Koran*, or *Gita* doesn't tally with the sant mat must be a perversion of the original teaching by later disciples. (2) The true teachings of the masters such as Buddha and Christ have been lost. We can't know what their teachings were "until we make intensive research." Maharaj Charan Singh claims that "if anyone with an unbiased mind will make a research, he will be told the same teachings."[20] But he also confesses, "I do not know much about the Bible. I have read here and there, but mostly I have read Matthew, John and Luke."[21] Without doing any intensive research himself, he uses the Bible to "prove" his teachings and has written a commentary on the Gospel of John. He operates this way because he believes that in order to understand scriptures such as the Bible he has to pick up things from here and there and interpret them mystically.[22]

Without being derogatory, one must say that few people read other scriptures with more biased minds than the followers of sant mat. For example: "In the beginning was the Word, and the Word was with God, and the Word was God."[23] The term *logos* (word) has been interpreted by them as the sound (shabd), and they argue that Jesus taught about the same shabd or sound current about which they teach. To begin with, there is no evidence to say that Jesus ever used the word *logos* Himself. His disciple John, while writing his gospel for thinking Greeks, used the Greek term *logos* to explain to them who Jesus was. John argued that Jesus Christ, who was born as man, was the Word of God, eternally coexistent with God. Jesus was the logos—the reason and revelation of God—through whom God created the entire universe. That John believed that Jesus existed as a person in a relationship with God—prior to His incarnation and not as a sound current—is obvious from passages like John 17:5.[24]

Another instance: "The Kingdom of God is within you."[25] This text from the King James Version of the English Bible is used to argue that Jesus taught that God or the divine sound current was within us. Anyone who does even a little research can see that this interpretation can't be substantiated. Jesus had started his ministry by preaching "Repent, for the kingdom of heaven is near."[26] About three years later—recorded in Luke 17:20-21—the Pharisees asked, "When will the Kingdom come?" Jesus replied that "the Kingdom of God is in the midst of you" (Revised Standard Version), or "within you," as the King James Version translates it. Jesus is saying that He—the King—has already come and that He is reigning over the lives of the disciples. In other words, the kingdom is here among you.

Not only is it impossible to show from the Bible that Jesus taught that the kingdom or divinity was within every man; there is also no evidence that He taught that one had to hear the sound or practice any kind of meditation to enter the kingdom. The way to enter the kingdom, according to Him, was through repentance and faith, described by phrases such as "Come to me"[27] and "Be born again."[28]

There is another misinterpretation. "If therefore thine eye be single, thy whole body shall be full of light."[29] This text is very frequently used to argue that Jesus taught about the third eye. One can hardly have a more biased interpretation of the text. In the passage, Matthew 6:19-34, Jesus is teaching that you can't serve both God and money. You have to choose one. You can either set your heart on the treasure below or on the treasure above: you've got to be single-minded, or single-eyed. As the treasure determines where the heart will be (verse 21), so the eye determines where the body will go. The eye is the lamp that shows the way. The rest of the body is dark by itself, Jesus says; therefore, your eye must be "single" (AV) or "sound" (RSV) if the body is to have light.

It has been necessary to expose the sant mat's false interpretation of other scriptures to show that their claim that all sadgurus have always taught the same "science" is at best completely unverified. The proof texts that are quoted from other scriptures are not handled fairly or honestly.

Expositors of the sant mat argue that only the sadguru can interpret any scripture correctly because he alone knows the truth. If this contention is true, then it means that the proof texts from other scriptures can never prove to the inquirer whether sant mat is true. They can never verify or falsify the interpretations given by the sadguru. Seekers have to accept the guru's interpretations blindly because they are not allowed to interpret for themselves. If we have no way of checking whether the guru's interpretations are true or not, then other scriptures can never be a proof of sant mat. Devotees have to accept things blindly on the authority of the guru himself. However, if we can't interpret the scriptures, including the books by Maharaj Charan Singh, why are they written at all?

Experience

C. W. Sanders argues in his book *The Inner Voice* that this science is "freely open to proof for each soul," because each one can go within and move up to higher planes during meditation. They can hear the sound and see the master in his radiant form. The Divine Light Mission also argues that the proof of their teaching is in the experiencing of it. Come and see the divine light for yourself.

Many people undoubtedly hear the sound and see the light, but this is not a meaningful proof because there is no way of knowing whether these experiences of light, sound, and astral travel are real or mere hallucinations.

An intelligent satsangi who meditated every morning from 4:00 A.M. to 6:00 A.M. once told me that he knows from his own experience that one doesn't need rockets to go to the moon. "Through this science, you can go to the moon or to America in a second." "Maybe," I replied, "but the only problem is that you can't bring back moon rocks from the journey for investigation!" How do we know whether these experiences are not hallucinations? Obviously, many schizophrenic patients see visions and hear sounds.

Alfonso Caycedo is a psychiatrist and a pioneer of the new branch of medicine known as "sophorology." He came to India to study the phenomenon of "sound and light" and its relation to schizophrenia. He asked many leading gurus about it. He has recorded his interviews and findings in *India of Yogis*. Swami Chidananda of Shivananda ashram and Mother Krishnabai of Ananda ashram said to him that many yogis experience the sound and light, but the highest yogis do not attach much importance to these experiences. Dr. Caycedo asked Swami Chidananda: "Is it possible that some relation exists between these visions of the yogis, this omkar [primordial] sound, this anhat [causeless] sound, and the characteristics of some mentally sick people, curing whom is our special job?"

Swami Chidananda replied, "Yes, hallucinations."[30] He went on to say that the visions always come in reference to what the yogi is seeking. "If he is a bhakta of Lord Rama his vision shall be associated with Lord Rama. And if he is a devotee of Lord Krishna, his vision will be of Lord Krishna." Swami Chidananda also added that the vision "depends on the temperament" of the yogi. "If the sadhak has a highly imaginative temperament, he will have visions."[31]

Maharaj Charan Singh agreed that the experiences of the yogis and mentally sick patients are "the same"[32] but added that the difference lies in the fact that while the patients get stuck with the nonessential details of the visions, the yogis go on in the spiritual journey to realize God.

When I gently asked a devotee how he would know whether his soul actually went out to see the worlds that are there or if it was all imagination, he got upset and replied, "These arguments will not help you; you start meditating and you will know." His manner suggested that he himself had doubts as to whether the experiences were imaginary but had suppressed the doubts in favor of the security which comes from blind belief.

"God made kal, right?" I asked the deeply committed satsangi.

"Yes," he said.

"And kal performed great religious austerities for 134 yugas, which pleased God?"

His reply was the same.

"Pleased with his austerities, God gave him souls that he might bind them with mind and matter and rule over them. Is that right?"

"Yes."

"Why should God put souls into bondage and suffering because of someone's religious austerities?" I asked. "Isn't this unjust? If God has made me blind to begin with, isn't he responsible for the evil karma?"

"I don't know why you got into this bondage," my friend replied. "But once you have fallen into a well, it is no use asking how you fell in. 'Why did I fall? What is this well? How deep is it? Are there other wells? Would I fall again if I got out?' These questions won't help you. What you need to do is take the help of the one who is willing to pull you out of the well, and get out."

"My problem," I said, "is that I don't even know whether I have fallen into a well. You tell me that I am imprisoned in the bondage of matter, mind, and illusory individuality. What if my individuality is not illusory, and what if my body and mind are God's gift to me as other saints have taught? If I presuppose that I am in bondage, then I must seek deliverance first. But if body and mind are not a prison, I don't need to be delivered from them. You are asserting that I am in bondage; I want to know if that is true. In any case, I am grateful that the sadguru is willing to help me get out of the well. But I don't understand your concept of guru either."

"What do you mean?" my friend asked.

"My soul is God, right?"

"Yes, but it's in ignorance at the moment."

"But it is God who becomes ignorant, right? And then he sends the guru who is also God to deliver himself from ignorance, right? And this God or guru has to labor very hard to deliver me (God) from ignorance. And in spite of all his labor, the great majority of these souls (God) stay in bondage? What sense does it make?"

"Your mind won't help; you have to give it up first," my friend patiently told me.

This reminded me that sant mat takes an avowed anti-intellectual stand: "The greatest enemy in the way of our spiritual progress and the conscious realization of our oneness with our Heavenly Father is our mind."[33] Devotees are forced to take an anti-intellectual stand because their "science" doesn't stand up to the scrutiny of reason. This doesn't mean that they don't have brilliant thinkers in their sects. The more intelligent ones would have replied to my objection about God being responsible for my bondage and evil by saying something like this: "You ask because you are still in ignorance, considering yourself to be apart from God. You are God. God has come into bondage himself and he is suffering in his own creation."

If God has decided to suffer in his own creation because of his own austerities, what is wrong with that? It is all acting, a one-man show! But this means that all suffering and evil is God's drama. There is nothing intrinsically wrong with suffering or evil. We need not fight the sufferings of our starving and sorrowful world, nor do we need to stand against the evils of crime and corruption.

Because of their monistic position, the Radha Soamis are driven to the conclusion that "there is really no such thing as evil. Good and evil are only comparative terms and evil is only a lesser good. Good and evil are like positive and negative electricity. . . . Good and evil are like the head and tail of the same coin."[34] If murder is no more regrettable than negative electricity, and if love and cruelty are only two sides of the same coin, then what good does talk about good and bad karma mean? Bad karma is not really bad.

PART VI

EVALUATION AND ALTERNATIVE

AT LEAST FROM the ninth century A.D., since the days of the great philosopher Shankaracharya, Advaitism or absolute monism has been billed as the "highest philosophy" in India, for our greatest minds have espoused it. To offer a critique is to invite the wrath of faithful followers. Most people believe in the monism of the gurus not because they can rationally prove it, nor because they have mystically perceived it, but because they have surrendered their minds to the authority of another.

A critical look at monism and its logical implications is needed. An alternative is proposed.

Chapter Twelve

Evaluating Monistic Gurus

ALL THE GURUS that we have looked at, except Swami Prabhupada,[1] share one fundamental belief. They agree that ultimately all reality is one. Stones, trees, animals, and humanity are only the diverse manifestations of the same one consciousness. This consciousness is "pure" in contrast to being "gross"—that is, it is beyond thought, reason, emotion, will, and morals. It is without attributes. It transcends personality and is therefore impersonal. It is called God, self, Brahman, shoonya, or void. This belief is called monism (oneness of all reality) or pantheism (all is divine).

These gurus also agree that the only way to see the oneness of all reality is to go beyond reason. Intellect is the "chief villain" which divides the one into many. Therefore we can't know God or the self through the mind. Realization has to come from an intuitive or mystic experience. It is claimed that there is a state of consciousness beyond deep sleep, dreams, or waking consciousness where you are wide awake and you actually "perceive" the pure consciousness; nay, you become it because you are pure consciousness. Pure consciousness becomes aware of itself. This is self-realization or God-realization.

But how do I know that the consciousness within me is the same as within you and within this stone or tree and that we are all one? These gurus teach that you can't know this intellectually—though Maharishi Mahesh Yogi is positive that the day is not far off when physics will prove it—but you can know it mystically.

Now it seems clear that those who may never have experienced the mystic oneness should in all fairness accept the claim that there is a state of consciousness where one experiences an "undifferentiated unity." Not only the Indian gurus but also many gentle souls in other cultures, in all ages, have testified to such an experience.

Our discoveries in physics indeed suggest that in its ultimate form energy may be one. But we have no scientific reason as yet to think that this ultimate form of energy is consciousness and that conscious energy is all that there is in the universe. Some of our leading physicists have admitted that ultimately reality may be beyond the reach of reason, but to declare it to be nonrational is only a philosophical assumption, not a scientific conclusion. We must also admit that to conceive of ultimate reality as consciousness gives a possible explanation of human consciousness, whereas on the basis of the hypothesis generally held at present—that the ultimate reality is unconscious energy—one doesn't know how consciousness could have arisen.

However, because monism is only a philosophical hypothesis of these gurus, it needs to be tested by the criteria for truth: Is this a consistent philosophy; does it give plausible answers to the problems it seeks to solve; and can we live by this philosophy?

Monism and Creation

While explaining creation, all monistic gurus almost inevitably slip into dualism or at least qualified, personalized monism. In this connection we can divide the monistic gurus into four categories.

First, there are those like Sivananda and Chinmayananda who take the standard Advaita (non-dualistic) position of Shankaracharya and explain away the world as simply an illusion. Then there are those like Mahesh Yogi who realize that such a position rules out science and participation in society and life, and therefore try to say that the creation is real and that it is a transformation of God through evolution (or involution and evolution). Then there is a third category of gurus like Muktananda and those of sant mat who are simply confused by such metaphysical subtleties. They sometimes declare the world to be real and at other times to be illusory; they do not see any need to be consistent. If pressed for consistencies, they just mock at intellect: "Don't think; just believe." Finally, there are those like Rajneesh who are wise enough to know that pure monism fails to explain creation. As a result they, like Buddha, practice silence on metaphysical questions: "Your intellect is the devil, the chief villain; it divides one reality into many. If you want to know the truth, stop thinking; just meditate."

Leaving the last two categories aside, as they don't really try to explain the why and how or even the what of creation, we should give a little thought to the first two.

If creation is illusion, a dream, then who is dreaming? Who is mistaking the rope for a snake? If the snake (the world) is not there, at least the rope is. What is the nature of the rope? The Advaitic answer is: God is the rope, and he himself is mistaking himself to be the snake. He is dreaming and ignorantly taking his dream to be real. But if God is pure consciousness, beyond thoughts, desires, and feelings, then how is he dreaming? Isn't dreaming a quality of personal beings? Moreover, if God is omniscient or all-wise, how does ignorance come upon him? The Advaitic answer is maya. Maya is God's own power that deludes him. It is "an inexplicable principle of unreality." Maya can't be real, for that would depose Brahman as the sole reality. But it can't be called unreal either since it produces the appearance of the world which seems so real. If it is neither real nor unreal, then what is it? Nobody seems to know anything about it, except that it's a supposition adopted by the Advaitins in their struggle to maintain an ideal unity. But does the concept of maya allow pure unity? It does not. Because even the illusory world is a product of Brahman plus maya and because the phenomenal world is an eternal process, it follows that there must be two eternal entities that coexist.

"Not at all!" the monistic gurus would no doubt argue. "Just as the possibility of the future tree preexists in the seed of the tree without the seed becoming any less the one and only seed, so Brahman, though associated with maya, is not less the one and only being." But this analogy actually argues against the Advaitins' position. Even though the seed is one and has the potential of the tree, the potential will never be actualized without the influence of soil, moisture, and heat. Thus even though the inert, passive, impersonal Brahman may be the seed containing the potential of the world, how can it be actualized without the active power of maya? Pure unity could never have existed even for the illusory creation to be there.

Even if one may be convinced that the belief in Brahman and maya is belief in absolute unity, one's explanation of empirical reality as illusory is indeed a very low view of nature. It destroys any basis for science or fulfillment in life. Many monists, like Mahesh Yogi, realize this and try to interpret the world as real, or at least mithya and not maya.

Mahesh Yogi gives up the doctrine of maya and attempts to interpret the world as real by postulating two forces, prana and karma. Karma is the actions of the individual which act as "wind" on prana, a tendency to vibrate and become an individualized "wave" in the ocean of pure being. Thus prana, when acted upon by karma, becomes individual ego. But where does karma come from? From a previous birth. But where did the previous birth come from? From still previous karma . . . ad infinitum! Mahesh Yogi is thrown back by his own logic to saying that the creation is eternal; individuals have always existed as pure being also has always existed. Where does the monism or pure unity go then? Here is pure plurality indeed! If souls have existed forever due to the influence of karma (or maya), then any hope of ultimate salvation, of getting rid of karma or maya, of merging into one, or getting rid of the plurality of consciousness is purely romantic. It has no intelligible basis within the monistic worldview.

Monism and Avatarism

The concept of avatar—or of a guru coming into the world to help ignorant souls—is inconsistent with monistic philosophy. If there is only one soul, which is God, and the human soul is also God, then it makes no sense for God to get into the bondage of ignorance, to forget that he is God, and to send God (a guru or avatar) to enlighten himself (God) from this ignorance, which exists in his own mind! The concept of avatar or guru makes sense only in theistic philosophy, according to which God and human souls are distinct, souls are in bondage, and God out of love for them takes incarnation or sends gurus.

A belief in reincarnation is inconsistent with absolute monism (Advaita Vedanta), as is Sai Baba's claim to be the reincarnation of Shirdi Sai Baba. For if Shirdi Baba has attained liberation and merged into God, then to believe that he has come back is to believe that rivers come out of the ocean after merging with it. The same applies to all the gurus who claim to be reincarnations of Rama, Krishna, or Christ.

Monism and Reality

What is this external universe—the world of variety and diversity which we have known from childhood and taken to be real? Is it real? From where has it come? For a monist the unity alone is real; the diversity ultimately is unreal. The world is either maya (illusion) or mithya (relatively real, ultimately unreal). It is to be looked down upon. Even the gurus who do consider matter to be real declare matter, the human body, mind, and ego to be "gross" and not pure. This indeed leads to a very low view of material reality.

Indian civilization has suffered greatly because of this low view of physical reality. In our history there have been scores of intellectual giants, persons of unmatched sacrifice, discipline, and devotion. But science and technology couldn't be taken beyond a very limited degree because of our low view of the reality which is the domain of science. Men like Whitehead, Oppenheimer, and Zaehner have pointed out that modern science grew because of the Christian cultural milieu in the West which was both otherworldly and this-worldly. India continues to suffer materially, partly because the best of her children still look down upon matter.

If the world is explained away as illusion, then another acute problem arises—the problem of the distinction between fantasy and reality. Are they really distinct? As Lao-tse says:

> If, when I was asleep, I was a man dreaming I was a butterfly, how do I know when I am awake I am not a butterfly dreaming I am a man?

This may not sound disturbing. But as Os Guinness says, to those "who have lost the ordinary reality through carelessly applied mental techniques or through repeated acid 'bummers,' the inability to distinguish fantasy and reality can become a living hell."[2] I realized the full force of the problem after meeting a girl in Switzerland who had been on drugs. For three weeks, she could not be sure whether the beautiful Alps and valleys were really there. She "saw" so many things that she did not know which were real and which were only in her mind. One wonders about the visions of men like Muktananda. Are they real or only mental fantasies? Monism gives no basis for distinguishing between the two.

In absolute monism there is also no basis for being interested or involved in reality any more than in fantasy. Here is the sum of the problem with the monistic view of the gurus on reality: it either explains the reality away or considers it "gross." It neither gives an adequate basis on which to ground continuing scientific investigation nor enables us to distinguish between fantasy and reality. The gurus who do declare the material world to be real do so at the expense of being inconsistent with their monism.

Monism and Abnormality

Just as monism fails to explain the reality of the phenomenal universe, it also fails to explain its abnormalities. If the entire universe is a manifestation of God (or the dance of God, as Bhagavan Rajneesh would say), then why are there all these disastrous floods and famines, diseases and deaths, fires and earthquakes? Why isn't there a perfect harmony? Is God such a poor dancer?

Some gurus will explain these natural calamities as illusory, too. Others who take the world as real and a manifestation of God will have to argue that these are not in any way bad calamities. God is both the creator and the destroyer. He destroys only to create anew. This is his play. We must not attach any importance to calamities.

Such an explanation destroys all basis for sympathy and compassion for those who are victims of the abnormalities of nature. No wonder that Hinduism, in spite of all her claims to spirituality, has no ancient tradition of humanitarian service—hospitals, leprosy clinics, schools for the blind, or orphanages—even though charity such as almsgiving has been practiced to earn merit. We have only recently learned to do some charity and relief work under the impact of other religions and cultures. But even now a great deal of the aid for relief work goes into the pockets of the rich and influential—and why not? There are any number of gurus and Godmen who teach that the miseries are illusory or are just the result of our karma.

Monism and Personality

If God or unity consciousness alone is all-important and the world of diversity is maya, then what about individuals? Who am I? Who are you? Once it is assumed that the ultimate reality is impersonal—as these gurus do—it is impossible to explain how personality comes out of impersonality. Though substituting consciousness in place of unconscious energy explains a little more of the universe, it still doesn't solve the problem, for personality is more than consciousness. Personality inspires rational creative communication in words and symbols. It has feelings of likes and dislikes. It has volitional, aesthetic, and moral feelings, which impersonality does not. Most gurus today explain the emergence of personality as evolution (that is, if they consider it real at all). But the question is, How can personality come out of impersonality at all—whether it is impersonal energy, sound, silence, or consciousness?

Suppose there are three parallel hills forming two valleys in between them. One valley has water; the other does not. As you are sitting and watching these valleys, let us imagine that water begins to rise up in the dry valley as well. After some time, the rising of the water level stops. If you took careful measurements and found that the water level was the same in both the valleys, you could conclude that the water in the second valley had come from the first. But if the water in the second had risen a hundred feet above the first, then no one could possibly conclude that it had come from the first valley—something higher does not come out of something lower. This being so, how can personality come out of impersonality?[3]

Most gurus, realizing that personality can't come out of impersonality, simply declare that personality is also illusory. Your ego is supposedly your bondage. Salvation consists of getting rid of your individuality. In merging back into impersonal consciousness, your aim must not be individual fulfillment but the annihilation of your individuality. Those gurus, like Mahesh Yogi, who are embarrassed by these conclusions and therefore declare that their aim is "to develop the full potential of the individual" do so by becoming inconsistent with their monistic presuppositions.

The gurus often demand total self-surrender to help deliver you from your ego. You are asked to surrender your intellect, body, emotions, and will. You must believe completely and without a doubt, obey the guru implicitly, and love him with complete devotion. It is this which makes the guru-chela relationship so authoritarian, so dehumanizing, so blinding, and so binding.

Because the monistic worldview is so depersonalizing and dehumanizing, our traditional culture—which is an outworking of our faith—is so dehumanizing as well. Children are totally under the authority of their parents. A wife is her husband's slave, and a man is controlled by his caste. Because the ultimate impersonality of philosophical monism in India rules out personality, our culture—especially in the ashrams—is very depersonalizing. This must sound a warning to those who are turning to gurus to find an alternative to the dehumanization of technological society. Guinness writes:

Communism may have betrayed its humanism in practice, making an arbitrary absolute of the state and so overriding the individual. Secular humanism may have so shown itself deficient in providing a basis for its optimistic view of man that it is floundering in the swift currents of technological dehumanization. But the East has never had a high view of man. In both philosophy and practice it exhibits a dangerous carelessness about the higher reaches of man's aspirations of humanness.[4]

To put it simply, a philosophy that denies any intrinsic worth to human personality can never provide a basis for building a humane society. This becomes alarmingly vivid in Bhagavan Rajneesh's views on love and sex. Sex, which is a God-given means for reinforcing and building a lasting love relationship between two persons, is depersonalized. Here is a kind of "love" which can forget the person completely and can transcend marriage or family, yet is quite consistent with monistic presuppositions.

Monism and Morality

If God alone is, then what is evil? Is it different from good? It can't be. As Muktananda says, "Even what appear to be opposites are in fact expressions of the same Reality."[5] Or as Rajneesh says:

> We have divided the world into the good and the evil. The world is not so divided. The good and the evil are our valuations. If there is no man on the Earth, there will neither be good nor bad. Things will be, but there will be no valuation. . . . There is no good, there is no bad. . . . These are two aspects of one reality.[6]

If reality is one, the duality of good and evil can't be maintained. You have to agree that "the conflict between right and wrong is the sickness of the mind."

Not only all monistic gurus, but also Swami Prabhupada (who teaches bhed-abheda), fail to find any genuine basis for a distinction between good and evil. They claim that in a relative sense things are good or evil, but nothing is ultimately evil. Dostoevski shows the implications of this position in *The Possessed*. Kirilov argues with Stavrogin:

> "Everything is good."
>
> "Everything?"
>
> "Everything. Man is unhappy because he doesn't know he's happy. That's the only reason. The man who discovers that will become happy that very minute. The step-daughter will die, the little girl will remain—and everything is good. I suddenly discovered that."
>
> "So it's good, too, that people die of hunger and also that someone may abuse or rape that little girl?"
>
> "It's good. And if someone breaks open that man's skull for the girl, that's good too. And if someone doesn't break his skull, it's equally good. Everything's good."

This amoral position is the only one which can be consistent with monism. So whenever the gurus pass moral judgments, they betray their own worldview.

India can have a million incarnations of deity today, but so far as they believe and preach amoral monism, our immoral corruption will remain. As Pandit Jawaharlal Nehru noted, our religions in thousands of years of teaching have never motivated anyone to plow a field, build a house, drain a swamp, or dam a stream. With such low views of reality, personality, and morality, we can be sure that our country will not progress very far even in another millennium.

Monism and Cruelty

Why is humanity often so cruel and horrible? Whether it is the Pakistanis committing genocide in Bangladesh or the American massacre in My Lai, whether it is the Russians torturing their own brothers in Siberia, or twice-born Indians burning harijans alive, mankind everywhere has displayed the same horrifying nature. True, humanity has risen to great heights of nobility, yet our philosophy has to account for our evil and cruel nature too.

Because monism presupposes that we are God, it fails to give a serious and credible explanation for our apparent (or real?) sinfulness. The Hindu gurus don't really think that anyone is a sinner. Because morality is illusory or at best relative, our problem is not considered moral at all. Our problem is metaphysical. Our main problem is not that we are sinners, but that we think of ourselves as human. We are divine but somehow have forgotten it. We are simply ignorant. All that we need is realization of our inner divinity.

Because monism doesn't explain our cruelty and sinfulness, the gurus are forced to put forward various superficial explanations. Rajneesh's view that the problem with unenlightened humanity is that we are mechanical, though true to an extent, doesn't stand up to reality. Don't we often deliberately choose and plan evil, in fact return evil for good? Or take Mahesh Yogi's explanation for the evil in us—that because we don't have inner rest and peace we become criminal. Teach us to meditate morning and night; this will give us peace, strength, and creativity, and we will become all right. Doesn't this sound utterly superficial and naive? Couldn't a criminal with greater inner peace, strength, and creativity become more dangerous?

Rajneesh, in fact, describes the bloody history of mankind as "madness." Maharishi, afraid of a nuclear holocaust, is working hard for world peace. Yet their philosophical position is that we are divine—not evil! Their own pronouncements and labors demonstrate that their philosophy is false. It is not true to life.

A philosophy or a worldview is like a map which is drawn or a theory which is propounded in order to sort out the perplexing problems of life and to tell us what life and the universe are all about and how we are to live. The universe and our lives already have a given nature, and this nature raises questions which philosophy is supposed to answer. A philosophy that is contradicted by the given nature of things can't be true. A map must be adjusted to the reality and not the reality to the map. But the monistic gurus ask us to change the reality of our nature in order to readjust it to their philosophical map. The intrinsic nature of our being, however, can't be changed.

The religious quest, for instance, is at its root a quest for meaning: Who am I? Why do I exist? What is the meaning of life and the world? Along with the search for meaning is the search for forgiveness, resulting from our moral dilemma. Our conscience tells us to do good and to shun evil. We spontaneously condemn evil when we see it and praise good. Yet often we don't know why anything is evil or good. We hate doing evil, yet often find ourselves yielding to temptation. The sense of guilt burdens our soul. We seek forgiveness of sin or bad karma. We go far and wide on pilgrimages, bathe in sacred rivers, sacrifice animals to deities, and surrender ourselves to the gurus, hoping thereby to be delivered from the guilt of sin. Added to this search for meaning and forgiveness is our search for immortality. Something within us refuses to believe that death is the final end. Some may fear the pain that often accompanies death; others may fear the unknown that awaits us beyond the grave; but most of us pray, "Lead me from death to immortality."

Meaning of Monism

Because the monistic gurus believe that reality is one and plurality is unreal and unity is true whereas diversity is illusory, they conclude that no particular thing or individual has any meaning. Our individuality is a play (lila) of God. He is playing hide-and-seek with himself. He became man, forgot for a moment that he was God, then sent gurus to help himself to become God again! Therefore, according to these gurus, our individuality is ultimately unreal. We should seek not meaningful, immortal existence but techniques of becoming nonexistent, of merging back into the ground of our existence, as a river in an ocean.

When I asked Swami Dayananda of Chinmaya Mission why he worshiped idols if the stone was maya and he himself was God, he replied that this relative world is just a drama. One can play any role in it. "You may be a millionaire but there is no harm in playing the role of a beggar in a drama. Likewise, we are God but there is no harm in playing the role of a devotee, so far as we know that it is a role."

This is perfectly logical within the monistic framework. But if one is to be honest and consistent, one must agree that there is no harm in playing the role of a murderer or an adulterer or of a non-devotee either. It is all a play which has no intrinsic significance or meaning. The only meaning or purpose to life which monism gives us is that we should try to get rid of our desire for meaning and authentic individuality. This is non-meaning.

Forgiveness in Monism

All the monistic gurus, as well as the non-monistic Hare Krishnas, deny that there is ultimately any duality of good and evil. Yet they all offer forgiveness for doing evil (bad karma). Why? Because to explain the apparent (or obvious) moral motions, they postulate a hypothetical moral law—the law of karma, which is supposedly independent of their God. At times they do suggest that it is an absolute, eternal moral law, but the fact that it is not considered absolute in their system becomes obvious from their view of forgiveness.

They say that when a devotee surrenders to the guru, the latter takes away the bad karma. What does he do with it? Nothing. Nobody takes the result or reaction of karma upon himself. The law of karma is just set aside. Why? Most gurus don't give any explanation, but some do. According to Sathya Sai Baba, the guru has such a vast bank of good karma that his good karma cancels out the bad of his devotee. According to Radha Soami, the law of karma is the law of kal (the devil). When you come under the shelter of the guru, you are no longer under kal's jurisdiction.

Neither of these is convincing. If the guru has lots of good karma and some of his devotee's bad karma, then, according to the classical theory, he should take the consequences of both before he can be liberated! Good acts don't cancel out bad ones. If a person is generally good but commits one murder, it doesn't mean that he or she will be forgiven in a court of law because that person's many good acts balance out one bad act.

The Radha Soami view that a guru just takes the devotee out of the jurisdiction of the law of karma implies that the law is not absolute—in the end it doesn't matter. It also implies that irreligious people need to abide by the moral law, whereas religious ones don't have to worry about it since they are no longer under its jurisdiction.

In forgiveness, according to these gurus, the law is not satisfied but set aside. But if the law can simply be set aside, it means that it is not real law and also that there is no real forgiveness. The law is hypothetical, and forgiveness, too, is hypothetical. At best, it is a trick to ease the guilty conscience of devotees who ignorantly assume that true moral law does exist and that they are truly guilty. At worst, this is a mockery of the devotee's search for forgiveness of sin.

Immortality In Monism

If we accept monism, our search for immortality takes an abrupt turn—instead of immortality, we seek final annihilation, a merging into the ocean forever. With this complete reversal of our search, we change the criterion for truth. We no longer consider that guru to be true who offers immortality but that one who offers the technique of final annihilation of one's individuality. How the followers of monistic gurus settle for something quite different from and lesser than what they started out to seek came home to me while reading Dr. Anthony Campbell's *Seven States of Consciousness*. Campbell, one of the most prominent followers of Mahesh Yogi, grew up as a Catholic. He turned away from his faith at an early age by uncritically accepting secular premises. Later, when he saw the folly of secularism, he started out on the search for a true religion. His search was primarily for immortality. He writes:

> The seeking for a way to this liberation from the fear [of death] became my guiding principle. Yet I had no idea how to attain it.[7]

Instead of reexamining Christianity, he looked for immortality in systems that taught that the very search for immortality was based on the illusory assumption of the reality of individuality. What did he finally find? He writes:

> Before I meditated, I used to be appalled by the thought of death. Now, so far as I can discover by introspection, this is no longer so. As far as I can tell I am curious about death but not afraid except insofar as it may entail suffering. Yet this loss of fear of death is not, I think, related to any new-found certainty about survival; rather it is part of a general increase in what can perhaps be described as a sense of inner security and stability.[8]

Isn't this tragic? He starts out by seeking the certainty of an afterlife, but without even considering the guru who does offer it, he gives up the quest and settles for temporary "inner security and stability."

Monistic Gurus Demand Intellectual, Moral, and Social Suicide

Every Hindu guru ultimately considers the intellect to be the chief villain. Each of these gurus propounds techniques for "killing the mind, transcending the mind." Reality is one, but the mind supposedly divides it like a prism. Therefore, to know the truth, "Thou shalt not think!" Using the analogy of the prism we can instead say the truth is that the rays are many but without the prism they appear as one. The prism helps us to know the truth.

We can ask how and why God, who is pure impersonal consciousness, forgot his reality and become a self-deluded personal ego. Shankaracharya explained it by his doctrine of maya, but modern gurus are often shy of that explanation. Their standard answer is, "Don't ask questions; try to liberate yourself." They ask, "Will a person who is drowning ask how and why he or she is drowning?" This way of reasoning is intellectual escapism. A philosophy that claims to be true ought to have the guts to face tough questions. Are we drowning? Could it be that we aren't deluded at all but are personal beings? If nothing is really evil; if life on earth is a metaphysical morass of bondage, ignorance, and rebirth; if my suffering is the result of my own karma from previous lives, why should I fight social injustices? Why shouldn't I just resign myself to my fate?

Because monism ultimately denies the dualism of good and evil, it leaves us with either moral silence or relativism. To be consistent, we must not say that anything is truly evil—be it individual evils such as murder, theft, or rape; economic evils such as black marketeering, smuggling, or adulterating; or political evils like wars or Watergates. Everything must be considered divine! However, nobody can live this way. Even our bhagavans and avatars, who have transcended the relative realm of morals, are forced to make moral judgments spontaneously. The moral conscience that is inherent in our nature contradicts the amoral monistic worldview.

Chapter Thirteen

The Sanatan Sadguru

IN THE MIDST of gurudom there stands a unique figure. He is active all around the world and commands a following far greater than that of all the other gurus put together. His devotees claim that He is always present with them personally. He guides, protects, and comforts them like a friend, and He rules over their lives as their king (maharaj). They claim that they can communicate with Him whenever they wish, wherever they may be. Though living in an invisible transcendental dimension, He is drawing literally thousands of devotees each day to Himself. At times He meets "visibly" with his devotees, though generally He meets with them spiritually. Yet whenever a person has an encounter with Him, he or she is transformed into a "new creation."

Dr. Sheela Gupta comes from a sophisticated Vaishya family of Agra. The guru appeared to her daily for several weeks during March and April 1955 while she was practicing medicine in Vellore. Finally, when she accepted Him as her guru, she was completely transformed. Today, much in demand as a religious preacher, she is also the medical superintendent of an unusual women's ashram—Pandita Ramabai Mukti Mission, Kedgaon (near Pune).

Mr. Bakht Singh was an orthodox Sikh who went abroad to study engineering. While holidaying in Canada in 1928, he met this guru while praying. This spiritual experience, he says, filled him with "joy unspeakable and full of glory." After the guru healed him of chronic nasal catarrh in response to a simple prayer, his faith in the guru became solid and his love for Him passionate. He returned to India as a preacher instead of an engineer. He has introduced thousands to his guru and healed many in the name of his guru. Today he has an ashram in Hyderabad and about four hundred centers all over India where the devotees of the guru gather for satsang.

Dr. K. N. Nambudripad, an outstanding neurosurgeon in India, comes from one of the most orthodox Brahmin castes in Kerala. He was introduced to this guru by a nurse. Today, though very busy as the director of a medical college in Ludhiana, he is always engaged in introducing others to his guru. He is also the president of a steadily growing student movement which is bringing university students in touch with the guru.

These are but a few examples to show how people of various backgrounds are becoming the followers of this guru. They testify that He who walked on this earth two thousand years ago, is active today, was crucified but rose again, and is alive. Who is He? His name is the Lord Jesus Christ!

The rationale for including a chapter on Christ in a study of contemporary gurus is obvious: His devotees claim that He is very much contemporary—He is the sanatan (eternal) sat (true) guru and maharaj (king). He is also God and the revelation (word or logos) of God. A critical study of His life, claims, and teachings is important because of the answers He gives to the questions that have been raised in this book.

We have seen that the basic reason men and women turn to gurus is that they have concluded that they can't know the truth by their own reason. Modern philosophy began with the rationalistic assumption that we could know the truth by our own reasoning and with the help of empirical experience. It was soon found that beginning with reason, we couldn't know God or the universe or even ourselves. We could neither make sense out of life nor derive any meaning or value from it if we were left alone to discover the truth.

Having failed to find truth through reason, humanity has often turned to the mysticism of the gurus, hoping to discover truth through intuition. But we have come to the conclusion that blind belief in a guru and in irrational mystic experience, however vivid, do not lead us to truth.

If we can't know the truth through reason or intuition, then how are we to know it? The answer is, through revelation. We can only know the truth if God, who knows the truth, reveals it to us. No human being can be the true guru or revealer of truth because all human beings are finite, and they see only a tiny part of reality. We are all like the five blind men of the Jain parable who are trying to know the truth about an elephant. Because blind men can't see the whole elephant, they can't make true propositional statements about it. Whatever they say about the elephant can only be "relatively true," or, strictly speaking, false. Only a sixth man who is sighted and sees the whole elephant can reveal the truth about it to the blind. Likewise, only if there is a God who knows the whole of reality and is willing to reveal truth to us can there be any hope of knowing it. An omniscient God alone can be the sadguru. The devotees of Jesus Christ claim that there is indeed a God who exists, who knows and who has revealed the truth; we don't have to accept this revelation blindly, but we can know it to be true using the same criteria which we used for examining the veracity of other things or theories.

Revelation

Christ's devotees claim that God has revealed the truth in nature and in our personality. But as this revelation is not enough, God has spoken to us through many prophets down through history. God especially chose to reveal Himself to the world through a righteous man, Abraham, and his descendants. God acted and spoke in Jewish history and inspired holy people to write down His words and acts. God has preserved these inspired writings in the Bible. That is not all; after preparing the Jews to receive His revelation, God became a man in Jesus Christ and came to dwell among us. In Jesus Christ, God has revealed Himself fully (not exhaustively, but uniquely) to the degree that finite individuals can and need to know the truth.[1]

The Bible, which contains sixty-six separate books, was written by about forty different authors during a period of some 1,600 years—from approximately 1,500 B.C. to 100 A.D. This is one continuous and consistent revelation which explains and supports each part. The Old Testament, which contains the first thirty-nine books of the Bible, was written before Christ's coming. In it, it is claimed that God was progressively revealing Himself to the Jews and preparing them for His final revelation in Christ. The Old Testament had taught that Christ would reveal the truth as a guru, become the savior who would save people from their sins, and be the king who would establish an everlasting kingdom of righteousness.

Moses had prophesied some fifteen hundred years before Christ that God would send the guru—this prophet-revealer of God's message—from among the Jews.[2] Jacob had prophesied two thousand years before Christ that He would come from the tribe of Judah,[3] which was one of the twelve Jewish tribes. King David was told around 1,000 B.C. that Christ, who would be the sanatan maharaj (everlasting king), would come from his line.[4] Micah prophesied six hundred years before the birth of Christ the exact place where He would be born—Bethlehem.[5] A little before Micah, the great prophet Isaiah had declared that Christ would be born of a virgin: "The Lord Himself will give you a sign: The virgin will be with child and will give birth to a son."[6] Isaiah further said that this coming child was in fact the "Mighty God" and "Everlasting Father" who would come to establish an everlasting kingdom of peace.[7]

Many more prophecies were made in the Old Testament. Besides prophesying about the coming Messiah, the saints who wrote the Bible also prophesied many things concerning different nations. Accurate fulfillment of these prophecies in history is often put forward by Christians as an evidence of the divine inspiration of the Bible. Perhaps it will suffice to point to some of the prophecies which the New Testament shows were amazingly fulfilled in Christ: that He would enter Jerusalem as a king on a colt,[8] that He would be betrayed by his own friend for thirty pieces of silver,[9] that lots would be cast for His garments,[10] that He would be crucified along with criminals,[11] that He would rise again and reign forever.[12]

The New Testament writers tell us that as the Old Testament had predicted, Jesus was in fact conceived by the Holy Spirit in the womb of a virgin called Mary who was engaged to Joseph, a carpenter. Christ's virgin birth was essential, it is argued, because Jesus was God.

According to the Bible, a human "soul" doesn't exist before a child is conceived. Human life begins at conception. But Christ claimed to have always existed as God. Therefore, He couldn't have been conceived by a human father. Also, the Bible teaches that because Adam—the first man—fell into sin, all his descendants thereby are born with a fallen nature. Since Jesus was to be the savior from sin, He had to be born sinless through God's Spirit. He became human but couldn't be born through natural conception because that would have given Him a fallen nature, too. As an incarnation, His birth was divine as well as human. The New Testament records many other remarkable incidents connected with His birth which impressed upon his contemporaries that He was an unusual child.

Soon after His birth, Jesus was taken to Egypt by Joseph and Mary because King Herod wanted to kill the boy. After Herod's death, the family returned to Palestine and settled in Nazareth in the province of Galilee. Jesus grew up there as a normal person, presumably working with Joseph as a carpenter.[13] At the age of thirty, Jesus began preaching His gospel (good news) and performing miracles in Palestine. He did so for over three years until He was crucified. During those years He was closely watched by His friends and enemies and was found to be faultless.[14] His heroic courage (without presumption or bravado) and tender gentleness (without sentimentality or weakness) made such a profound impact on His followers that it comes through even in a casual reading of their writings. His youthful enthusiasm and vigor combined with the equanimity, dignity, and wisdom of age can't fail to impress the readers of the New Testament. A passionate love for God and man was uniquely combined in Him. He could spend days and nights in fasting and prayer in rapt communion with His Father, yet His love for God didn't drive Him to the solitary confinement of a cave. Rather, it drove Him out to ceaseless service for others. He preached, fed and healed the multitudes, comforted the sorrowing, and, it is claimed, even raised the dead to life.

His heart was moved to compassion when He saw the multitudes hungry for truth; tears rolled from his eyes when He saw suffering humanity or cities lost in the darkness of sin and rebellion. Yet the keynote of His life was peace and joy: "The Son of Man came eating and drinking," He said of His own lifestyle, in contrast to John the Baptist who was an ascetic.[15] A life beautiful because of the balance between absolute authority and utter humility, great sorrow and amazing peace, love of God and compassion for humanity, and spotless purity yet friendship with sinners could not but draw devotees to Himself. However, these qualities of life were not the focus of His immediate disciples' teaching. Their preaching centered on the death, resurrection, and second coming of Jesus Christ.

The Jewish leaders who arrested Christ and persuaded Pilate to crucify Him were motivated by two frustrations. The orthodox Pharisees among them were infuriated because Jesus claimed that He was the Son of God and that He and the Father were one. "Anyone who has seen me has seen the Father," claimed Jesus.[16] The Jews understood that Jesus was claiming to be God. This was an unbearable blasphemy to them because they were strict monotheists. The more liberal Jews, the Sadducees, wanted to get rid of Christ because of the political implications they foresaw in His movement. Jesus claimed to be the Messiah—the liberator—sent from God. He said, "The Kingdom of God is at hand."[17] The masses who were longing for liberation from the Roman rule rallied around Him. They wanted to make Him their King. The Sadducees knew that if the movement grew, the Roman authorities would take notice and consequently even their own limited autonomy would go. So they reasoned that it was better for Jesus to die than for the whole nation to suffer, and they persuaded the Roman governor to crucify Him.

Jesus, and John the Baptist before Him, however, gave completely different reasons for His death. Isaiah had prophesied seven hundred years before Jesus' birth that He would die for the sins of the people.[18] In the Old Testament, Moses had instituted the law of sacrifice for the forgiveness of sins. The Jews were to sacrifice various animals regularly as a propitiation for their sins. But when Jesus came, John the Baptist declared that He was the "Lamb of God who takes away the sin of the world."[19] Jesus repeatedly foretold His coming death as well. The night before He was betrayed He asked for a special meal with His disciples and explained to them the meaning of His death. He said that He was going to shed His blood as the remission for the sins of many.[20]

Therefore, after Christ's death, His disciples proclaimed Him to be the savior. They explained from the Old Testament scriptures that God had put the penalty of all our sins on Christ. He had suffered as our substitute. Now if we believe in His death on our behalf and repent of our sins, God will forgive us because Jesus has already paid the penalty of our sins.

Initially, Christ's death had thoroughly shaken His disciples. This one who they thought would deliver the Jews from Roman captivity had died as a helpless victim in the hands of the Jews themselves. The disciples were afraid that they, too, would be arrested for following this rebel. They were sorry, fearful, and dumbfounded. Two days after Christ's burial, some of their women went to His grave to anoint His body with spices according to the Jewish custom. But they came back with astonishing news—"He is risen! Two angels have told us that He is risen!"

At first, naturally, the disciples couldn't believe it. But then they had the shock of their lives when their dead guru came and stood before them. For forty days, He met with them and explained the meaning of His death and resurrection and talked of the coming Kingdom of God. Then He took them to a high mountain and asked them to go back to Jerusalem and wait there in prayer. "You will receive power when the Holy Spirit comes upon you; and you will be my witnesses in Jerusalem and in all Judea and Samaria, and to the ends of the earth."[21]

While they were watching and talking with Him on that mountain, the New Testament records that

> He was taken up before their very eyes, and a cloud hid Him from their sight. They were looking intently up into the sky as He was going, when suddenly two men dressed in white stood beside them. "Men of Galilee," they said, "why do you stand here looking into the sky? This same Jesus, who has been taken from you into heaven, will come back in the same way you have seen Him go into heaven.[22]

If the crucifixion of Jesus indicated to His disciples that He was indeed the savior who takes away the sin of the world—by being sacrificed like a lamb—then His resurrection vindicated to them His claim of divinity.[23] They claimed that they saw Him ascend into heaven and that He is alive today. One day He will return to establish His kingdom on earth. Meanwhile, He has assigned the task to His Church of going into all the world and summoning people to turn away from their sins and submit their lives to His reign.

His disciples waited and prayed in Jerusalem in obedience to His last command. Ten days later, as the New Testament records, the Spirit of God came upon them. They were filled with the power of God and went out preaching that Jesus was the savior and Lord, and they performed many miracles in His name.

Christ's teaching no less than His life attracted masses to Him. People would stay on for days in the wilderness to hear His discourses. People sought Him in houses, synagogues, and mountains, in the temple and by the sea. They found both the manner and the content of His message unique. "No one ever spoke the way this man does," they said.[24]

The authority with which Jesus spoke startled His hearers. His use of simple parables drawn from their daily lives held them transfixed. The insights in His teaching made them wonder where this man got His wisdom.

Philosophical Tenets

God, according to Jesus and the Bible, is infinite and personal. This doesn't necessarily mean that He has a bodily form, for Jesus taught that "God is spirit."[25] Animals have flesh, life, and consciousness, but according to Christianity, they are not "personal."

Because we, according to the Bible, are made in God's image, we too are personal. What is it that distinguishes us from the animals, plants, and other matter? We are self-conscious, creative, moral, and aesthetic beings who communicate with propositions, images, and concepts, and enter into relationships with other beings. According to Christianity, God has revealed Himself to be personal in this same sense. Within the Christian framework, the concept of God is not anthropomorphic, but the concept of humanity is theomorphic.

When Christianity teaches that God is "infinite," it doesn't mean that He is "unlimited," that He incorporates everything within Him and transcends everything, as most of the other gurus believe. Christians believe that God has revealed Himself in the Bible and in Christ to be infinite in who He is. He has a definite character—He is limited to that—but He is infinite in what He is. That is, He is holy in contrast to being unholy. He is infinite in His holiness. He is limited to being wise and powerful in contrast to being weak and foolish. He is infinite in His wisdom and power. Because Christ taught that God has a definite and real moral character, He also taught that sin is real and definite—and that which is contrary to God's character is sinful.

Christians believe that God has revealed Himself to be one, but He has also revealed that He has eternally existed as a community of three distinct persons called Father, Word (or Son), and Spirit. These three persons have existed eternally as one God—one in substance and one in a perfect bond of interpersonal unity. This doctrine of the three-in-one God is called the Trinity. So Christian monotheism (one God) is Trinitarian. From this concept of God flow the Christian views of the universe, humanity, revelation, incarnation, creation, sin, and salvation.

Through His revelation God affirms both the reality and the rationality of the universe. The belief that the world is really there and is not maya or illusion is based on the fact that God in the Scriptures says that He has in fact created a physical universe. Philosophers like Berkeley and Hume have argued that from our empirical experience we can't know whether the world really exists or not. We have an experience of the world, but whether it is caused by a real world or mere illusion is beyond our scope of knowledge—if we begin with the assumption that we have to obtain knowledge by ourselves. But if we allow the possibility of a God who may reveal the truth to us, then within these epistemological presuppositions we can know that the world is really there. For God has revealed to us the fact that He has created an external world. So when we experience it, we have a basis for believing that our experience is not illusory but real.

The Christian belief in the reality and meaningfulness of the material world is also based on the doctrine of the Trinity. A strict monist like Shankaracharya could not logically accept the diversity of the physical universe. If Brahman or unity alone is real, then diversity must be illusory—with unity disguising itself under a mantle of diversity. Existentialists who only see the diverse particulars in the universe but no ultimate unity find that the universe is meaningless because, as Jean Paul Sartre said, no particular can have any meaning without a reference to a universal. But within the Trinitarian concept of God, there is no problem of unity and diversity.

The Christian is not forced to choose between unity or diversity, to join the monist or the existentialist. If God—the ultimate reality—is three in one, if at the heart of God's own being there is a diversity within unity and unity around diversity, then it means that when God created the world it wasn't an extension of His essence. The world is distinct and yet not divorced from Him. There is a balance. If the world is in fact created by a reasonable God (in contrast to being a blind accident), then it is perfectly valid to infer that it is governed by reasonable laws which are discoverable by human reason. This belief in the reality, rationality, and meaningfulness of the universe was the faith that propelled Christians like Francis Bacon and Isaac Newton into scientific inquiry. Thinkers like Whitehead and Oppenheimer have acknowledged that modern science grew not in a Greek, Hindu, or Buddhist milieu, but in a Christian one.

Jesus Christ strongly affirmed human personality, its dignity as well as its fallenness. Our personality is not illusory within the Christian system because the personal God has created humanity in His own image.[26] As a created being, we are finite and related to the rest of creation. But as persons, our relationship is upward toward God. Our personality can only be explained with reference to God, and it can only be fulfilled in relationship with Him.

To be personal, in the Christian sense, means to have subjective, objective, and relational dimensions. I have an objective dimension in that I am known by others. I don't exist purely subjectively, and it is when I get into relationships with others that I become fully personal. Personhood emerges in relationships. To be human means to be in proper relationship with God, others, and the nature over which God has made us ruler. But sin has broken our relationship with God. Jesus never taught that we are divine. According to Christ, we were created good but chose to do evil. Out of a bad heart arise

> evil thoughts, sexual immorality, theft, murder, adultery, greed, malice, deceit, lewdness, envy, slander, arrogance, and folly. All these evils come from inside and make a man 'unclean.'[27]

Because of our sin, we are morally guilty. The important thing is not that at times we feel guilty, but that we actually are guilty of having broken God's moral law. We justly deserve punishment. Because we have sinned against an infinitely holy God, we have sinned infinitely and deserve infinite punishment—eternal separation from God. That is hell.

Though the Bible teaches that all people are the offspring of God in that they owe their existence to Him, it doesn't teach that all are also children of God. Jesus said to the Pharisees, the most religious people of His day,

> If God were your Father, you would love me, for I came from God. . . . You belong to your father, the devil, and you want to carry out your father's desire. He was a murderer from the beginning, not holding to the truth, for there is no truth in him. When he lies, he speaks his native language, for he is a liar and the father of lies.[28]

Sin is not avidya (ignorance), but real moral guilt. It is the cause of our separation from God, others, and nature. The whole world has become abnormal because of humanity's fall. Even within the individual, sin has created remorse, worry, tension, and much emotional and psychological sickness. Sin, both individual and corporate, is the root cause of all suffering, illness, sorrow, and death in this world—and ultimately hell itself.

However, even though Jesus often talked about our sinfulness, He also had a high respect for our dignity. To whatever depths we may fall, we still bear the image of God, though it is marred by sin. Consequently, we are still the object of God's love. God seeks to save us from sin and longs for the prodigal child to return home.

Because of our intrinsic dignity, we are worth loving and serving. No one was too low for Jesus to stoop down and touch or even to wash their feet. He would accept and even make friends with social outcasts or untouchables—be they Samaritans, tax collectors, lepers, or the demon-possessed.

The whole person is created by God and is the object of His love. Jesus never despised the body or the mind. He healed the body and fed it. He respected intellectual doubts and answered them. The Bible warns people of the evil tendencies of the flesh and the darkness of the human heart. But the body and mind are not something to be cast aside. Jesus wants to save the whole person— body, mind, and soul.

According to Christ, our problem is not that we are ignorant, but that we are sinners. Salvation in His teaching means forgiveness of sin and deliverance from it and its results.

Because God is righteous, He can't overlook sin. It must be punished. Our infinite guilt must mean infinite punishment. Either we have to take this punishment ourself (and be separated forever from God in hell) or someone else must pay the penalty for our sin. But who can pay an infinite penalty? Only a person who is infinite in His love and being can pay it. The Bible teaches that this is exactly what God has done:

> For God so loved the world that He gave His one and only Son, that whoever believes in Him shall not perish but have eternal life.[29]

God the Father sent the second person of the Trinity, His unique and only begotten Son, to come and die in place of us. When Jesus Christ, who had eternally existed with the Father as God, hung upon the cross at His death, He cried out, "My God, my God, why have you forsaken me?"[30] The Bible says, "God made Him who had no sin to be sin for us."[31] Jesus took the punishment of sin—separation from God—upon Himself. So now if sinners repent of sin and believe in Jesus, which means accepting Him as guru (as savior and Lord), they can be forgiven. This salvation is a gift of grace because the full penalty of sin has already been paid by Jesus.

But salvation doesn't simply mean forgiveness of sin. The Bible teaches that when we accept Jesus as our guru, our sins are forgiven, we are accepted as a child of God, and Jesus comes to dwell in us through His Spirit. The indwelling Spirit of God produces deep peace and joy because the Spirit gives assurance that our sins have been forgiven and that we have been accepted by God. The Holy Spirit gives power to overcome sinful temptations. He exposes hidden sins and gives strength to remove them. Indeed, when individuals truly come to Christ, they become a "new creation,"[32] with a new nature and restored relationships.

The Holy Spirit is only the beginning[33] of what the Father has planned for those that love Him. The Bible talks of salvation in past, present, and future tenses. When we repent of our sin and put our faith in Christ, we are saved in the sense that our sins are forgiven, we are reconciled to God, and we have become His adopted child. But daily we are being saved from the power of sin and transformed into the moral likeness of Jesus Christ. Our emotional and spiritual problems are being healed. We are becoming whole and growing in a proper relationship with God, others, and nature. We are becoming fully human again. The Holy Spirit is giving us new powers and gifts to love and serve God.

But there is more. The risen Christ promised that one day He would return in glory and power. He will judge both the living and the dead. Those who have continued to live in sin to the end of their lives will be separated from God forever. But those who have repented, asked forgiveness, and received the gift of the Spirit will enter the kingdom of heaven. Then salvation will be total because Christians will be completely delivered from sin and all its results. Their bodies and minds and even the material world will be saved. Jesus Christ, who came as a guru, teacher, and savior, and who at present rules over the lives of His disciples, will become the eternal king of all creation. "Every knee should bow . . . and every tongue confess that Jesus Christ is Lord."[34]

Such a grand conception of salvation; such high views of God, the universe, humanity, and morals; such realistic views of sin, suffering, and death naturally fascinate a seeker. No wonder Jesus of Nazareth still continues to draw thousands. However, to those who refuse to believe blindly, the teaching Christ proclaimed presents many intellectual problems.

Does a Personal God Exist?

Christians argue that this is their primary presupposition or theory, that we can accept it to be true because it alone gives plausible answers to basic philosophical questions, and that it is the only presupposition with which we can live consistently.

Christians agree with Sartre that the fundamental question before us is, Why is there something rather than nothing? There are only two possible answers. First, that everything has come out of nothing. In the beginning, there was absolutely nothing—no gas, no energy, no sound, no light, no God, and no vibration—and out of this nothingness everything has come. Obviously, this is incredible. So the only other alternative is that something has always existed and out of this something everything has come.

The next question is, What is this something out of which everything has come? Again, there are only two main possibilities. Either something impersonal (energy, sound, silence, or Brahman) or someone personal (God), out of which everything has come, has always existed. If we hold ultimate reality to be impersonal, we have the problem of explaining how personality came out of impersonality. In spite of over a hundred years of scientific investigation, no one has given us any clue as to how this might happen. Moreover, even if someone did, how could personality be fulfilled if the ultimate environment of the universe were impersonal? If God were impersonal, then we would be like a fish that has suddenly developed lungs. It can't survive or be fulfilled in water. It needs an environment of air to be fulfilled as a being with lungs. Likewise, we as personal beings with aspirations for love, meaning, purpose, beauty, morals, creativity, and interpersonal communication can only be fulfilled if the ultimate environment is personal. Only if we presuppose a personal God can we have an explanation for the existence of personality as well as the possibility for its fulfillment.

But Can a Personal God Also Be Infinite?

The Indian mind has traditionally distinguished between impersonal God (Brahman) and personal God (Ishvara). The infinite God (Brahman) is called nirguna (unattributed) and is therefore impersonal. The infinite, according to traditional Indian reasoning, must incorporate everything within it. It can't have some attributes and not others. So it must have everything within it: good and bad, love and cruelty, strength and weakness. In other words, it must be beyond all attributes. Personality implies definite, limited attributes, and the infinite can't be limited. But because the human mind can't comprehend or worship a faceless, formless, infinite God, the Indian philosophers have postulated a limited, personal Ishvara, who has a definite form. He can be pictured, loved, and worshiped. But Ishvara is not ultimate truth, according to monists, because God must be infinite and thus can't be personal.

Christians argue that infinite and personal are not mutually exclusive categories. In geometry, there is talk of an infinite straight line. If a line can be infinite and not include everything in it, then why can't God be infinite and not include everything within Him? Just as a line is infinite within the limitation of what it is, so also God can be infinite within the limitation of that which He is.

Christ's devotees also argue that the concept of God as infinite and personal alone is credible because if God is impersonal, He offers no basis for the value of human personality. If He is finite (as Ishvara or other avatars and deities are), then He is not sufficient to carry philosophical unity as a universal being. The failure of finite deities becomes obvious in Greek and Hindu mythologies. Not only are there flaws in their characters, but there is always the confusion of whether fate is behind the gods or the gods behind fate. Also, only a personal God can provide a basis for true morals.

Isn't It Inconsistent to Believe in One God Who Exists in Three Persons?

The Christian belief in a triune God is based essentially on God's self-revelation in history. The Jews were the strictest of all monotheists because God so revealed Himself to them and forbade worship of all other gods. Yet all through the Old Testament, we see the "Spirit of the Lord" (the third person of the trinity) active as a person in His own right. The prophets talk about a coming child who will be the Messiah (God's anointed) and call Him the "Mighty God, Everlasting Father."

When Jesus Christ came, He claimed to be the Messiah, the Son of God, and one with the Father—"I and the Father are one. . . . Anyone who has seen me has seen the Father."[35] His enemies and His friends alike understood that He was claiming to be God. His enemies decided to kill Him because He claimed to be God, and His disciples worshiped Him as God when they saw Him risen from the dead.

At first, the disciples didn't fully articulate the doctrine of the Trinity. They accepted both Jesus and His Father as God, as John has written: "In the beginning was the Word, and the Word was with God, and the Word was God."[36] During His lifetime, Jesus had promised that after His death He would rise again and send His Spirit to come dwell in His disciples. He said that this Spirit was to be just like Him, a "comforter," who would be sent by the Father in Jesus' name.[37]

The New Testament records that on the day of Pentecost, fifty days after Christ's resurrection, the Holy Spirit came upon the disciples and filled them. They received divine power to heal, to prophesy, and to speak in tongues they had not learned. This experience of the Holy Spirit convinced them that the Spirit was God, too. So out of God's self-revelation in history and Christian experience as one God, eternally existing in three persons—Father, Son, and Holy Spirit—came the doctrine of the Trinity.

Is It Intellectually Acceptable?

Christian theologians have argued that the doctrine of a tripersonal God alone is intellectually credible for two reasons. First, God can't be both personal and unitarian. For what does it mean to be personal? If the chief distinguishing mark of personality is the ability to engage in rational, propositional communication and interpersonal relationships, then an isolated being can only be a subpersonal entity. Personhood has a subjective, objective, and relational dimension. One is subpersonal without all three of these dimensions. If God has existed eternally as a unitarian individual without anyone with whom He can communicate, then He is not eternally personal. Without love and communication, at best He can only be an unfulfilled person who needs to create other personal beings in order to love and communicate with them. Such a God who needs something outside of Himself is not self-sufficient or autonomous and therefore can't be the final absolute in the universe. But if God has existed eternally as three persons in a mutual relationship of love and communication, then He can be self-sufficient and autonomous. The Bible teaches that this love and communication have gone on forever in the Godhead.

Second, Christ's devotees argue that the Trinitarian concept of God is alone credible because it alone gives the basis for accepting both unity and diversity as real in the universe. All philosophers and religious thinkers have to face the problem of unity and diversity. We see water, vapor, and ice as three distinct things, yet we know they are also one and the same. Is the diversity real or is the unity real? We have seen that all philosophers move to one or the other extreme, depending upon their view of ultimate reality. Existentialists see things as random and unrelated, while at the other extreme many Hindu gurus see everything as one. But the Christian presupposition of a Trinitarian God provides a basis for accepting both unity and diversity as real.

Thus Christians believe in a tripersonal God because He has so revealed

Himself, because the concept of a unipersonal God is logically inconsistent, and because the Trinitarian concept of God alone solves the problem of unity and diversity.

Is God Good?

Seeing the sin and evil in the world, many people have concluded that there can't be a God or that at least He can't be a good God. "If there is a God, he is the Devil," said Charles Baudelaire. Many others, including all the Hindu gurus, have concluded that God contains both good and evil within Himself (or Itself). But if this is so, then ultimately evil is not bad because it is also divine.

Christians argue that people who feel that the presence of evil in the world precludes the existence of a good God should realize that, logically, if they don't believe in the existence of a good God they can't call anything evil, either. Existence of evil presupposes the existence of a good God in contrast to whom evil is evil. In order to believe in the reality of evil, one has to believe in a good God. But if the creator of the world is good, then where does evil come from?

According to God's revelation in the Bible, evil originates in our free will. God made us good and free—free to love and obey God or to disobey Him. The Bible teaches that we chose to disobey God, to act contrary to God's character and commands. This naturally severed our relationship with God and consequently from others and nature as well. This rebellion against God's law is the source of all sin and suffering in the world. Not only has there been rebellion against God in this world, but the Bible also teaches that there is a spiritual world of angels. Some of them have chosen to live contrary to God's will. These are called demons, and they too tempt and influence us toward evil.

But if God gave us the free will to begin with, why does He punish us when we exercise this will to do whatever we like? Or if God gave the free will, then isn't He responsible for the entrance of sin into the world?

"Not at all," Christ's devotees argue. It is like saying, "Because the constitution of India guarantees our fundamental right of freedom, the government should not punish us no matter what we say or do." Obviously, this is ridiculous. Freedom is always given to be exercised within the boundaries of the law. Suppose a father left a million rupees in his will for his son. In the company of some friends the son started drinking and gambling with this money. Could he plead innocent before a court of law on the basis that it was all his father's fault for giving him this vast sum?

The biblical answer is that Jesus Christ has indeed paid the penalty of our sin by His death on the cross. But we have to appropriate the benefits of His death individually through repentance and faith. It is as if we have been found guilty in a court and fined one million rupees for the crime. A rich friend comes along and offers us the sum we need. We have to accept it thankfully and go to the authorities and say, "Here is the fine; please let me go free."

The punishment of sin is death, or separation from God. The Lord Jesus Christ has paid this penalty on the cross on our behalf. We now have to accept this by faith, to kneel before God in humility, and to confess before Him that we acknowledge that we are guilty and deserve punishment. But because the Lord Jesus has died in our place, we pray that we may be forgiven for sins we've committed and that our broken relationship with Him may be restored.

If we choose to remain in sin, away from God, we will find His death meaningless, even though Christ has died in our place and opened a way for forgiveness and reconciliation with God.

Isn't Belief in the Miraculous Outdated?

If there is no almighty God who can act in the universe, then surely miracles and the Resurrection are myths, and the belief in the second coming of Christ mere fancy. But if there is a God who has created this universe out of nothing and who has put life into lifeless matter, then it is not impossible that He would put life into a dead body.

Many individuals have set out to study all the historical data available about Christ to disprove that Jesus ever rose again from the dead. General Lew Wallace was one; Frank Morrison was another. After years of research, they both independently concluded that all the historical evidence pointed to the fact that Jesus did rise again from the dead. Lew Wallace then wrote his classic *Ben Hur*, and Frank Morrison wrote *Who Moved the Stone?*

The problem is this: on the day of Pentecost, exactly fifty-three days after Christ's death, Peter stood up before a crowd of Jews and proclaimed that Jesus, whom they had crucified, had risen again. Peter was preaching in the same city where Christ had been condemned. Many of his hearers had been part of the crowd that killed Him. Yet that day, three thousand of these Jews believed Peter and accepted the risen Christ as their guru. Shortly after this, two thousand more Jews became followers of Christ. The number of Christians started growing rapidly in Jerusalem. Many of the Jewish leaders also became Christians. But other leaders were angry and arrested Peter and the other disciples, threatened them, beat them up, and killed many in an attempt to stop them from preaching that Jesus had risen again.

All this was taking place just about two miles from where Jesus had been buried after His death. His grave was still there, and it was empty. Everybody knew that it was empty. His disciples proclaimed that it was empty because Jesus had risen. Their enemies said that it was empty because the disciples had stolen His dead body.

But the explanation of their enemies was so flimsy that few of their contemporaries could believe it. First, they had absolutely no proof for the charge of theft. Second, the disciples soon became known as saints—persons of unusually high moral standards. Anybody who knew them couldn't believe that they were thieves and liars. Third, these disciples were so convinced that Jesus had risen that they gladly died for their faith instead of backing out. Who could die for a lie, especially if telling the truth would save them? Finally, what about St. Paul? He was not a disciple when Christ died and rose again. He was not part of the "theft." Why did he start preaching that Christ had indeed risen? Was it because it was as he testified that the risen Christ had appeared to him? The theory that the disciples had stolen Christ's body has never appealed to the thoughtful.

However, those who don't believe that there is a God and consequently can't accept miracles have tried over the centuries to put forward various theories to solve the riddle of the empty tomb.

Some have argued that the Roman or Jewish authorities themselves must have removed the body to another tomb so that Christ's tomb wouldn't become another holy shrine. The absurdity of this theory is obvious. If they had done so, then the simplest way to stop the growth of Christianity (which they desperately wanted to do) would have been to assure the people that they had removed Christ's body; He had not risen. But they never even dreamed of doing so.

Others have argued that resurrection is impossible; some animal must have taken away Christ's body. When the women went to anoint His body on Easter Sunday, they found the tomb empty, so they went back to spread the rumor that He had risen. This theory completely overlooks the incidental historical data that we have about Christ's burial. Matthew records that "Joseph took the body, wrapped it in a clean linen cloth, . . . placed it in his own new tomb that he had cut out of the rock," and "rolled a big stone in front of the entrance to the tomb."[38] It doesn't seem possible that Joseph would have made such a costly tomb for himself, cut out of rock, if an animal could get in.

St. John records in his Gospel that after the women reported to the disciples that the tomb was empty he and Peter ran to the tomb:

> Then Simon Peter . . . arrived and went into the tomb. He saw the strips of linen lying there, as well as the burial cloth that had been around Jesus' head. The cloth was folded up by itself, separate from the linen.[39]

Why would an animal (or a human thief, for that matter) remove clothes and fold up a burial cloth before dragging the body away?

In 1899, Mirza Ghulam Ahmad, the founder of the Ahmadiyya movement, wrote his treatise *Masih Hindustan Mein* (Christ in India), in which he argued that Jesus didn't die on the cross, but later came to Kashmir and then died and was buried in Srinagar.

Few of Mirza Ghulam's contemporaries, apart from his own followers, paid much attention to his thesis because it didn't have any evidence whatsoever to support it. The Ahmadiyya movement, however, has kept asserting loudly that the theory is true, with the result that over the past decades some non-Ahmadiyya Muslims and Hindus have begun to believe it. The following have been the important popularizers of this theory: Mufti Muhammad Sadiq of Shahpur, who published *Qabr-i-Masih* (The Tomb of Christ) in October 1936; Khwaja Nazir Ahmad of Lahore, who in 1951 compiled his monumental work, *Jesus in Heaven on Earth*; Dr. Aziz Ahmad Qureshi, who published his *Asrar-i-Kashmir* in 1957; Maulana Jalal-ud Din Shams, ex-Imam of the London Mosque, who wrote the book *Where Did Jesus Die?* in 1959; Dr. Mohammed Yasin, who wrote *The Mysteries of Kashmir* in 1972; and Akshy Kumar Jain, who in December 1973 wrote a series of four articles in *Dharmyugh*, a Hindi weekly, trying to prove that Mirza Ghulam's theory was true.

The "evidence" put forward by these scholars need not be examined because no such evidence actually exists. The inscription on the tomb in Srinagar, which is said to be that of Christ, itself says clearly that it is the tomb of one called Yus-Asaf. The majority of Muslim scholars and authorities don't believe it to be the tomb of Christ.

In recent years, some have suggested that perhaps Jesus didn't die on the cross but merely fainted. Soldiers thought He had died, so they allowed Him to be buried. When He regained consciousness, He walked out of the grave and pretended that He had risen from the dead.

To believe that Jesus had merely fainted on the cross, later walked out of the tomb, and convinced His disciples that He had conquered death requires more "faith" than to believe that He actually rose from the dead. To believe the former requires that we believe that a man who had been brutally lashed on His back, whose head had been "crowned" with thorns, who had been nailed to a cross for three hours, in whose stomach a soldier's spear had been thrust, who had suffered so much and bled so much that He had become unconscious, who had been put in a tomb which was sealed with a stone so heavy that it couldn't be removed by three women, and who had been hungry and thirsty for three days could walk out of the grave without being seen by the guards who were specially commissioned to see that His body wasn't stolen. Not only did He get out of the grave, but this man who desperately needed first aid walked at least two miles into the city without being seen by anyone and convinced His disciples that He had conquered death and not merely escaped it. His disciples became so sure that He had risen from the dead that they ceased to be afraid of death anymore; instead they went all over the world to proclaim this good news at the cost of unparalleled persecution, torture, and death.

And what was the good news that they proclaimed? They declared that God exists and that He loves us and has revealed Himself to us, that He has taken our sin upon Himself and suffered in our place, and that we can, through repentance and faith in Him, receive forgiveness of sin and be reconciled with Him. Also, that He offers the gift of the Holy Spirit and that of everlasting life in the kingdom of heaven, which He is establishing and is going to reveal at the end of the age. His disciples went forth proclaiming that God, who had come as a human guru, who had died for our sins, is risen again and is alive forevermore. Anyone, at any time and at any place, can receive Him as guru, obtain the free gift of salvation, and live in an eternal love relationship with Him.

I myself am a devotee of Jesus Christ. Why? Because the teachings of Jesus Christ alone make sense to me. I believe that the revelation, the philosophy, the worldview, and the map of reality given by Christ alone stand up to the test of reason. They alone can be upheld with total intellectual integrity.

Also, I have found Him to be a true guru. He has been my friend, my comforter, my guide, my protector, and my provider—one who dwells in me and one to whom I can turn at any time for help, love, joy, peace, and power.

Finally, I believe that Jesus Christ alone can fulfill our spiritual and cultural aspirations.

NOTES

CHAPTER 1: *Understanding Guruism*

1. Secularism has different connotations in India. Here it simply means religious neutrality of the government.
2. See "One Dimensional Man" in Os Guinness, *Dust of Death* (Downers Grove, Ill.: IVP, 1973), for a survey of the important critics of the mechanistic society.
3. Ibid., 130.
4. For a treatment of the failure of drugs, sex, and the occult from an Indian point of view see Captain F.D. Colaabavala, *Hippie Dharma* (Delhi: Hind Pocket Books, 1974).
5. John R. Yale, ed., *What Vedanta Means to Me* (London: Rider and Co., 1961), 29.
6. Dr. B. B. Chaubey, "The Nature of Guruship According to Hindu Scriptures." (A paper presented at the Christian Institute of Sikh Studies, Batala.) This and other papers referred to in this chapter have been published by the Institute in a book entitled *The Nature of Guruship.*
7. Ibid.
8. Prof. G. S. Talib, "The Concept of Guruship in the Sikh Tradition" in *The Nature of Guruship.*
9. I. C. Puri, "Guru According to Radha Soami Teachings" in *The Nature of Guruship.*
10. With the exception of Keshab Chandra Sen, who allowed his followers to worship him as guru.
11. J. N. Farquhar, *Modern Religious Movements in India* (New York: Macmillan, 1951), 199.
12. Swami Sivananda, *Bliss Divine* (Sivananda Nagar: Divine Life Society, 1974), 202-3.
13. Peter Brent, *Godmen of India* (Harmondsworth: Penguin Books, 1973), 72.
14. Ibid., 60.
15. Ibid, 41-42.
16. A. C. Bhaktivedanta Prabhupada, *On Chanting Hare Krishna* (Los Angeles: ISKCON), 5.
17. *Back to Godhead* (Magazine of the Hare Krishna Movement), no. 51, 11.
18. Ibid., no. 34, 15.
19. A. L. Basham, *The Wonder That Was India* (London: Fontana Books, 1971), 164.
20. Chaubey, *Nature of Guruship*, 9-10.
21. C. O. McMullen, "The Nature of Guruship: Sociological Approach" in *The Nature of Guruship.*
22. Brent, *Godmen*, 287.
23. Ibid., 185.
24. Not all gurus preach complete otherworldliness. Some, like Mahesh Yogi, try to reconcile Western materialism with Eastern spirituality.
25. R. C. Zaehner, *Mysticism: Sacred and Profane* (London: Oxford University Press, 1961), 17.

CHAPTER 2: *The Intellectual Impulses Behind Guruism*

1. Descartes argued that because he doubts, he must exist. But from the fact that doubting goes on, we can only conclude that thinking exists, not that the thinker also exists. To establish the latter, we will have to prove causation, which is impossible on the premise of modern philosophy, as Hume showed.
2. Guinness, *Dust of Death*, 202.
3. Swami Sivananda, *Bliss Divine*, 555.

4. For a detailed treatment of epistemological problems, see Francis Schaeffer's *He Is There and He Is Not Silent.*

5. *Rig Veda*, 129, quoted in A. L. Basham, *The Wonder That Was India*, 249-50.

6. Sivananda, *Bliss Divine*, 379.

7. Basham, *The Wonder That Was India*, 251.

8. William James, *The Varieties of Religious Experience* (London: Fontana Library, 1971), 373-74.

9. R. D. Laing, *The Divided Self* (New York: Penguin Books, 1974), 23.

10. Quoted by Anthony Campbell in *Seven States of Consciousness* (London: Gollanoz, 1973).

11. Ibid.

12. Ibid.

13. Marvin Harper, *Gurus, Swamis and Avataras*, 241-42.

14. Campbell, *Seven States.*

15. Carl Jung in a foreword to D. T. Suzuki's *An Introduction to Zen Buddhism*, 26.

16. J. S. Neki, "The Nature of Guruship: A Psychological Perspective" in *The Nature of Guruship.*

17. Quoted in Guinness, *Dust of Death*, 207.

CHAPTER 3: *Criterion for Evaluating Guruism*

1. R. C. Zaehner, *Mysticism: Sacred and Profane*, xiii, 7.

2. William James, *The Varieties of Religious Experience*, 374.

3. Martin Buber, *Between Man and Man* (London: Fontana Library, 1969), 43.

4. Quoted by Zaehner, *Mysticism*, 69.

5. Ibid., 83.

6. Ibid., 88.

7. Ibid., 91.

8. Ibid., 92.

9. Ibid., 157-58.

10. Swami Krishnananda, *Short History of Religious and Philosophic Thought in India* (Sivananda Nagar: Divine Life Society, 1973), viii.

11. Swami Chinmayananda, *Kindle Life* (Madras: Chinmaya Publications Trust), 36.

12. I am indebted to Francis Schaeffer for the general perspective of this chapter. See his principle of verification in *The God Who Is There* (London: Hodder and Stoughton, 1969), 109.

13. Some religious systems like Islam and Christianity claim to have been revealed by God and not thought up by humanity. We can't rule out the possibility of divine revelation, but because these are also rational systems that answer basic philosophical questions, we can still call them theories, and our criterion applies to them as well. If they are truly revealed by God, then our criterion will show them to be true.

14. Aldous Huxley, *What Vedanta Means to Me*, 28-29.

CHAPTER 4: *The Divine Life Society and Chinmaya Mission*

1. Swami Sivananda, *Ten Upanishads* (Sivanandanagar: Divine Life Society, 1973), 19.

2. Swami Sivananda, *Bliss Divine* (Sivanandanagar: Divine Life Society, 1974), 539-540.

3. Ibid., 375.

4. Ibid., 538.

5. Ibid., 97.

6. Quoted by H. K. Vissanji, *Bhavan's Journal* (April 30, 1972). Most of the biographical data of Swami Chinmayananda comes from this article.

7. Ibid.

8. Swami Chinmayananda, *Kindle Life*, 27-28.

9. Ibid., 37.

10. Ibid., 1.

11. Ibid., 20-21, 42.

12. "Pure" consciousness is not to be understood in contrast to impure or unholy consciousness, but in contrast to "gross" consciousness. "Gross" means that consciousness which has thoughts and feelings.

13. Swami Sivananda, *Ten Upanishads*, 67.

14. Ibid., 6.

15. Ibid., 76-77.

16. Swami Chinmayananda, *Kindle Life*, 97-99.

17. R. C. Zaehner, *Mysticism: Sacred and Profane*, xiii.

18. Swami Sivananda, *Bliss Divine*, 420.

19. Ibid., vii.

20. Zaehner, *Mysticism*, 167.

21. Sivananda, *Bliss Divine*, xxv.

22. Swami Chinmayananda, *Kindle Life*, 50.

23. Swami Sivananda, *Bliss Divine*, 459.

24. Ibid., xvii, xxx.

25. Ibid., 202.

26. Swami Chinmayananda, *Kindle Life*, 79.

27. Ibid., 80.

28. Swami Sivananda, *Bliss Divine*, 377.

29. Ibid., 398.

30. Ibid., 106.

31. Ibid., 206, 236, 392.

32. Swami Krishnananda, *Resurgent Culture* (Sivanandanagar: Divine Life Society, 1972), 38.

33. Swami Chinmayananda, *Kindle Life*, 145.

34. Swami Sivananda, *Bliss Divine*, 531.

35. Ibid., 288, 502.

36. Ibid., 34.

37. Ibid., 35.

38. Ibid., 629.

CHAPTER 5: *Hare Krishna*

1. *Back to Godhead*, no. 34 (Allston: ISKCON Press, 1970), 25.

2. Ibid., 2.

3. A. C. Bhaktivedanta Swami Prabhupada, *Krishna*, vol. 1 (New York: Bhaktivedanta Book Trust, 1970), xvii.

4. Prabhupada, *On Chanting Hare Krishna*, 11.

5. D. S. Sharma, *Hinduism through the Ages* (Bombay: Bharatiya Vidhya Bhavan, 1973), 51.

6. J. N. Farquhar, *Modern Religious Movements in India*, 293.

7. Ibid., 294.

8. J. Stillson Judah, *Hare Krishna and the Counter-Culture* (New York: John Wiley and Sons, 1974), 43. I am indebted to this book for some of the ideas expressed in this section.

9. Irving I. Zaretsky, foreword to Judah,*Hare Krishna and the Counter-Culture*, v.

10. Judah, *Hare Krishna and the Counter-Culture*, 76.

11. Dr. S. Radhakrishnan, *The Bhagavad Gita* (London: George Allen & Unwin Ltd., 1963), 14. See also Sharma, *Hinduism*, 37.

12. *Back to Godhead*, no. 34, 2.

13. Ibid., no. 34, 15.

14. Ibid., no. 56, 15.

15. Ibid., 16.

16. Ibid., 19.

17. Prabhupada, *The Nectar of Devotion* (New York: Bhaktivedanta Book Trust, 1970), 59. See also *Back to Godhead*, no. 51, 11.

18. Prabhupada, *Krishna*, vol. 1, 152. See also *Back to Godhead*, no. 56, 21.

19. Judah, *Hare Krishna and the Counter-Culture*, 60.

20. *Back to Godhead*, no. 51, 27.

21. Ibid., 17.

22. Ibid., 11.

23. *Back to Godhead*, no. 34, 3.

24. Prabhupada, *The Nectar of Devotion*, xviii.

25. Ibid., xx.

26. Prabhupada, *On Chanting Hare Krishna*, 9.

27. Ibid., 8.

28. Prabhupada, *Krishna*, 21. See also *Back to Godhead*, no. 51, 1.

29. Sharma, *Hinduism through the Ages*, 53.

30. *Back to Godhead*, no. 56, 28.

31. Ibid., no. 34, 14.

32. Ibid., no. 51, 11.

33. Prabhupada, *Krishna*, 155.

34. Faye Levine, *The Strange World of Hare Krishnas* (New York: Fawcett, 1974), 35.

35. Judah, *Hare Krishna and the Counter-Culture*, 86.

36. Prabhupada, *Krishna*, 7.

CHAPTER 6: *Transcendental Meditation*

1. Maharishi sometimes uses the word "God" not for the ultimate reality but for a special state of our consciousness which is inferior to the absolute.

2. Forward to the "First International Symposium on the Science of Creative Intelligence."

3. Mahesh Yogi, *The Science of Being and the Art of Living* (London: International SRM Publications, 1966), 26-27.

4. Ibid., 36.

5. Ibid., 45.

6. Ibid., 46.

7. Ibid., 30.

8. Ibid., 42-43.

9. Ibid.

10. Ibid., 236.

11. Ibid., 275.

12. Mahesh Yogi, *Science of Being*, 278.

13. Anthony Campbell, *Seven States of Consciousness*, 99.

14. Mahesh Yogi, *Science of Being*, 287.

15. Ibid.

16. Ibid., 291.

17. Ibid., 301.

18. Ibid., 302.

19. Mahesh Yogi, *Bhagavad Gita* (Middlesex: Penguin Books, 1969), 469. English translation from *Special Report of Christian World Liberation* (Berkeley: June 25, 1975).

20. Mahesh Yogi, *Science of Being*, 19.

21. Ibid., 43.

22. Mahesh Yogi, *Bhagavad Gita*, 105.

23. David Haddon, "New Plant Thrives in a Spiritual Desert" in *Christianity Today*, 1973.

24. "The TM Craze: Forty Minutes to Bliss," *Time*, (Oct. 13, 1975).

25. Quoted by David Haddon, *Transcendental Meditation: A Christian View*, 3.

26. Mahesh Yogi, *Science of Being*, 106.

27. *TM: Penetrating the Veil of Deception* (Berkeley: Spiritual Counterfeits Project).

28. Ibid.

29. Quoted in William James, *Varieties of Religious Experience*, 370.

30. "The TM Craze," *Time*.

31. Quoted by David Haddon, *Transcendental Meditation*, from a letter sent by Berkeley SIMS center to the parents of students at area high schools.

32. Mahesh Yogi, *Bhagavad Gita*, 317-19.

33. Mahesh Yogi, *Science of Being*, 310.

34. Mahesh Yogi, *Bhagavad Gita*, 224.

CHAPTER 7: *Acharya Rajneesh*

1. Dr. Ramachandra Prasad, *The Mystic of Feeling* (New Delhi: Motilal Banarsidas, 1970), v.

2. Foreword to Acharya Rajneesh, *Path to Self-Realization* (Bombay: Jeevan Jagruti Kendra, 1971).

3. Ibid., 1.

4. Prasad, *Mystic of Feeling*, 197.

5. See chapter two.

6. Prasad, *Mystic of Feeling*, 91.

7. Ibid., 50.

8. Ibid., 134.

9. Ibid., 190, 214.

10. Rajneesh, *Path to Self-Realization*, 13-14.

11. Acharya Rajneesh, *Satya Ki Pahli Kiran* (Bombay: Jeevan Jagruti Kendra, 1971), 15. Translation mine.

12. Ibid., 20.

13. *Neo-sannyasa* vol. 2, no. 4, 3.

14. Acharya Rajneesh, *Beyond and Beyond* (Bombay: Jeevan Jagruti Kendra, 1970), 14-15.

15. Ibid., 12.

16. Ibid., 18.

17. Acharya Rajneesh, *Seeds of Revolutionary Thoughts* (Bombay: Jeevan Jagruti Kendra, 1969), 30.

18. Rajneesh, *Path to Self-Realization*, 12.

19. Acharya Rajneesh, *From Sex to Super Consciousness* (Bombay: Jeevan Jagruti Kendra, 1971), 134.

20. Ibid., 26-30.

21. Rajneesh, *Satya Ki Pahli Kiran*, 47-48.

22. Ibid., 48-49.

23. Ibid., 52-53.

24. Rajneesh, *Path to Self-Realization*, 15.

25. Ibid., 11.

26. From a leaflet entitled "Bhagwan Shree's Meditation."

27. *Neo-Sannyasa* vol. 2, no. 4 (1973), 5.

28. Ibid., 7.

29. Ibid., 12.

30. Ibid, 20.

31. Ibid., 27.

32. Acharya Rajneesh, *The Mustard Seed*, 140.

33. Rajneesh, *Beyond and Beyond*, 12-14.

34. Rajneesh, *Sex to Super Consciousness*, 24, 34, 78.

35. Acharya Rajneesh, *Dharm Aur Rajniti* (Bombay: Jeevan Jagruti Kendra, 1972), 17.

36. Acharya Rajneesh, *Pragati Sheel Kaun?* (Bombay: Jeevan Jagruti Kendra, 1971), 16.

37. Prasad, *Mystic of Feeling*, 214.

38. Rajneesh, *Dharm Aur Rajniti*, 13.

39. R.C. Zaehner, *Mysticism: Sacred and Profane*, 173.

40. Scotta Callister, James Long, and Leslie L. Zaitz, "For Love and Money," *The Oregonian*, 2 July 1985, sec. A6.

41. Quoted in *The Oregonian*, 1 July 1985.

42. *The Book of Books* vol. 2, quoted in *The Oregonian*, 11 July 1985.

CHAPTER 8: *Sathya Sai Baba*

1. V. K. Gokak, *Sri Sathya Sai Baba* (New Delhi: Abhinav Publications, 1975), 61-66. Sathya Sai Baba, after thirty-five years of claiming to be the reincarnation of Shirdi Baba, narrated these "facts" about him, which no one has known for the last hundred years or more.

2. Howard Murphet, *Sai Baba: Man of Miracles* (Delhi: Macmillan, 1972), 54.

3. Gokak, *Sai Baba*, 4.

4. Ibid., 304.

5. Ibid., 219-20.

6. Ibid., 304.

7. Ibid., 24.

8. Ibid., 37.

9. Murphet, *Man of Miracles* 195.

10. Ibid.
11. Gokak, *Sai Baba,* 229.
12. Ibid., 31.
13. *Sanatan Sarathi* (August-September 1969), 127.
14. Murphet, *Man of Miracles* 197-98.
15. John Hislop, *Conversations with Bhagavan Shri Sathya Sai Baba* (Ratlam: Bhagavan Shri Sathya Seva Organization, 1976), 16.
16. Ibid., 9.
17. Ibid., 12.
18. Matt. 24:26-27.
19. Matt. 25:31-46.
20. *Illustrated Weekly of India* (December 28, 1975).
21. C. S. Lewis, *The Screwtape Letters* (New York: Macmillan, 1961), xi.
22. Hislop, *Conversations,* 13.
23. Gokak, *Sai Baba,* 216.

CHAPTER 9: *Swami Muktananda Paramahansa*

1. Amma, *Swami Muktananda Paramahansa* (Ganeshpuri, 1971), 5.
2. Ibid., 19-20.
3. Peter Brent, *Godmen of India,* 274.
4. Amma, *Swami Muktananda,* 30.
5. Ibid.
6. Ibid., 49.
7. *Sree Gurudev Vani,* vol. 2, 12.
8. Amma, *Swami Muktananda,* 32-43.
9. Ibid., 35.
10. Ibid., 36.
11. Ibid., 37.
12. Ibid., 41.
13. Ibid.
14. Ibid., 45.
15. Ibid., 46.
16. Ibid., 47.
17. *Sree Gurudev Vani.*
18. Ibid., 6.
19. Ibid., 6-7.
20. Amma, *Swami Muktananda,* 60.
21. Ibid., 71.
22. Ibid., 77.
23. *Sree Gurudev Vani,* 31.
24. Ibid., 23.
25. Ibid., 3-4.
26. Amma, *Swami Muktananda,* 69.
27. *Sree Gurudev Vani,* 22.

28. Charles S. J. White, "Swami Muktananda and the Enlightenment through Sakti Pah" *History of Religions (University of Chicago), vol. 23, no. 4, 319.*

29. *Ibid., 329.*

30. R. C. Zaehner, *Mysticism: Sacred and Profane,* 96.

31. 2 Cor. 11:14.

32. William James, *Varieties of Religious Experience,* 410–11.

CHAPTER 10: *The Divine Light Mission*

1. C. L. Tandon, *Satgurudev Shri Hansji Maharaj* (Delhi, 1970), 18.

2. Charles Cameron, *Who Is Guru Maharaj Ji?* (New York: Bantam, 1973), 35.

3. *The Statesman,* 4 April 1975.

4. Ibid.

5. The following information regarding initiation and "knowledge" is kept strictly secret by the Divine Light Mission. I am indebted to Bobby Cumiskey for revealing it to me. He was one of the first in Scotland to take initiation into DLM in 1971. Later, he left the Mission because it failed to satisfy his spiritual longings. Instead of giving him a spiritual relationship with God, it taught him that the experiences derived from autosuggestion and the physiological manipulation of eyes, ears, and tongue were experiences of divinity.

6. The point between the two eyebrows on the forehead above the nose.

CHAPTER 11: *Radha Soami Satsang (Beas)*

1. Those interested in knowing the early history of the movement can refer to J. N. Farquhar's *Modern Religious Movements in India.*

2. Julian P. Johnson, *The Path of the Masters,* (Beas: Radha Soami Satsang, 1965), 207.

3. Ibid., 208.

4. Ibid., 207.

5. Ibid., 209.

6. Maharaj Charan Singh, *St. John: The Great Mystic* (Beas: Radha Soami Satsang, 1974), 4.

7. Johnson, *Path of the Masters* 214.

8. Maharaj Charan Singh, *The Master Answers* (Beas: Radha Soami Satsang, 1973), 334.

9. Charles Cameron, ed., *Who Is Guru Maharaj Ji?,* 91.

10. Charan Singh, *The Master Answers,* 335.

11. Johnson, *Path of the Masters,* 216.

12. Charan Singh, *The Master Answers,* 342.

13. Johnson, *Path of the Masters,* 186.

14. Ibid., 187–88.

15. C. W. Sanders, *The Inner Voice* (Beas: Radha Soami Satsang, 1970), 15.

16. Ibid., 15.

17. Johnson, *Path of the Masters,* 229.

18. Ibid., 373.

19. Charan Singh, *The Master Answers,* 18.

20. Ibid., 47.

21. Ibid., 27.

22. Ibid., 20.

23. John 1:1.

24. See also John 1:14.
25. Luke 17:21.
26. Mark 1:15.
27. Matt. 11:28.
28. John 3:3.
29. Matt. 6:22 (KJV).
30. Alfonso Caycedo, *India of Yogis* (Delhi: National Publishing House, 1966), 58-60.
31. Ibid.
32. Ibid., 110-11.
33. Sanders, *Inner Voice*, 16.
34. Narain Das, *Sant Mat and the Bible* (Beas: Radha Soami Satsang, 1971), 63.

CHAPTER 12: *Evaluating Monistic Gurus*

1. See chapter five.
2. Os Guinness, *Dust of Death*, 214.
3. See Francis Schaeffer, *He Is There and He Is Not Silent*, 12.
4. Guinness, *Dust of Death*, 218.
5. Amma, *Swami Muktananda Paramahansa*, 77.
6. Rajneesh, *Beyond and Beyond*, 12-13.
7. Anthony Campbell, *Seven States of Consciousness*, 22.
8. Ibid., 163-64.

CHAPTER 13: *The Sanatan Sadguru*

1. See Heb. 1:1-2, 2 Pet. 1:20-21.
2. Deut. 18:15.
3. Gen. 49:10.
4. See 2 Sam. 7:12-16, Isa. 11:1-10.
5. Mic. 5:2.
6. Isa. 7:14.
7. Isa. 9:6-7.
8. Zech. 9:9.
9. Zech. 11:12-13.
10. Ps. 22:18.
11. Isa. 53:12.
12. Ps. 16:10, Ps. 2:6-12, etc.
13. Since the publication of Nicolas Notovitch's *Unknown Life of Christ* (1895), many have believed that Jesus came to India between the age of twelve and thirty. Notovitch was shown to be a fraud soon after the publication of his book, but many still hold to his beliefs without any evidence whatsoever.
14. Matt. 27:23, 24, Heb. 4:15.
15. Matt. 11:19.
16. John 14:9
17. Mark 1:15 (KJV)
18. Isa. 53.
19. John 1:29.

20. Matt. 26:28.
21. Acts 1:8.
22. Acts 1:9-11.
23. Rom. 1:4.
24. John 7:46
25. John 4:24.
26. Gen. 1:26.
27. Mark 7:21-23.
28. John 8:42-44.
29. John 3:16.
30. Matt. 27:46.
31. 2 Cor. 5:21.
32. 2 Cor. 5:17.
33. Eph. 1:13, 14.
34. Phil. 2:10, 11.
35. John 10:30, 14:9.
36. John 1:1.
37. John 14:26.
38. Matt. 27:59, 60.
39. John 20:6-7.

INDEX

Abu Hamid al-Ghazili, on mystic ecstasy, 31
Acharya Rajneesh. *See* Bhagwan Rajneesh
Acharya guru and Indian education, 10-11
Acharya, Srinivasa and Chaitanya's movement, 58
Advaita and avatar concept, 118-19; discussion on, 48-50; philosophy of, 46-48. *See also* Monism
Advaitins, 39; and reasons, 52-53; justification of, 49-50
Ahmad, Mirza Ghulam, 182
Alvars and bhakti, movement, 57
Anda. concept of, 145-46
Arya Samaj, 9
Asamprajnata samadhi, state of, 47
Ashram system, 7, 10
Asthul sharir, concept of, 145
Aurobindo, 9. *See also* Ghose, Sri Aurobindo
Avatars, Hindu belief of, 117-18
Ayer, A. J., 20

Baba Jaimal Singh and Radha Soami Satsang, 141
Bal Bhagavan, as leader of Divine Light Mission, 137
Balyogeshwar, 7, 21, background of, 135-37; claims of, 135-37; downfall of, 136-37; phenomenal popularity of 136
Bangalore University committee on superstitions and miracles and Sathya Sai Baba, 121
Baudelaire, Charles, 180
Benson, Dr. Herbert and Transcendental Meditation, 31
Bergman, Ingmar, *Silence* (film), 20
Berkeley and Western philosophy, 19
Bhagavad Gita, 12; dating of, 63
Bhagwan Rajneesh, 8-9, 156; and Zen Buddhism, 89; background of, 89; concepts and ideas of, 89-94; illegal activities of, 99-104; influences on, 87-88; meditation techniques of, 94-97; on history of man, 162; on love and sex, 161; on meditation through sex, 96-97; synthetic stance of, 71; teaching of, 49
Bhagvantham, Dr. S. and Sathya Sai Baba's miracles, 112-14
Bhakti movement, streams of, 57
Bhaktimarga, 12

Bhaktivinode and Gaudiya Vaishnava Mission, 58
Bhakti Siddhanta Goswami, 58
Bhed-abheda, concept of, 57
Bible, the prophesies of, 169-70; on God, 173-74. *See also* Christianity; Jesus
Biology and mysticism, 26
Brahmanda, concept of, 144
Brahmin dominance and guruism, 12
Brahmo Samaj, 1, 9; sankirtana, revival by, 58
Brent, Peter, on Swami Muktananda, 125
Brooke, Tal and Sathya Sai Baba, 115-17
Buddha, 22, 53
Buber, Martin, mystical experience of, 30; testimony of, 49

Cage, John, *Silence* (biography); 20
Campbell, Dr. Anthony, on consciousness, 76-77, 165
Caycedo, Dr. A., study of mystic experiences by, 149
Chaitanya, 56; sankirtana movement of, 57; Krishna-Rukmini, worship of, 57; philosophy of, 57
Charan Singh, Maharaj, 141; on mystic experiences, 150
Chetramis, 9
Chinmaya Mission, 39; activities of, 45-46; formation and growth of, 44; founding of, 45; philosophy of, 46-48
Christianity, beliefs of, 173-74; overthrow of, 14-15. *See also* Bible; Jesus
Chowdhury, Amiya Roy (Dadaji), miracles of, 117
Class system and guruism, 12
Consciousness and reality, 23; pure, 46-47, 155-57; seven states of, 76
Cosmos, Sant Mat's divisions of, 144-45
Counterculture, 5; inadequacy of, 59; means of, 21
Creative intelligence, meaning of, 74
Cultural awareness, implications of, 4
Custance, John, experience of, 128; manic experience of, 30-31

Dada Guru and Shri Hans Ji Maharaj, 135
Dada Lekhraj and Brahma Kumari Ishwariya Vishv Vidhyalaya, 71

Darwinism and Christianity, 14
Das, Shyamananda and Chaitanya's movement, 58
Datta, Narottama and Chaitanya's movement, 58
Dayal, Sant Mat concept of, 143
de Chardin, Teilhard, and mysticism, 26
Descartes and Western philosophy, 19
Dev Samaj, 9
Diabolical mysticism, nature of, 129
Divine Life Society, 20, 39, 43; founding of, 41-43; philosophy of, 46-48
Divine Light Mission (DLM), 7, 13, 133; background of, 135; claim of, 29; controversy in, 136-37; initiation techniques in, 138-39; success of, 136; techniques of realization in, 138-39
Divine reality, 9; and words, 20; merger into, 8
Divine revelation, 35n; possibility of, 23
Divine sound, 32
Dwaitins, 39

Ecology and pantheism, 28
Ekankar, concept of, 143
Eknath, Krishna-Rukmini worship of, 57
Ellul, Jacques, and protest movement, 4
Emerson, and Indian thought, 14
Epistemology, mystical, 23; subject matter of, 19
Existentialism, failure of, 16-17
Extrasensory perception, 28

Free speech movement, 5
Freud and love, 37; on religion, 34

Galileo, Christian world view of, 24
Gandhi, Mahatma, 1, 9, 53
Gaudiya Vaishnava Society, 55; succession controversy in, 56
Ghose, Sri Aurobindo, 9, 26; impact on West, 14
God, Christian concept of, 173-74; concept of, 10, 123; in Sant Mat, 143
Godman, concept of, 9-10
Goodman, Paul and protest movement, 4
Godmen of India (by Peter Brent), 13
Goethe, and Indian thought, 14
Gokak, Prof, on Sathya Sai Baba, 108-9
Goswami Maharaj, 56
Gunas, classification of, 49
Guinness, Os, on God, 20
Guru Govind Singh, 8
Guru Nanak, 7-9

Gurus and absolute surrender, 165; and God, 51; concept of, 6-7; contemporary impact of, 3; history of, 6-7; Sikh concept of,7-9
Guruism and epistemology, 19; and India, 3-4; as an alternative, 5; elements of, 31-32; revival of, 1, 3-4

H. H. Swami Tapovan Maharaj, 44
Hans Ji Maharaj, background of, 135
Hare Krishna movement, 39, 49, 164; appeal of, 59-62; beginning of, 55; claims of, 56; contribution to West, 67. *See also* International Society for Krishna Consciousness
Harigiri Baba and Swami Muktananda, 124-25
Harper, Marvin Henry, 5
Hedonism, reaction to, 15
Hegelian Philosophy and Christianity, 15
Heidegger, and existentialism, 17
Hinduism, 1; and America, 5; impact on West, 14
Hippyism, failure of, 59-60
Holy Trinity, concept of, 176-77
Humanism. *See* secularism
Hume, David, impact of, 20; on knowing, 19-20
Humphreys, Christmas, on spiritual healing, 27
Huxley, Aldous, 21, 28, 35, 36; and protest movement, 4; conversion of, 16; drug experience of, 49; on Godhead, 6
Huzu Sawan Singh Ji Maharaj and Radha Soami Satsang, 141

Indian cultural heritage, search for, 4
Indian education and guru concept, 11
Indian family structure and guruism, 13
Indian religions, esoteric character of, 11-12
Indian society, repressive puritanism of, 13
International Congress of Brain Researchers Vatican (1966), 25
International Society for Krishna Consciousness (ISKCON), 5, 10; centers in India, 58; criticism of, 67-68; formation of 55-56; growth of, 58-59; philosophy and teachings of, 63-66; regulations of, 61-62. *See also* Hare Krishna movement
Ishvara, concept of, 51

Jai Gurudev Dharm Pracharak Sangh, 133
James, William, 42; experience of, 23; on mystical experience, 30; on diabolical mysticism, 129; testimony of, 49

Jesus, as Sadguru, 168-70; death and resurrection of, 171-72, 181-84; life of, 170-72; on God, 169-74; teachings of, 172; on God, 169-74; teachings of, 172. *See also* Bible; Christianity

Jivan mukta, state of, 127

Jnaneshvar, Krishna-Rukmini worship of, 57

Jung, Dr. Carl, 27

Kabir, philosophy of, 7, 8

Kal, concept of, 144

Kal niranjan, concept of, 143-44

Kant, Emmanuel, 16, 20

Karan sharir, concept of, 145

Karma, concept of, 157; law of, 46, 50

Karmamarga, 68-69

Kierkegaard, and existentialism, 17

Krishna, Sri, and *Bhagavad Gita*, 11

Krishnamurti, 9; impact on West, 14

Kundalini shakti, awakening of, 126; passage through chakras, 126

Laing, R. D., on mechanistic view of man, 24

Laragh, John, on Transcendental Meditation, 81

Leary and LSD, 21

Lewis, Prof. C. S., on spirit possession, 119

Lila, concept of, 163

Locke, and Western philosophy, 19

Logical positivists and Western philosophy, 19

McMullen, C. O., on guru tradition, 12

Madhava, philosophy of, 39, 57

Mahesh Yogi, 21, 26, 29, 155, 156, 157; background of, 73; criticism of, 80-81; popularity in West, 73; synthetic approach of, 71; world plan of, 5. *See also* Transcendental Meditation

Mantras, 11; and guru, 7

Marcuse, Herbert and protest movement, 5

Marxist philosophy and Christianity, 15

Materialism and soul, 22; reaction to, 15-16

Maya, concept of, 23, 157, 158; influence of, 46; spell of, 51

Meher Baba and Shirdi Sai's tradition, 108

Millenium Festival (Houston, 1973) and Balyogeshwar, 136

Mills, Cyril Wright and protest movement, 4

Mind and matter, research on, 25; in Sant Mat system, 145-46

Modern science, changing of, 14; mechanistic world view of, 24

Moksha, attainment of, 46; interpretation of, 51; meaning of, 48

Monism, 23; absolute, 39; and abnormality, 159; avatarism/guruism, 158; and creation, 156-57; and cruelty, 162-63; and Godmen, 9, 10; and immortality, 164-65; meaning, 163; and morality, 161-62; and personality, 159- 60; and reality, 158-59; forgiveness of, 164; on pure consciousness, 155; qualified, 39. *See also* Murphet, Howard, on Sathya Sai Baba, 108

Mysticism and modern science, 24

Neel Kanth Thataji, Sri, 8, 118

New Left, 5; disillusionment with, 73-74; failure of, 59

Newton, Christian world view of, 24

Nietzsche, impact of, 14

Nimbaraka, Krishna-Rukmini worship of, 57

Nirankar, concept of, 143; Sikh concept of, 8

Noumenal reality, 16; and phenomenal, 20

Otis, Dr. Leon S. and Transcendental Meditation, 81, 82

Pantheism, 23; on God, 123; on pure consciousness, 155

Paramahansa, Ramakrishna, 9

Parapsychology, researches of, 28

Patanjali, on ashtanga, yoga, 47

Pauranika religion and concept of guru, 7

Physics and irrationalism, 24-26

Pinda, concept of, 145

Prana, concept of, 157

Prarthana Samaj, 9

Prasad, Dr. Rama Chandra, on Bhagavan Rajneesh, 88

Prashanthi Nilayam (Puttaparthi), Sai Baba's ashram, 109

Psychology and Vedanta, 27

Pyrrhonists, ideas of, 22

Quantum theory, 26

Radha, myth of, 67

Radha Soami Satsang, 9, 133; and concept of guru, 8; ashram of, 141; founding of, 141; initiation ceremony of, 142-43. *See also* Sant Mat

Radhakrishnan, Dr. Sarvapalli, 1, 6, 9, 14

Ramakrishna Mission, impact on West of, 14

Ramananda and Kabir, 7

Ramanuja, 39; qualified monism of, 10; philosophy of, 57

Rationalism, failure of, 16-17; vs. guruism, 4, 5

Reactionism, failure of, 16
Reason vs. randomness, 26
Religion and philosophy, 33-35; elements of, 31-33; need of, 34; quest of, 163; test of, 35-37
Rig Veda, "Hymn of Creation" quoted from, 21-22
Riesman, David, and protest movement, 4
Rimbaud, Arthur, and mystical experience, 30
Rishikesh, Academy of Meditation at, 78
Rodarmor, William, and Swami Muktananda, 129-30
Roy, Raja Ram Mohan, 1

Sachidananda, state of, 47
Sahasra dal kanwal, concept of, 145
Sai Baba of Shirdi, 107-8
Samkhya yoga, theory of, 49
Samskaras and successive births, 47
Sanders, C. W., on meditation, 149
Sant Mat, criticism on, 147-49; on cosmos, 144-45; on sadguru, 146; on soul in bondage, 145-46; philosophic system and teachings of, 142-47. *See also* Radha Soami Satsang
Sat desh, concept of, 144
Sat purush, concept of, 143
Sathya Sai Baba, 9, 28, 105, 164; and Jesus, 118-19; and Sathya Sai samitis, 110; avatarhood, claim of, 117-19; background of, 107-9; claims of, 108-10; criticism and exposure of, 118-21; disillusionment with, 114-17; life-style of, 119; miracles performed by, 109, 112-14; philosophy and teachings of, 111-12; popularity of, 107, 109, 110; reincarnation claims of, 118-19; secret sessions of, 115-16
Shabd, concept of, 144
Shaivism, 39
Shankaracharya, 39; philosophy of, 46
Sartre, and existentialism, 17
Sati Godavari Mataji, and Shirdi Sai's tradition, 108
Schaeffer, Francis, 24
Schopenhauer, and Indian thought, 14
Schrodinger, Erwin, on mind and matter, 25
Secularism, and overthrow of Christianity, 14-15; and rationalism, 4; failure of, 4-5; vs. guruism, 6; worldview of, 36-37
Shaivite sect and guru, 9
Shaivites and Bhakti movement, 57
Sharma, D. S., on Bhakti movement, 57; on Radha myth, 67

Sharma, Subramanya, 10
Shoonya, Bhagwan Rajneesh's interpretation of, 94, 98
Shuksham sharir, concept of, 145
Siddha yoga, path of, 127
Sidharudha Swami, and Swami Muktananda, 124
Sikhism, and human gurus, 9; philosophy of, 7-8
Simran and dhyan, Sant Mat techniques of, 146-47
Sivananda ashram, founding of, 42; present state of, 43
Skinner, B. F., 27
Slater, Philip E., on stable culture, 59
Soul bondage, in Sant Mat concept of, 145-46
Spirit possession, phenomenon of, 105, 119
Srila Bhaktisiddhanta Saraswati Maharaj and Swami Prabhupada, 55
Surat-shabd yoga, features of, 133, 146-47
Suzuki, D. T. and Zen Buddhism, 21, 89
Swami Akhananda of Vrindaban, on guru, 10
Swami Chidananda, foreign tours of, 43-44; on mystic experiences, 149
Swami Chinmayananda, 156; and Sandeepany Sadhanalaya, 46; background of, 44; influences on, 44-46; discourse of, 48; technique of gnana yagna, 44; on good and bad, 51; on philosophy, 33; teachings of, 44-48; and Advaita Vedanta, 45
Swami Krishnananda, 33; Allahabad lectures of, 4; on objective thinking, 53; scholarship of, 44
Swami Muktananda, 105, 156, 159; background of, 123-24; quest of, 124-25; blue pearl vision to, 126-27; evaluation on, 128-29; on morals, 128-30; on realization, 126-27; spiritual experiences of, 126-27
Swami Nityananda, and Swami Muktananda, 124
Swami Prabhupada, 5, 10, 21, 155; and Nimbareka's dualism, 57; background of, 55; on morality, 257. *See also* International Society for Krishna Consciousness
Swami Saraswati Dayananda (Chinmaya Mission), 46
Swami Sivananda, death of, 43; escapism of, 42; on attitude to work, 53; on good and bad, 50-51; on guru, 10; on human wit,

22; on law of karma, 50; on physical universe, 52; on preaching Vedanta, 54; on spiritual experience, 49; pessimistic view of, 42; philosophy of, 4; on silence, 20

Swami Viswananda, 41
Swami Vivekananda, 9, 14, 43
Swamy Shyham Sunderdass, 10
Sykes, Gerald, on Vedanta, 27

Tagore, Rabindranath, 14
Talib, Prof. Gurbachan Singh, on guru, 8
Tantrika religions and concept of guru, 7
Tantrism, 22
Tennyson, Lord, and Transcendental Meditation, 82-83
Theosophical Society, 28; impact on West, 14
"Third eye," concept of, 142
Thoreau, and Indian thought, 14
Transcendental Meditation (TM), 5; alleged advantages of, 78, 81; in the appellate court, 84; growth of, 73; dangers from, 82; initiation into, 78-79; meaning of, 74; as medicine, 84-85; philosophy of, 74-77; practice of, 76; popularity of, 74. See also Mahesh Yogi
Transmigration, doctrine of, 51
Tukaram, Krishna-Rukmini worship of, 57

Tulsidas Ji Maharaj, Sri, 133
Turya, state of, 48

Upasani Baba and Shirdi Sai's tradition, 108

Vaishnavism, 39
Vaishnavite sect and guru, 9, 39
Vaishnavites and Bhakti movement, 57
Vasishtha and Tantrism, 22
Vallabha, Krishna-Rukmini worship of, 57
Vishishtadvaitins, 39
Vishnu, avatars of, 117-18
Vishnuswami, Krishna-Rukmini worship of, 57
Voltaire, impact of, 14

Waddington, C. H., on consciousness, 25
Wallace, Dr. Keith, and Transcendental Meditation, 81
White, Charles S. J., on mystic experiences, 128
Whyte, William H., and protest movement, 4
Wittgenstein, philosophy of, 20

Yoga techniques, 46-47

Zaehner, Prof. R. C., on mystical experience, 29; on Aldous Huxley, 16; testimony of, 49
Zen Buddhism, 21, 89
Ziprauanna, and Swami Muktananda, 124-25